THE PHILOSOPHICAL
FOUNDATIONS OF
SOCIAL WORK

The Philosophical Foundations of Social Work

FREDERIC G. REAMER

COLUMBIA UNIVERSITY PRESS

NEW YORK

COLUMBIA UNIVERSITY PRESS
NEW YORK   OXFORD
COPYRIGHT © 1993 COLUMBIA UNIVERSITY PRESS
ALL RIGHTS RESERVED

LIBRARY OF CONGRESS CATALOGING-IN-PUBLICATION DATA

REAMER, FREDERIC G., 1953–
THE PHILOSOPHICAL FOUNDATIONS OF SOCIAL WORK
FREDERIC G. REAMER.
P.   CM.
INCLUDES BIBLIOGRAPHICAL REFERENCES (P.   ) AND INDEX.
ISBN 0-231-07126-4
I. SOCIAL SERVICE—PHILOSOPHY. I. TITLE.
HV40.R35 1993 361'.001—DC20 92–28971
CIP

CASEBOUND EDITIONS OF COLUMBIA UNIVERSITY PRESS
BOOKS ARE SMYTH-SEWN AND PRINTED
ON PERMANENT AND DURABLE ACID-FREE PAPER

BOOK DESIGN BY AUDREY SMITH
PRINTED IN THE UNITED STATES OF AMERICA

C 10 9 8 7 6 5 4 3 2 1

For Deborah and Emma

Philosophy, the lumber of the schools.
—JONATHAN SWIFT

CONTENTS

PREFACE

I recently read a book—*The Examined Life: Philosophical Meditations* (1989)—by the acclaimed philosopher Robert Nozick. Toward
the end of the book Nozick includes a chapter with a curious title:
"What Is Wisdom and Why Do Philosophers Love It So?" For
Nozick, philosophy's ultimate aim is an understanding of what is
fundamentally important and a grasp of life's central issues. Nozick
argues that this sort of understanding takes the form of wisdom:
"Philosophy means the love of wisdom. What is wisdom? How shall
it be loved? Wisdom is an understanding of what is important,
where this understanding informs a (wise) person's thought and
action. Things of lesser importance are kept in proper perspective"
(267).

One of social work's principal virtues is that its practitioners tend
to have a certain wisdom about life's important issues. Seasoned
social workers have come up against life's most compelling circumstances and clients' struggles with them. Social workers have much
to be philosophical—and wise—about. My purpose here is to identify and explore the core philosophical issues in social work and
speculate about their relevance to practice. As I will argue in some

detail, this sort of exploration is particularly important at this point in social work's history, as the profession closes in on the end of its first formal century.

Throughout social work's evolution, practitioners have made a concerted effort to deepen and broaden the profession's knowledge base. Even a cursory survey of the profession's expanding literature demonstrates that social work's own scholars and practitioners have added increasingly to what we know about such phenomena as mental illness, poverty, aging, crime and delinquency, child welfare, health care, substance abuse, community development, social policy, administration, and evaluation research.

Although social work is still in the relatively early stages of the cultivation of its own knowledge base—reflecting the unique value base, conceptual principles, and practice methods of the profession—it is clear that knowledge is expanding rapidly with respect to social work's various fields of practice (for example, children and family services, mental health, aging, and health care) and methods of intervention (for example, casework, group work, community organization, advocacy, and research).

What is curiously lagging in this evolution, however, is sustained, scholarly examination of the philosophical foundations on which the profession rests. Admittedly some progress has recently been made in this regard, especially with respect to philosophical questions bearing on social work research and ethics. Yet, a careful review of the profession's literature demonstrates clearly that this foundation-level inquiry is nascent at best and is developing at a rather modest pace.

The principal aims of any profession rest on core assumptions about mission, methods, and conceptual orientation. In short, the heart of any profession consists of a philosophically oriented statement of purpose and perspective. The central goal of *The Philosophical Foundations of Social Work* is to help lay the groundwork for such a statement.

Such an endeavor is an essential component of a profession's maturation, and it is especially important to social work's continued development. Careful consideration of philosophical issues related to the profession is essential if social workers' practice-based decisions are to be anchored in core values and tenets that uniquely frame and characterize the profession, emanate from its central mission, and are not derived in hybridlike fashion from allied disciplines and professions. Examination of relevant philosophical issues is necessary if social workers are to critically examine the aims, methods, and motives that surround their day-to-day duties.

In some respects the pursuit of philosophical questions and issues may seem like an exercise in intellectual gymnastics, removed from the more immediate, pressing, and daunting demands faced by contemporary social workers. (The British playwright, John Osborne, said, in *Epitaph for George Dillon:* "It's easy to answer the ultimate questions—it saves you bothering with the immediate ones.") At least since the time of Socrates and the Greek thinkers of the seventh and sixth centuries B.C., Western philosophers have been known for their tendency to wrestle with remarkably abstruse concepts that may seem quite distant from the compelling problems today's social workers face. After all, what social worker can afford to dwell for hours on Plato's conception of justice when one of her clients does not have enough food for her own children? As Hunt (1978) aptly notes, "In a real sense the sometimes urgent business of social work cannot be suspended while a careful analysis of its assumptions is carried out by philosophical analysts concerned about the veracity of any claims for justification" (24).

In the end, however, we cannot ignore the primary questions, questions that move social workers in the first place to be concerned about starving children, or any other vulnerable group. If social work is to enhance its own knowledge base as it continues to mature as a profession, it is essential for the profession to examine, shape, and clarify its key philosophical assumptions. Moreover, social workers must learn how to think philosophically, to know what it means to critically examine an argument and claims about practice. As Kaelin (1989) says, "Experience, reflection, criticism; renewed experience, reflection, and criticism describe the never-ending round of the philosophical enterprise, which begins in a relatively confused experience and, if it attains to any degree of felicity, ends in a richer, clearer, more enjoyable experience of the values to be found in living" (3). If such inquiry is to be meaningful to the social work professional, clear links must be made between underlying philosophical issues and the mission, skills, and practical decisions of today's social workers.

For our purposes, philosophy can be defined as "the rational, methodical, and systematic consideration of those topics that are of greatest concern" to humankind (The History of Western Philosophy 1989:742). Among the many areas of inquiry within philosophy, several are particularly relevant to social work. In *The Philo-*

sophical Foundations of Social Work I focus on five major philosophical themes that are especially germane to contemporary practice. First I explore a series of issues related to political philosophy,
in particular those related to the role of the state in social welfare,
distributive justice and equality, welfare rights, and the concepts of
the public interest and common good (chapter 1).

From there I move to an overview of issues raised by moral
philosophy. My major purpose in chapter 2 is to acquaint readers
with the rudiments of ethical theory and to show how they are
relevant to practice. I focus mainly on the nature of ethical inquiry,
ethical conflict, and the emergence of applied and professional
ethics.

I then move from discussion of overarching issues concerning
social work's mission (those raised by political and moral philosophy) to an examination of how social workers think, in the philosophical sense, about their practice. In chapter 3 I concentrate on
the branch of philosophy known as logic, acquainting readers with
traditional ways of thinking about valid forms of argument and
logical fallacies. My aim here is to alert readers to the importance
of precise, logical argumentation in social work—especially as it
relates to claims about the effectiveness of practitioners' interventions—and to a number of logical fallacies encountered in the
profession.

Chapter 4 addresses a series of issues that have received considerable attention in the social work literature in recent years. They
concern the role of science in social work and ways of knowing. In
philosophy, such questions typically fall under the heading of epistemology. In this section I provide an overview of the substantial
and ever-increasing debate about the status of empiricism and
positivism in social work, as compared to other ways of knowing.

The book concludes with a discussion of aesthetics, that is,
issues pertaining to the ways social workers perceive, judge, and
critique their work. Aesthetics as a branch of philosophy has a
great deal to offer social workers, mainly with respect to the ways
in which practitioners evaluate their work and perform artistically.
Hence, in chapter 5 I provide a survey of various schools of thought
in aesthetics and explore a variety of concepts that, in my view, can
be usefully incorporated into social work practice.

I make no claim that this book constitutes a comprehensive,
exhaustive review of all philosophical issues relevant to social work.
One could make a case, for example, that a volume such as this
might have also explored the philosophy of religion and existential

philosophy. I have no particular quarrel with this. Instead, I have chosen to limit my discussion to those areas of philosophy that are applicable to social work in the broadest sense, including the "micro" *and* "macro" domains of the profession. As we shall see, the subjects of political philosophy, moral philosophy, logic, epistemology, and aesthetics are relevant to casework, group practice, family intervention, community organization, social policy, administration, and social work research. In contrast, philosophy of religion and existential philosophy, while certainly important, have narrower relevance, pertaining mainly to direct practice and individual casework.

My hope is that my speculation about the philosophical foundations of social work will generate considerable discussion and debate about the profession's central aims and will help, at least in some modest way, to deepen the grasp of the profession's conceptual anchor. This is hard intellectual work, but I suspect the effort will pay off. As Carlyle said, "Knowledge conquered by labor becomes a possession—a property entirely our own."

CHAPTER ONE

ย/ร

POLITICAL PHILOSOPHY

The culminating point of administration is to know
well how much power, great or small, we ought to
use in all circumstances.

—MONTESQUIEU

Since its inception as a profession, social work has had complex
ties with the state. Although many social work functions have been
offered under private-sector auspices, no one questions that the
profession's mission is inextricably linked to government, in the
form of public laws, policies, regulations, and funding.

Certainly the ties between social work and the state have been
loosened and tightened at various points in the profession's history.
Particularly during the Progressive Era, the New Deal era, and the
War on Poverty years, social work was an integral participant in
federal, state, and local government's efforts to design and implement novel and ambitious social welfare programs. During other
periods, however, including the years immediately following World
War II and the 1980s, social work has been more peripheral to the
formulation of government's social welfare mission.

Even during quiescent periods, when social work has not been
central to social welfare policy design, the profession still, by necessity, has been linked to government programs that offer social
services and benefits to clients. No social worker can avoid drawing connections between clients' needs and publicly sponsored

programs, regulations, or benefits pertaining, for example, to public assistance, elder or child welfare services, community-based programs for the mentally ill, or shelter care for the homeless.

Thus social workers have had a long-standing interest in the role of the state in social welfare. For nearly a century, social workers have been involved in intense debate about the division of responsibility between the public and private sectors for the welfare of vulnerable and disadvantaged citizens. Considerable discussion has taken place in the social work literature about the nature and limits of government obligation to meet social welfare needs, the ability of the private market to provide social services, the functions of public assistance, welfare rights, and various models of a welfare state (see, for example, Atherton 1989; Blau 1989; Gilbert 1983; Gilbert and Gilbert 1989; Jansson 1988; and Martin 1990).

Clearly, much of our current thinking about the role of the state and distributive justice has its origins in classic theories of political philosophy. By and large, however, little recognition has been given to the philosophical roots and assumptions embedded in contemporary statements about the role of government in social welfare. Examining the philosophical origins of modern-day policies and conceptual frameworks can enhance our understanding of prevailing approaches to social welfare and enable us to examine their merits critically.

PHILOSOPHICAL UNDERPINNINGS

Although social workers' ordinary responsibilities tend to focus on practical aspects of government's role in their clients' lives—related, for example, to changing eligibility requirements or benefits for welfare clients, provisions contained in new affordable housing legislation, a state agency's regulations concerning reimbursement rates, or the impact of a recent court decision on deinstitutionalization—publicly sponsored social welfare activities are ultimately shaped by deep-seated beliefs about the goals of government, the rights of citizens in relation to the state, the obligations of the state toward its citizens, the nature of political or civil liberty, and the nature of social justice. For social workers to adequately understand the determinants of their contemporary thinking about such issues, they must have some appreciation of the historical and philosophical origins:

Political philosophy is not merely unpractical speculation, though it may give rise to highly impractical myths: it is a vitally important aspect of life, and one that, for good or evil, has had decisive results on political action; for the assumptions on which political life is conducted clearly must influence what actually happens. . . . Questions concerning the aims of government, the grounds of political obligation, the rights of individuals against the state, the basis of sovereignty, the relation of executive to legislative power, and the nature of political liberty and social justice have been asked and answered in many ways over the centuries. (Political Philosophy 1988:972)

Questions concerning the role of the state, for instance, have been addressed at least since Greco-Roman times. Although there is evidence of speculation about some aspects of government in earlier cultures (for example, the laws of Hammurabi of Babylon, c. 1750 B.C., concerning trade and irrigation and the sixth-century B.C. writings of Confucius), the most focused and sustained inquiry concerning the role of government and political power began in ancient Greece (Political Philosophy 1988).

The most significant work of this era was Plato's renowned *Republic* (c. 378 B.C.). Plato grew up in the midst of the devastating, twenty-seven-year-long war between Athens and Sparta and sought in the *Republic* to formulate a utopian view of political life. Social workers can find in this work a compelling forerunner of contemporary debate about the use of authority to meet the public's needs, the relationship between elite rulers and the citizenry, and the conflict between public corruption and social welfare. The *Republic* also represents one of the earliest efforts to grapple with questions with which today's social workers continue to struggle: How should an ideal society function? Is such a society possible? How can a society best be governed and best meet the needs of its most vulnerable citizens? Although Plato has been properly criticized for being elitist, he nonetheless broached a variety of compelling issues that continue to resonate among social workers.

One of Plato's principal concerns, for example, was with class conflict. Based on his own experience in conflict-torn Athens, Plato was preoccupied with the deleterious effects of strife and tension between competing factions. Like today's conflicts among ethnic, religious, and cultural groups, and between the wealthy and the poor, the conflicts during Plato's time threatened to tear asunder the very fabric of civilization.

Like some social workers, Plato was inclined to analyze his society's troubles reductionistically, by comparing it to the development of an individual who matures and deteriorates—the so-called biological analogy (Stroll and Popkin 1979:194). For Plato, the society was little more than "the individual writ large." Hence, Plato believed that by studying individual human beings, rules and patterns could be identified that would help us understand the broader culture.

Plato argued that the state needs to be governed in much the same way an individual is "governed," that is, by its cognitive abilities, its spirit, and its passions. For the state to be governed adequately, it would require a hierarchical class structure made up of (1) leaders, (2) soldiers to defend the state, and (3) workers who provide necessary labor. Thus, the ideal society would consist of three distinct classes, the members of which would accept their fate and mission and would not attempt to usurp the responsibilities or privileges of the other classes. This, for Plato, would offer the greatest stability. This arrangement, of course, is reminiscent of modern-day citizens who believe that members of each social class should understand and "know" their place.

To ensure this tripartite division, Plato advocated administering tests of citizens' ability. Ideally, children would be raised together until age twenty, at which time they would take tests of their inherent intellectual, physical, and "moral" abilities. The results of the tests would determine whether one would be placed in the class of rulers (to be subdivided later into soldiers and legislators) or workers.

Thus, Plato favored a highly centralized form of rule, with the general citizenry having relatively little autonomy concerning their ultimate role in society. This perspective clearly clashes with most social workers' vision of the role of government, the importance of individual self-determination, and the value of social services designed to enhance individual skill, opportunity, and capacity.

At the same time, one can see in Plato's work the seeds of contemporary criticism of generous and ambitious social service programs. Conservative criticism of social welfare spending often seems couched in an elitist view, according to which the state is not obligated to provide opportunity and assistance to the least capable and advantaged. Instead, as in Plato's ideal world, government's principal task is to distribute responsibility and resources to ensure stability and to identify the "proper place" for its citizens. The state's resources should be channeled primarily to train the most capable, intelligent members of society. Those who pass the various tests and training should be rewarded, while those who fail should be cast aside. In many respects, Plato's perspective was decidedly undemocratic.

Aristotle's *Politics* provides another example of a reductionistic approach to analysis of society. Aristotle, who was a student in the Academy of Plato, analyzed society as if he were a physician and prescribed remedies accordingly. This was perhaps the first formal expression of what we now know as the "medical model."

Like Plato, Aristotle believed that only a minority within society could lead a high quality of life and, further, that some individuals are "slaves by nature" (Political Philosophy 1988:973). He also argued that a hierarchical, aristocratic, and undemocratic form of government is essential to preserve social order.

Among the most patronizing, contemptuous, and undemocratic sentiments toward the masses—which foreshadowed some contemporary characterizations of the poor—are found in Machiavelli's sixteenth-century writings:

> Since this is to be asserted in general of men, that they are ungrateful, fickle, false, cowards, covetous, and as long as you succeed they are yours entirely; they will offer you their blood, property, life, and children . . . when the need is far distant; but when it approaches they turn against you. . . . [And] since the desires of men are insatiable, nature prompting them to desire all things and fortune permitting them to enjoy but few, there results a constant discontent in their minds, and a loathing of what they possess. (Political Philosophy 1988:976)

Thomas Hobbes's seventeenth-century views were also rather contemptuous of the masses. In his classic, the *Leviathan,* Hobbes presented a point of view quite at odds with social work's vision of the community's need to care for its most vulnerable members. He argued that the true law of nature, its central imperative, is self-preservation, which can be achieved only if all citizens agree to transfer, through a social contract, their individual power to the "leviathan" (ruler). Like Machiavelli, Hobbes assumed that human beings are basically depraved and self-interested. Society's principal function is to provide opportunity for gain and glory, and the only form of equality possible or desirable among people inheres in their ability to kill each other. In "the state of nature," Hobbes writes in his best-known passage, life is "solitary, poor, nasty, brutish, and short."

A much more enlightened—by social work's standards—and somewhat more democratic perspective on the role of the state appeared in John Locke's seventeenth-century work, particularly his *Two Treatises on Civil Government*. For Locke, government authority depends on a contract between rulers and citizens, a limiting of power by mutual consent, "directed to no other end but the peace, safety, and public good of the people" (Political Philosophy 1988:977). Government depends on law, not force, people enjoy certain fundamental rights with which government should not interfere (to life, freedom, and property), government is the servant of the people and not its master, and the people's will should be determined by majority vote. A limited, constitutional state is necessary to protect citizens' rights to life, liberty, health, and possessions (Moon 1988:31). One of the practical consequences of Locke's staunch defense of property rights is the persistent linkage between capitalism and democracy.

Some of the most severe criticism of Locke came from John Stuart Mill, whose nineteenth-century writings have had an enormous—albeit frequently indirect and unrecognized—influence on contemporary social work and social welfare. Although Mill agreed with Locke in many respects, he had difficulty with Locke's views on natural rights and majority rule. In his essay, *Utilitarianism,* Mill argued that it can be shortsighted to regard some rights as inviolable. Since, according to utilitarianism, the rightness of any action is determined by the nature of its consequences, it would be a mistake to hold that certain rights should never be violated. We can say, for example, that one should never break a law, but what if a friend's life can be saved by breaking a law? Would it not be foolhardy to obey that law? For Mill, it would be. Similarly, one might argue that while individuals ordinarily have a right to their own property, taxation is justifiable if it provides necessary services and public assistance to needy citizens. Hence, for Mill there are no absolute rights; whether a right can be exercised depends on the consequences likely to obtain.

Mill was particularly troubled by Locke's emphasis on majority rule, and Mill's concerns are quite comparable to those expressed by today's social workers. Mill argues that the principle of majority rule needs to be limited, and sometimes trumped, by consideration of minority interests. As social workers know well, majority rule can be tyrannical, such as when it prohibits establishment of community-based facilities for special needs populations, deprives homeless citizens of shelter, or legislates racist policies.

Mill was particularly troubled by the prospects of gratuitous or paternalistic government interference in citizens' lives. Although Mill recognized that some offensive or destructive behaviors cannot be tolerated in a civilized society, he was concerned about unwarranted government intrusion into individuals' privacy (Spicker 1988:44–57). In modern times, Mill might be concerned about government's right to force homeless people into shelters or mentally ill but competent individuals into psychiatric institutions against their wishes. Mill's famous passage from his essay *On Liberty* clearly states his bias:

> The sole end for which mankind are warranted, individually or collectively, in interfering with the liberty of action of any of their number, is self-protection. That the only purpose for which power can be rightly exercised over any member of a civilized community, against his will, is to prevent harm to others. His own good, either physical or moral, is not a sufficient warrant. He cannot rightfully be compelled to do or forbear because it will be better for him to do so, because it will make him happier, because, in the opinions of others, to do so would be wise or even right. These are good reasons for remonstrating with him or reasoning with him, or persuading him, or entreating him, but not for compelling him, or visiting with him any evil in case he do otherwise. To justify that, the conduct from which it is desired to deter him must be calculated to produce evil to someone else. The only part of the conduct of anyone, for which he is amenable to society, is that which concerns others. In the part which merely concerns himself, his independence is, of right, absolute. Over himself, over his own body and mind, the individual is sovereign.

Among the clearest precursors of social workers' contemporary thinking about the welfare state and about the common good was Jean-Jacques Rousseau's eighteenth-century writings, particularly his *Social Contract*. Rousseau was a champion of egalitarianism and a critic of social hierarchies that oppressed the masses. He promoted what he called the "general will," a sort of moral will concerning the common good expressed by the community. Rousseau was particularly sensitive to the tension between individual freedom and equality, as reflected in what is perhaps his most famous comment, "Man was born free, but is everywhere in bondage." Rousseau recognized that property rights lead to inequality, and that enhancing equality is one of the principal challenges of a civilized society. He favored the formation of what he calls a "collective moral body" that is primarily concerned about the collective interest or good of society.

This brand of humanism, particularly its awareness of the tension between individual freedom and equality, is also reflected in the nineteenth-century works of the French writer Alexis de Tocqueville (*Democracy in America*) and the English philosopher T. H. Green (*Lectures on the Principles of Political Obligation*). Concerning equality, Tocqueville wrote, "We cannot prevent the conditions of men from becoming equal, but it depends upon ourselves whether the principle of equality will lead them to servitude or freedom, to knowledge or barbarism, to prosperity or wretchedness." Green was particularly concerned about securing the "common good" of society and minimizing inequality. Helping to lay the foundation of the British welfare state, Green favored a strong, centralized role for government in the provision of health care, housing, education, unemployment relief, and town planning.

No review of the philosophical underpinnings of contemporary thinking about social welfare would be complete without some discussion of Marxism. Although only a small percentage of social workers identify themselves as ideological Marxists, Marx's work has unquestionably had a significant influence on social work throughout its history.

Marx, of course, was primarily concerned about class struggle, oppression, and exploitation that are a function of capitalism—concerns that continue to preoccupy social workers. Marx's theory was couched in the concept of the "dialectic" as formulated by the nineteenth-century German philosopher G. W. F. Hegel. For Marx, capitalism is a passing stage in human history and is destined to be replaced by socialism. Like Hegel, Marx believed that nations must follow in lawlike, stepwise fashion a dialectical process where they first come into existence (the "thesis"), then develop an "opposing" nation that espouses fundamentally different values (the "antithesis"), and, finally, from the conflict between the two factions they produce a new nation (the "synthesis"), and so on. Friedrich Engels, who collaborated with Marx on *The Communist Manifesto*, provides a succinct summary of this phenomenon:

> In every historical epoch, the prevailing mode of economic production and exchange, and the social organization neces-

sarily following from it, form the basis upon which is built up, and from which alone can be explained, the political and intellectual history of that epoch; that consequently, the whole history of mankind (since the dissolution of primitive tribal society holding land in common ownership) has been a history of class struggles, contests between exploiting and exploited, ruling and oppressed classes. (Marx and Engels 1955:5)

Marx's economic theory contains the seeds of what has evolved into growing concern among many social workers about the baneful by-products of capitalism, where a profit-driven society has minimal regard for employment security or the welfare of the masses. For Marx, capitalists are motivated primarily to generate profits. To do so, they must continually enhance the means of production, either by refining existing forms of production or inventing new ones. In principle, these improvements increase production and reduce labor costs, thereby increasing profits. Another consequence of these improvements, however, is that jobs become obsolete or are eliminated. Entrepreneurs who are unable to improve their productivity and reduce their labor costs are not able to compete successfully with competitors' prices and, therefore, are likely to go out of business (further eliminating jobs). Hence, as capitalism evolves the wealthy tend to become wealthier and the poor tend to become poorer, with a consequent shrinking of the middle class. Social workers will recognize that today much concern is evident among some groups that this scenario is precisely what we are experiencing in the United States (Martin 1990:51–52; Primus 1989; Smith 1986).

According to Marx, over time workers will become increasingly resentful of this bifurcation of wealth, leading eventually to workers' (or the proletariat's) expropriation of owners' (or bourgeoisie's) wealth. A new society will emerge where the means of production are owned by the masses who do not exploit workers.

THE EMERGENCE OF THE WELFARE STATE

These various conceptions of the nature of society—in its social, political, and economic forms—have had substantial influence on contemporary thinking about social welfare, particularly with respect to the role of government, the private sector, and market forces. It is essential for social workers to appreciate the close connection between these philosophical perspectives on welfare and modern-day efforts to address citizens' needs.

Debate concerning the obligations of the state, or government institutions, to promote and maintain welfare has an ancient history. The balance between private and public responsibility for welfare has shifted over time and across nations, reflecting widely varying philosophical views concerning the state's proper role.

The growth of government responsibility for social welfare problems began largely out of concern for the poor. At the end of the Middle Ages, the developing nation-states of Western Europe had to contend with the problem of poverty. As economies and governments developed on a national scale, poverty became a national problem. National laws and ordinances concerning the treatment of the poor, vagrancy, and begging were enacted and ordinarily administered by local authorities (Rimlinger 1971). They frequently cited the individual's duty to work, the community's duty to provide work for the able-bodied and relief for the disabled, and forms of punishment to be inflicted on those who failed to comply.

Substantial changes in the treatment of the poor came about during the second half of the eighteenth century as a result of the Industrial Revolution and the American and French revolutions. National governments had to become increasingly concerned about problems resulting from large concentrations of poor people. As a result, national strategies were developed throughout Western Europe and the United States in an effort to respond to the needs of the poor. The welfare programs and poor laws that resulted were regarded for the most part as concessions that eighteenth- and nineteenth-century life required. Though certain individuals supported national welfare strategies for altruistic reasons, widespread support depended on arguments that aid to the poor was necessary to preserve the social order.

It is in these early attempts to devise national welfare programs that contemporary programs have their roots. For example, what is frequently referred to as the *welfare state*—where a national government accepts responsibility for some basic level of economic security and health of its citizens—has its origins in eighteenth-century Prussia and the *Landrecht,* or civil code, of 1794. This document, which is at least somewhat reminiscent of modern welfare legislation, stipulated that:

(1) It is the duty of the State to provide for the sustenance and support of those of its citizens who cannot . . . procure subsistence themselves; (2) work adapted to their strength and capacities shall be supplied to those who lack means and opportunity of earning a livelihood for themselves and those dependent upon them; (3) those who, for laziness, love of idleness, or other irregular proclivities, do not choose to employ the means offered them by earning a livelihood, shall be kept to useful work by compulsion and punishment under proper control. . . (6) the State is entitled and bound to take such measures as will prevent the destitution of its citizens and check excessive extravagance . . . and (15) the police authority of every place must provide for all poor and destitute persons, whose subsistence cannot be ensured in any other way. (Rimlinger 1971:94)

Since the earliest attempts at national policies, the growth of governmental involvement in social welfare has been accompanied consistently by considerable ideological debate concerning the proper limits of intervention by the state. This was especially apparent, for instance, during the period in which social insurance was formally introduced in Imperial Germany by Bismarck in the late nineteenth century, following, as it did, the laissez-faire policies of the eighteenth century discouraging the provision of aid to the poor.

The philosophical debate specifically concerning the role of the state in welfare matters has endured for centuries, stemming at least since the time of Plato and from the time of the decline of the kinship system in ancient Athens under the statesman Cleisthenes. The most significant chapter in the debate for social welfare was in the early nineteenth century, when mercantilist and laissez-faire doctrines clashed. Mercantilism was then the dominant economic principle in Great Britain and other major European nations. A central assumption under mercantilism was that the primary sources of a nation's power were a large population and precious metals. As a result, activities of the economic market were highly regulated, emigration was prohibited, and protective tariffs were imposed. It was assumed that "*Under prevailing conditions,* increases in heads would increase real income per head" and that, in order to discourage idleness, repressive poor laws needed to be imposed (Schumpeter 1963:251–52).

In contrast to mercantilism, the laissez-faire doctrine was based on an assumption that human welfare could be promoted and sustained if labor were allowed to find its own price in the market, if the creation of money were subject to a gold standard, and if goods and services were allowed to be freely exchanged between nations (Pinker 1979). Adam Smith trusted, for example, that some of the increases in wealth that resulted from a free-market economy and a laissez-faire policy would eventually find their way to the poor. Critics of Adam Smith and the laissez-faire perspective argued, however, that social welfare and national security brought about by government intervention were more important than the pursuit of profit under conditions of a free market:

> The prosperity of a nation depends on the achievement of a balance between the several productive processes of that nation, and only extensive government intervention can assure the achievement of such an equilibrium between the interests of agriculture, commerce, and manufacturing. The free market could not be relied upon to bring about a natural reconciliation of individual and national interests. Only governmental regulation could ensure that the long-term needs of the nation were not jeopardized by the short-term interests of individuals and sectional groups. (Pinker 1979:80)

The English Poor Law Reform Bill of 1834 represents what is perhaps the best example of the importance of this philosophical debate to those who were interested in poor relief in the nineteenth century. The Royal Poor Law Commission for Inquiring into the Administration and Practical Operation of the Poor Laws was dominated by a laissez-faire philosophy that—in the spirit of Adam Smith and David Ricardo—was critical of the Elizabethan Poor Law of 1601. The so-called classical economists believed that poverty was "the natural state of the wage-earning classes"; the poor law was an artificial creation of the state which taxed the middle and upper classes in order to provide care for the wayward needy (Trattner 1979:42–47).

One result of the commission's report was an end to public assistance for able-bodied persons, except in public institutions. Moreover, poverty was described in the report as a condition that resulted from the moral inferiority of individuals. As a consequence, poor relief was designed to increase "fear of insecurity, rather than to check its causes or even to alleviate its problems. At best, it would prevent starvation or death from exposure, but it would do so as economically and unpleasantly as possible" (Trattner 1979:47).

The growth of the state's role in welfare can be attributed in part to a declining confidence, following the Great Depression of the 1870s, in the ability of a free market to promote and sustain individual welfare. It is interesting to note that the Passenger Acts passed between 1842 and 1855, which were designed in part to discourage the mistreatment of paupers shipped to the United States by private firms, represent a significant move toward the development of government regulation. The European nations that began to industrialize in the late nineteenth century—most notably France, Prussia, Italy, and Russia—did so with extensive governmental involvement in the formulation of economic and social welfare policy (MacDonagh 1961). Government intervention was much more moderate in Great Britain, which was still attached to a laissez-faire and free-trade doctrine. Germany, on the other hand, which had a history of government involvement in economic policy, became under Bismarck the first so-called welfare state in Europe.

The development of contemporary national welfare programs has been influenced greatly by the early twentieth-century economic theories of John Maynard Keynes. Keynes drew on his understanding of mercantilist principles and applied them to problems of economic and social welfare in Great Britain. Keynes suggested that employment and investment could be stimulated by creating a system of flexible exchanges and international cooperation (Pinker 1979:113). He argued that the "outstanding faults of the economic society in which we live are its failure to provide for full employment and its arbitrary and inequitable distribution of wealth and incomes" (Keynes 1960:372). In response, Keynes claimed, government must become actively involved in economic and welfare policy: "The State will have to exercise a guiding influence on the propensity to consume, partly through its scheme of taxation, partly by fixing the rate of interest, and partly, perhaps, in other ways" (Keynes 1960:378). As Pinker (1979) has pointed out, these "other ways" included extensive social services, public investment programs, and, in general, a close association between the state and private enterprise (such as cooperative enterprise sponsored jointly by public and private organizations).

The spirit of some of Keynes's proposals was later carried forth by Sir William Beveridge who, in his classic 1942 study of British social security, foreshadowed and influenced the development of social welfare policy in every major nation of the world. The Beveridge Report outlined a comprehensive plan of social programs as "an attack upon want" (Beveridge 1942:6). The central concept of the report was the principle of a national minimum income needed for subsistence and was based on an assumption that individuals have a right to freedom from want to which the state must respond. His plan differed somewhat from the one in most other nations in that the level of benefit was to be determined by need rather than past contributions or past earnings (Rimlinger 1971). Beveridge was, at the same time, however, concerned about harmful effects of governmental involvement in welfare: "The State in organizing security should not stifle incentive, opportunity, responsibility; in establishing a national minimum, it should leave room and encouragement for voluntary action by each individual to provide more than that minimum for himself and his family" (Beveridge 1942: 6–7).

Beveridge's concern about the possibility that welfare benefits would discourage "incentive" and "responsibility" also crossed America's shores. Although welfare capitalism was gaining favor in the United States, it was with considerable ambivalence. As Gilbert (1983) notes:

> These early welfare measures were embraced with mixed motives. In extending their concern for the conditions of employee life beyond the production line, business leaders were certainly influenced by their need to mold a disciplined industrial work force out of the immigrant masses—an unpredictable, sometimes dangerous lot . . . The rise of welfare capitalism was fueled as much by these self-interests as by any altruistic desires to ameliorate the conditions of working people. (3)

IDEOLOGICAL CONCEPTIONS OF THE WELFARE STATE

The extent to which national governments intervene in welfare matters has grown considerably since the innovations of the nineteenth and early twentieth centuries. In the United States, for example, between 1929 and 1975 spending on social welfare bureaucracies increased (in constant dollars) from $12 billion to $286 billion. Between 1950 and 1975, financing of social welfare activities by the public sector moved from 65.9 percent to 72.7 percent. Per capita social welfare expenditures increased from $405 in 1950 to $1,775 in 1978 (in constant 1978 prices). The percentage of the

gross national product spent on social welfare also increased dra-
matically, from 3.9 percent in 1929 to 18.5 percent in 1985 (Gilbert
1983:4–7, 139, 142; Gilbert and Gilbert 1989:xi; Gutmann 1988:3;
Martin 1990:21).

Clearly, the welfare state has expanded in the United States—
and in nearly all other industrialized nations (Jansson 1988). Like
the blind men and the elephant, however, in spite of the welfare
state's obvious size, conceptions of its nature vary widely. Over the
years various models have emerged with respect to the welfare
state's philosophical foundation.

Perhaps the most familiar and simplistic model consists of conservative, liberal, and radical interpretations of the welfare state
(Atherton 1989; Blau 1989). As was hinted in the Beveridge Report, conservatives argue that the welfare state encourages personal and social irresponsibility more than it provides some measure of defense against poverty, unemployment, sickness, and so
on. From this perspective, generous welfare benefits encourage
sloth, teenage pregnancy, and other forms of dependence (Friedman 1962; George and Wilding 1976; Gilder 1981; Hayek 1944).
As the conservative critic Charles Murray argues, referring to recent social welfare spending, "We tried to provide more for the poor
and produced more poor instead. . . . We tried to remove the barriers to escape from poverty, and inadvertently built a trap" (Murray
1985:9).

The liberal perspective, in contrast, argues that social welfare
spending has been insufficient, and that this is one of the principal
reasons why current social problems are so vexing. Liberal critics
claim that stingy funding of social services has resulted in anemic
efforts to address such persistent problems as poverty, crime, unemployment, homelessness, and mental illness (see, for example,
Reich 1983).

The radical perspective, in contrast, is uniquely complex. As
Gutmann (1988) suggests, radicals tend to agree with conservatives that liberals demand too much of the welfare state, while also
agreeing with the liberals that the welfare state has not gone far
enough (also see Abramovitz 1988; Gough 1979; Piven and Cloward 1971, 1982). In contrast to liberals and conservatives, radicals
argue that the fiscal policies of a capitalist welfare state contradict
their own purposes:

> The capitalist welfare state either temporarily succeeds in
> providing a safety net for its citizens but consequently fails to

maintain a sound economy, or it temporarily succeeds in maintaining a sound economy but fails to protect those citizens most at the mercy of market forces. In both situations, private ownership of commercial property impedes the self-realization of citizens, especially those most vulnerable to fluctuations in the labor market and therefore least in control of their working lives. Welfare and capitalism are therefore a socially unsavory as well as economically unstable combination. (Gutmann 1988:5)

A more complex typology of philosophical perspectives on the welfare state, with richer texture and more subtlety, is offered by Gilbert (1983). Like most analyses, Gilbert's initially separates extant views into those of the "Left" and "Right." Critics on the Left perceive the welfare state as a "cunning device that takes just enough of the edge off the hardships of capitalism to keep the masses in check without altering the basic inequities of the market economy. . . . The low dose of collectivism injected through the welfare state acts to preserve rather than transform the capitalist order." In contrast, critics on the Right perceive the welfare state as "an insidious agent slowly corroding the work ethic and the spirit of capitalism" (Gilbert 1983:164).

From this rather typical bifurcation, however, Gilbert outlines various philosophical schools of thought concerning the appropriateness of government intervention, distributed along a bell-shaped curve of tolerance for the welfare state. Tolerance for the welfare state is low at both ends of the curve (relatively pure forms of socialism and capitalism), rising toward minimal acceptance up to strong endorsement at the apex (in the form of a mixed economy).

The harshest critics of the welfare state are Marxists (or socialists) and social Darwinists (capitalists), although their respective reservations are based on diametrically opposed ideological foundations. For Marxists, the modern welfare state simply does not go far enough in its efforts to provide for those in need. Marxists prefer a "welfare society" to a welfare state, where all economic matters occur in a social market for the common good, consistent with the oft-cited maxim, "From each according to his ability, to each according to his needs." Modest reforms of the welfare state—or tinkering—cannot change the fundamental defects of capitalism that produce daunting economic inequality and related social problems. Moreover, whatever domestic calm we experience is, to a great extent, a function of coercive measures exerted by government bureaucracies (for engaging discussion of the social control functions of public welfare policy see Hawkesworth 1985 and Piven and Cloward 1971).

Social Darwinists, in contrast, view the welfare state as unwarranted and counterproductive interference with natural evolution. The competitive forces of the free market ultimately encourage perfection and progress, by weeding out the weak and cultivating the economic garden that allows the "fittest" to survive.

Between these extreme—and familiar—views are several intermediate ones. *Syndicalist socialism*, for example, supports various forms of collective intervention to enhance social welfare, although it shares with laissez-faire capitalism considerable suspicion of the state and centralized government bureaucracy. From this perspective, industrial society should be organized in such a way that workers have direct control over the means of production, through worker management and local authority over centralized government programs.

This more moderate position on the Left is counterbalanced by the views of *classical capitalists* on the Right. For classical capitalists, such as Adam Smith and Jeremy Bentham (and the more recent versions offered by Milton Friedman and Friedrich Hayek), government should properly assume a range of functions that go beyond law enforcement and other forms of peacekeeping. Friedman (1962) recognizes the need for government to address poverty, and Hayek (1944) concludes, "There can be no doubt that some minimum of food, shelter, and clothing sufficient to preserve health and the capacity to work can be assured to everybody" (cited in Gilbert 1983:168). Both these welfare state critics, however, urge forms of assistance that minimize the need for and presence of government bureaucracy.

As Gilbert notes, both the syndicalist socialist and classical capitalist views share a distrust of centralized state bureaucracy, and this bias has found expression in the design of a number of major welfare state initiatives in recent decades. The doctrine of "maximum feasible participation" fostered under the Economic Opportunity Act of 1964, the mandate for "widespread citizen participation" in the Demonstration Cities and Metropolitan Development Act of 1966, and the emphasis in the Reagan and Bush administrations on self-help and voluntary-sector responsibility for social welfare all reflect this orientation.

Stronger support for state-sponsored intervention comes from *Fabian socialism* and *interest-group liberalism*. Fabian socialism—based on the strategy of gradual change embraced by the Roman general, Fabius Maximus—assumes that collectivist ideas and reforms will lead eventually to widespread acceptance of socialist ideals and principles. Fabians, who have had considerable influence on the design and operation of the British welfare state, typically support expansion of the boundaries of the welfare state (including the provision of social services and public assistance) without calling for radical dismantling of capitalism (see Titmuss 1958).

Interest-group liberalism, on the other hand, while also supporting an expanded role for government social services and public assistance, is not inspired by socialist ideals. Rather, it is the product of humanistic values and practical recognition of the need to improve social conditions produced by capitalism.

The true middle-ground view—which is not to say the most enlightened, necessarily—is held by supporters of a *mixed economy*, which combines a respect for capitalism with significant collectivist instincts. This is the perspective that seems to be embraced by today's mainstream social workers. As Gilbert suggests, the result is a "liberal creed" that includes an "almost negative prescription: not too much public, not too much private" (Gilbert 1983:171). He goes on to say that the mixed economy view strives to:

> achieve the proper balance between competing values that enhance the human condition. Liberty and security are among the most prominent of these values. If the balance is tipped too far in one direction liberty may be smothered in a thick blanket of collective security, too far in the other direction and collective security may be shattered by the unrestrained clash of individual interests. In the balance between freedom and security the social market lends its weight to security. The advancement of communal security, however, represents a narrow view of the social market's purpose in a mixed economy. A broader conception of purpose would further encompass the competing notions of equality: equality of material conditions and equality of opportunity, that mighty precipitator of material inequality. Here the social market leans toward reducing material inequality through the redistribution of resources. (172)

THE LIMITS OF GOVERNMENT INTERVENTION

Clearly, a central theme in political philosophy concerns the state's proper role in the provision of social welfare. An enduring tension exists between those who view the state as a burdensome, intrusive, paternalistic, and counterproductive beast and those who see in the state the potential (albeit often unfulfilled) to provide essential succor to those who are poor, disabled, or otherwise disadvantaged.

The philosophical debate concerning the limits of state intervention has centered historically on the compromises that necessarily inhere in systems of government that simultaneously value individual freedom and social security or equality. Typically, attempts by nations to design programs to care for its poor and disabled have required some sacrifice of individual freedom, either as a result of regulations that prohibit certain activities—such as subjecting people to harsh working conditions or unsafe living conditions—or those that require certain activities—such as paying taxes to support welfare programs or sending one's children to school.

Thoughtful arguments have been offered over the years both in favor of and opposed to extensive government intervention in welfare matters. Supporters of government sponsorship of welfare programs have argued that an economic system based entirely on principles of free enterprise does not provide adequate protection to individuals who suffer the sometimes tragic effects of unemployment, abuse, poverty, physical and mental disability, and old age. Proponents of government sponsorship of welfare programs frequently point to the turbulent and unsettling Depression years following 1929 as evidence of the misery that can result from an unpredictable and insufficiently restrained system of free enterprise unsupported by national welfare policies. They point out that when Western nations moved from agrarian to industrial economies, individuals lost control over much of their economic well-being (Bruce 1965; Furniss and Tilton 1977; Pinker 1979; Wilensky 1975). Workers became subject to factors such as structural and cyclical unemployment, market fluctuation, and harsh labor practices and working conditions. As Goodin (1988) argues in his insightful and vigorous defense of, *at the very least,* a "minimal welfare state":

Perhaps it is permissible to depend upon the state for certain aspects of our welfare, but not others. Perhaps the point is

that, in a market society, you should be able to provide basic
food, clothing, and shelter for yourself and your family through
your own efforts. That explains why it is deemed shameful to
depend upon the state to do so on your behalf: it constitutes
an admission of inadequacy, "a notarized manifestation of
misery, of weakness, or misconduct on the part of the recipient" (Tocqueville).

Sometimes, however, it is simply untrue that you can provide for your family's basic welfare needs through your own
efforts. . . . [This] is an argument that the state *should* provide
for people's basic needs. Furthermore, it is an argument that
the state should do that much *at the very least*. There is
nothing in the positive case for a minimal welfare state that I
shall be developing (as there is in the New Right's negative
case for a minimal welfare state) to debar the state from doing
more than relieving the destitute. (365–366, 18–19)

Opponents of government involvement in welfare programs argue that government interference in the private market inevitably
results in a series of unwanted consequences that, in the long run,
jeopardize welfare rather than safeguard it. In particular, such
critics frequently claim that attempts by government to guarantee
employment, provide generous public assistance benefits, subsidize
housing and food, and impose price controls weaken communal
ties and mutual aid and increase the likelihood that incentives to
work will be destroyed, taxes will increase, and incentives for individuals to train and seek advancement will diminish. In addition,
critics argue, government-sponsored welfare programs will con-
strain individual freedom. Opponents of extensive government involvement in welfare programs generally claim that both individual
freedom and well-being are best protected and promoted under
conditions of a competitive market that is not subjected to regulations imposed by public-sector welfare policies (Friedman 1962;
Hayek 1944). As Nozick (1974) argues in his provocative book,
Anarchy, State and Utopia:

Our main conclusions about the state are that a minimal state,
limited to the narrow functions of protection against force,
theft, fraud, enforcement of contracts, and so on, is justified;
that any more extensive state will violate persons' rights not
to be forced to do certain things, and is unjustified; and that
the minimal state is inspiring as well as right. Two noteworthy
implications are that the state may not use its coercive appa-

ratus for the purpose of getting some citizens to aid others, or in order to prohibit activities to people for their *own* good or protection. (ix)

PUBLIC- AND PRIVATE-SECTOR RESPONSIBILITY

Critics of substantial state involvement in welfare often make several additional points to supplement their concern about gratuitous government intervention. First, they argue that bloated public-sector spending exacerbates economic problems. The Reagan administration, for example, argued that public spending on social welfare needed to be reduced to shrink the federal deficit, thereby reducing taxation and enhancing incentives and capital for private individuals and firms to invest in economic production. According to administration officials, this attempt to reduce the federal deficit, increase productivity, and lessen intervention in the private sector, consistent with "supply side economics," was the only sensible response to the "demand side" doctrine of economics that characterized earlier administrations (Hawkes 1982). In addition, the administration claimed, reduced government spending would result in weaker government purchasing power, which would increase the private money supply, investment in new plants and equipment, employment, and—because of lower tax rates and consequent financial rewards for hard work—productivity (Reamer 1983a).

In addition, critics of extensive public responsibility for social welfare argue that attempts to deliver welfare-related services typically are less efficient than comparable private-sector efforts. The assumption here is that the "invisible hand" of the private market and free enterprise will encourage private providers to generate and sustain services of high quality in order to obtain an initial contract, and competition from other providers will impose "natural" incentives to control costs without resorting to complex and burdensome government regulations. Private agencies can also expand and contract their payroll as the demand for services changes, unlike public agencies that may have difficulty terminating or quickly hiring civil servants.

According to this perspective, social welfare clients or "consumers" should also be encouraged to shop for services provided to them, much as customers shop for goods and services in stores. Promoting choice among clients presumably increases their control over their own lives and presents providers with incentives to create and maintain quality services. In the end, clients who have the freedom to choose and purchase services—with government-subsidized vouchers, perhaps—will vote with their feet (Reamer 1983a).

A number of these contemporary concerns have their roots in nineteenth-century political philosophy. In his *The Philosophy of Right,* published in 1821, Hegel commented on the tendency of a market economy to produce great poverty alongside great wealth, and that this can ultimately threaten the stability of a culture:

> The poor still have the needs common to civil society, and yet since society has withdrawn from them the natural means of acquisition . . . their poverty leaves them more or less deprived of all the advantages of society, of the opportunity of acquiring skill or education of any kind, as well as of the administration of justice, the public health services, and often even of the consolations of religion. (in Moon 1988:28)

Hegel suggested several possible responses to the inadequacies and cruel by-products of the market, although he stopped short of a simple redistribution of income or wealth to the poor. One proposal, for example, was for the state to regulate the prices of essential commodities to enable the poor to purchase them. This suggestion, of course, is frequently criticized because of concern that such price regulation would cause damaging distortions in the market.

Hegel also suggested the development of "corporations" that would maintain funds contributed by their members, who would use them in times of crisis (a form of private insurance). These corporations would consist of "producer organizations" in each industry or trade and would link the state and private society (Moon 1988:29–30).

Whatever the merits of Hegel's specific proposals, his perspective represents widespread sentiment among many political philosophers that, at minimum, some form of state-sponsored intervention is essential to assuage the effects of private-market capitalism on human welfare. This sentiment is represented well by Goodin's (1988) conclusion:

> The problem to which the welfare state is the solution is the risk of exploitation of dependencies. Such exploitation could well occur in the course of interactions in ordinary economic markets. By removing a wide range of interactions from the market, the welfare state aims to prevent that form of exploi-

tation. Similar exploitation could equally well occur in the course of interactions between benefactor and beneficiary in the context of old-style public or private charities. By tightly defining the legal rights and duties of welfare claimants and welfare dispensers, the welfare state aims to prevent that form of exploitation, too. (21–22)

Richard Titmuss's modern classic, *The Gift Relationship* (1972), offers an unusually valuable, insightful, and influential case study of the risks and benefits associated with private-sector delivery of a valued social service. Titmuss set out to study these well-known trade-offs in his comparative analysis of blood donation in Great Britain, the United States, the Soviet Union, South Africa, and Japan. He used blood donation as a prototypical case of a critically important service whose supply and distribution are dependent on public- and private-sector involvement. Titmuss points out that in the United States, private-sector responsibility for blood donation and distribution is defended on the grounds that market forces, in the form of competition and the pursuit of profit, lead to greater efficiency and higher standards of care. Titmuss concluded that such a system "is highly wasteful of blood, [that] shortages, chronic and acute, characterize the demand and supply position and make illusory the concept of equilibrium," and that "the so-called pluralism of the American market results in more bureaucratization, avalanches of paper and bills, and much greater administrative, accounting and computer over-heads" (Titmuss 1973:232). Titmuss also claimed that blood banks in which donors are paid are far more likely to obtain and distribute contaminated blood, since such an arrangement is likely to attract individuals who are substance abusers, malnourished, or who have hepatitis. Consequently, individuals receiving blood from paid donors allegedly face much greater risk of disease and death than do those receiving blood from unpaid donors (Higgins 1981:145–46). In the end, Titmuss (1972) argues, the private-market consumer fares less well than his or her counterpart who receives assistance from nonmarket sources:

> In commercial blood markets the consumer is not king. He has less freedom to live unharmed; little choice of determining price; is more subject to shortages in supply; is less free from bureaucratization; has fewer opportunities to express altruism; and exercises fewer checks and controls in relation

to consumption, quality and external costs. Far from being
sovereign, he is often exploited. (233; cited in Higgins
1981:146)

Although Titmuss's methodology and conclusions have been challenged by a number of scholars (see Reisman 1977; Sapolsky and
Finkelstein 1977), his novel study certainly raised a series of critical questions about the various trade-offs generated by private-
market efforts to deliver social services.

Titmuss's concerns are particularly noteworthy and sobering in
light of the dramatic resurgence in recent years of a market-based
orientation throughout the world. Contrary to Joseph Schumpeter's
assertion that "the ethos of capitalism is gone" (1950:410), we saw
by the late 1980s that a number of socialist and communist nations
seriously considered and even embraced a variety of market-ori-
ented reforms—epitomized by the stunning collapse of the Soviet
Union in 1991. Moreover, Margaret Thatcher's election to a third
term—built on a platform of capitalist reform—was the second
largest conservative victory since World War II and the first con-
secutive three-term victory by a British prime minister since the
1820s (Gilbert and Gilbert 1989:33). And, of course, all of this
occurred during politically conservative presidential administrations in the United States that evoked a variety of market reforms
designed to return many services previously provided by the public
sector to the private sector, including health care, psychiatric care,
day care, homemaker services, employment training, and even
corrections.

Much of the contentious debate about the privatization of social
welfare has focused on the concept of profit. Not surprisingly,
ardent supporters of private-sector involvement in social welfare
argue that profit incentives ultimately enhance efficiency and quality of service. From this point of view, the profit motive helps to
streamline the delivery of services, minimize wasted resources, and
focus agencies' effort on demonstrating the quality of care they
offer. As Nathan Glazer notes, particularly strong ideological support exists in American society for profit-oriented services, even in
the social welfare arena, and

> a remarkably strong sentiment that problems should be taken
> care of by autonomous, independent institutions, and even by
> profit-making businesses, rather than by the state. That one
> can handle social problems, such as the problem of the poor,
> through profit making might seem bizarre; yet this is widely

believed to be a reasonable approach and not only by Repub-
licans. (quoted in Gilbert and Gilbert 1989:40)

Putting aside the remarkably complex debate concerning the
relative effectiveness and efficiency of social services offered by the
for-profit and nonprofit sectors (for illustrative discussions see
Abramovitz 1986; Fottler, Smith, and James 1981; Gilbert and
Gilbert 1989; Judge and Knapp 1985; Mendelsohn 1974; Weisbrod
1988; and Wooden 1976), the resolution of this debate rests to a
considerable extent on philosophical sentiment. In short, although
profit-driven incentives may offer economic benefit, many critics of
proprietary involvement in social services view as anathema profit
generated by attempts to respond to human need and misery. Gilbert (1983) captures this sentiment eloquently:

> As previously suggested, the social market to some extent can
> accommodate to and benefit from an infusion of competition,
> choice, profit, self-interest, and other methods and incentives
> of the market economy. Values inhere in these means as
> much as in their ends. Employed too vigorously, however,
> these methods and incentives eventually must vitiate the val-
> ues and purposes of the social market. Competition and self-
> interest seldom cultivate equality of material conditions and
> communal security. The elevation of consumer choice inhib-
> its thoughts of individual sacrifice for the common good.
> Stringent concerns for economic efficiency lend brief consid-
> erations to the adequacy of social provisions. The pursuit of
> profit engenders little compassion for the economic circum-
> stances of others. In essence, this issue hinges on the contra-
> dictory potential of these methods to undermine the broad
> values of the social market while enhancing the efficiency of
> its distributive activities. (178)

DISTRIBUTIVE JUSTICE

A central theme that runs throughout philosophical literature on
welfare concerns the allocation of resources, such as wealth, health
care, housing, and other social services. For social workers, gross
inequality is a deeply troubling phenomenon that exacerbates the
chronic disadvantage experienced by many of the profession's clients.
Distributive justice has been of enduring concern among politi-

cal philosophers. Aristotle offered one of the earliest conceptualiza-
tions of justice when he distinguished between *corrective* justice,
relating to punishment and retribution, and *distributive* justice,
relating primarily to the allocation of resources.

As Spicker (1988) suggests, distributive justice can be defined
and understood in several ways. The eighteenth-century philosopher David Hume, for example, viewed justice rather conserva-
tively as an extension of property rights. That is, justice is determined in part by defensible principles related to the acquisition of
property, transfer of property, occupation of property, and so on.
For Hume, extreme concentrations of wealth and property may not
be a problem as long as established property rights are respected
(see Nozick 1974 for a more recent defense of the relevance of
property rights).

In contrast, Herbert Spencer defined justice in terms of *desert*,
in that what people have a right to is a function of what they
contribute to the broader society. For Kropotkin, the Russian anar-
chist, justice is determined by need and may require some form of
redistribution.

Theorists who view justice in terms of property rights tend to be
critical of any sort of redistributive program designed to reduce
inequality. Aside from their various economic arguments concerning disincentives introduced by redistribution of property or wealth
(for example, related to hard work or financial investment in production), these critics tend to claim, as Spicker (1988) does, "In
the simplest terms, redistribution would be theft" (138). Schoek
argues, in addition, that redistribution is nothing more than envy—
the envy of people who want the possessions of others (cited in
Spicker 1988:138; also see Hayek 1976).

Clearly, the concept of equality is central to any discussion of
distributive justice. It strikes at the heart of social workers' concern
about disadvantage, oppression, and exploitation. As R. H. Tawney
(1964) observed in his classic, *Equality:*

> What is repulsive is not that one man should earn more than
> others, for where community of environment, and a common
> education and habit of life, have bred a common tradition of
> respect and consideration, these details of the counting house
> are forgotten or ignored. It is that some classes should be
> excluded from the heritage of civilization which others enjoy,
> and that the fact of human fellowship, which is ultimate and
> profound, should be obscured by economic contrasts, which

are trivial and superficial. What is important is not that all men should receive the same pecuniary income. It is that the surplus resources of society should be so husbanded and applied that it is a matter of minor significance whether they receive it or not. (113)

The concept of equality has been defined in a variety of ways, particularly as the concept pertains to social work and social welfare (Dworkin 1981). First, there is what might be called *absolute equality*, where resources (wealth, property, access to services, and so on) are divided equally among all people. This is sometimes known as *equality of result* (Spicker 1988:127). There is also *equality of opportunity*, which is concerned less with the ultimate outcome of distributive mechanisms than with the opportunity individuals have to gain access to desired resources. Examples include the use of a lottery or the principle of "first come-first served" to distribute resources. The concept of equality of opportunity also might entail the provision of remedial services to enhance opportunities for disadvantaged individuals to compete for scarce or limited resources (Reamer 1990:49–50).

In a penetrating analysis, Rae (1981) suggests that four practical (and somewhat overlapping) mechanisms can be used to enhance equality and minimize inequality. The first is the *maximin* policy (maximizing the minimum), where minimum standards for housing, education, health care, and so on, are raised. A second approach is to address the *ratio* of inequality, or increasing the resources of those who are worst off in relation to those who are best off. A third policy aims for the *least difference*, where the goal is to reduce the range of inequality. And the fourth is the *minimax* principle, whose goal is to reduce the advantage of those who are most privileged, that is, minimize the maximum (Spicker 1988:130).

It is impossible, not to mention inappropriate, to discuss the nagging problem of inequality without confronting the debate concerning affirmative action. This is, of course, a central issue for social workers. In principle, affirmative action strategies are designed to provide disadvantaged individuals with greater access to resources and equal opportunity (and the requisite skills) to compete for available resources. Critics of affirmative action claim, however, that this form of distributive justice is, in fact, unjust in that it simply stimulates a new form of discrimination against the more privileged. As Spicker (1988) says, "If positive discrimination is egalitarian, it is because it compensates people in one sector for disadvantage in another, or because it makes up for past disadvantage. It may achieve equality of result overall, but it does so at the expense of equal treatment and equal opportunity. The argument is that inequality in one respect may lead to greater inequality in others" (132).

A considerable portion of contemporary social workers' thinking about distributive justice has been influenced, or at the very least stimulated, by John Rawls's modern philosophical classic, A Theory of Justice (1971). Rawls bases much of his argument on the concept of a "social contract" that is to be used to establish a just society. He derives two core principles to enhance justice: First, liberty is the most important rule of social justice, and a just society must preserve liberty. Second, whatever inequalities exist must be acceptable to everyone.

Rawls's rather abstract theory assumes that individuals who are formulating a moral principle by which to be governed are in an "original position" of equality and that each individual is unaware of his or her own attributes and status that might represent relative advantage or disadvantage. Under this "veil of ignorance" it is assumed that individuals will produce a moral principle that protects the least advantaged. Rawls's "difference principle," which states that goods must be distributed in a manner designed to benefit the least advantaged, includes a requirement to aid those in need and provides an important safeguard against applications of classic utilitarianism that might sacrifice the needs of the disadvantaged for a greater aggregation of good (Reamer 1990:51). In a just society, according to Rawls, some differences in wealth and assets would be acceptable only if those less well off benefit as a result. In addition, all offices would be open to all under conditions of equality of opportunity.

Rawls argues that these principles of justice can best be practiced under a regime of competitive markets and some degree of state intervention to correct market imperfections and to ensure equal opportunity. Although Rawls favors competitive markets for the usual reasons related to economic efficiency, he sees competitive markets as an important device for ensuring equal liberty and equal opportunity. For Rawls, markets protect the "important liberty" of free choice of occupation, since "in the absence of some differences in earnings as these arise in a competitive scheme, it is hard to see how . . . certain aspects of a command society inconsistent with liberty can be avoided" (quoted in Krouse and McPherson 1988:81).

Rawls is particularly concerned about income derived through labor. Ideally, Rawls says, in a democracy that accommodates privately held property, full employment is maintained by what he dubs the "stabilization branch." This branch seeks to ensure full employment and to avoid "wage slavery" by promoting strong aggregate demand and tight labor markets. Further, since most workers would derive part of their income from property ownership and a minimum income would be guaranteed, no class of workers would be easily exploited. By investing in educational and training opportunities, the supply of skilled individuals would increase, thereby limiting their income (as a function of the laws of supply and demand); at the same time, the supply of persons who, for whatever reason, must take unskilled jobs would decrease, thereby increasing their income (Krouse and McPherson 1988:91–92). As Rawls (1971:307) says, with many more persons receiving the benefits of training and education, "the supply of qualified individuals is much greater. When there are no restrictions on entry or imperfections on the capital market for loans (or subsidies) for education, the premium earned by those better endowed is far less. The relative difference in earnings between the more favored and the lowest income class tends to close."

For Rawls, the economic and social advantages some people enjoy because of the "natural fortune" into which they are born—with accompanying initial endowments of natural talent, property, skill, and luck (Krouse and McPherson 1988:95)—are morally arbitrary. Ensuring greater equality in the initial distribution of property and skill level would lessen the need for significant redistribution of wealth by tax and transfer programs administered by the welfare state. This is Rawls's (1971) principal argument for an adequate "social minimum," progressive inheritance taxation across generations, some degree of income redistribution, public policies that promote equal opportunity in education, and so on:

> The social system is to be designed so that the resulting distribution is just however things turn out. To achieve this end it is necessary to set the social and economic process within the surroundings of suitable political and legal institutions. Without an appropriate scheme of these background institutions the outcome of the distributive process will not be just. . . . [In] addition to maintaining the usual kinds of social overhead capital, the government tries to insure equal chances of education and culture for persons similarly endowed and

motivated either by subsidized private schools or by establishing a public school system. It also enforces and underwrites equality of opportunity in economic activities and in the free choice of occupation. This is achieved by policing the conduct of private firms and private associations and by preventing the establishment of monopolistic restrictions and barriers to the more desirable positions. Finally, the government guarantees a social minimum either by family allowances and special payments for sickness and unemployment, or more systematically by such devices as a graded income supplement (a so-called negative income tax). (275)

Rawls's conceptualization of social justice has been viewed by some as "a philosophical apologia for an egalitarian brand of welfare-state capitalism" (Wolff 1977:195; also see Barry 1973; Buchanan 1982; and Daniels 1975). Others (Krouse and McPherson 1988) argue that the degree of equalization of property entailed by Rawls's framework moves society considerably beyond existing examples of welfare-state capitalism and is seriously flawed. Nonetheless, whatever the ultimate merits of his ambitious set of proposals, Rawls's provocative statement has clearly served to rivet much needed attention on the concept of distributive justice and its implications for social welfare and the welfare state.

WELFARE AND RIGHTS

Much of the philosophical analysis of welfare, the welfare state, and distributive justice is anchored in the concept of *rights,* or specifically what Hohfield (cited in Spicker 1988:58) aptly refers to as *claim-rights,* which imply duties on other people. A number of scholars (see, for example, Block et al. 1987; Piven and Cloward 1982) have argued that welfare should be viewed as a fundamental right that offers essential protection against the destructive by-products of a capitalist system (for example, poverty, unemployment, and high-cost housing and health care), and that society has a correlative duty to respond to these rights. Plant expresses somewhat similar sentiments when he argues that because welfare rights can be counted among our fundamental rights as humans, a legitimate state would have to be a welfare state (Plant 1985; Plant, Lesser, and Taylor-Gooby 1980; also see Moon 1988).

Debate about the concept of welfare as a right is rooted in two distinct philosophical traditions (Blau 1989). According to one relatively conservative tradition, most closely associated with John Locke, individual citizens acquire rights by virtue of their financial stake—in the form of property held to counterbalance the state's power—in the society. As Moon (1988) observes:

> From this perspective, we can see the welfare state as an essentially internal development of the idea of human rights that is basic to the liberal tradition. Just as Locke asserted that a limited constitutional state is necessary to protect our rights to life, liberty, health, and possessions, proponents of this view argue that the welfare state is required to guarantee a wider set of rights, including the "social" rights to employment, economic security, health care, and education. (31)

In contrast, a more radical democratic tradition holds that people need protection from both the power of government and the power of private property. As Blau (1989) notes, "Invoking the communitarian vision of personal rights and popular democracy, this tradition declares that commodities such as medical care and affordable housing are a natural right" (36).

From the conservative vantage point, social welfare benefits represent a form of charity organized by the state; they are not based on any assumption about rights. At the other, more radical extreme, welfare rights are absolute and unconditional. The intermediate view is that welfare is neither charity nor an absolute entitlement; rather, individuals' welfare claims must be balanced and weighed against competing political, social, and economic claims.

It is particularly useful to speculate about the implications of a rights-based view of welfare with respect to a concept that is fundamental to social work clients' well-being: work. Work has certainly been one of the lightning rods in debate about the social welfare state, welfare rights, and various social welfare models. In short, the chronic challenge social workers and policy analysts have faced has been to devise a strategy that provides support to the needy without undermining their incentive to work (assuming, of course, that we are focusing on the nondisabled needy).

Attempts to strike a balance between a level of benefits that is sufficient to ensure a reasonable standard of living and one that discourages work date back at least to the English Poor Laws. During that period, debate about the relationship between welfare and work was couched in moralistic language concerning religious views about the inherent value and virtue of work as a means of character building, in addition to being influenced by fear of violence and social disruption that unemployment might foment (Higgins 1981:101). European nations and the United States, in particular, struggled to design welfare programs that balanced these trade-offs as much as possible, as evidenced by the various distinctions among "deserving" and "undeserving" poor, "impotent" and "able-bodied" poor, "indoor" and "outdoor" relief, and so on. Two central questions here are relevant to social work. One concerns whether able-bodied individuals have a *duty* to work, particularly in exchange for welfare benefits; the second concerns whether individuals, particularly in a capitalist nation, have a *right* to work.

As noted above, debate concerning welfare benefits and the extent to which individuals have a right to them represents one of the most persistent themes in social welfare history, dating back at least to the Elizabethan Poor Law of 1601. Funds to administer the original Poor Law were raised through taxes and administered by local parishes. The law was designed to provide aid to three categories of individuals who were dependent and had no relatives to support them: those who were involuntarily unemployed, helpless adults (the old, sick, and disabled), and dependent children. Work was to be provided by the community for individuals who were involuntarily unemployed, and helpless adults were to be cared for in private homes or almshouses. Dependent children were to be apprenticed.

It is clear that as early as the seventeenth century, sharp distinctions were made between individuals who, through no particular fault of their own, required, and had a right to, assistance (such as those who suffered unemployment because of unstable market conditions, the old, and the infirm), and those who were considered to be largely responsible for their own destitute state. These so-called undeserving poor generally included beggars, vagrants, and other able-bodied individuals who were unwilling to work. Jailing and physical punishment were not uncommon treatments for them.

Distinctions between the deserving and undeserving poor have persisted ever since the Elizabethan era. They were evident in debate around the English Poor Law reforms of 1834, the development of the first Charity Organization Society, the settlement house movement, the social insurance programs proposed early in the twentieth century, the creation of the first state department of public welfare in 1917, and the spate of social security, public assistance, and welfare programs created following the tragic era of the Great Depression of the 1930s.

At the heart of the welfare debate has been the issue of whether benefits should be regarded as a right or a privilege. The concept of welfare benefits as a right suggests that people have a duty or obligation to assist those who are destitute (Marshall 1981). As Spicker (1988) observes:

> The movement, in the United Kingdom and the United States, for "welfare rights" has been in part an attempt to convert moral rights into positive ones [rights which have a sanction of means of enforcement], but it has also used existing positive rights, in the legal system, to establish a moral position. The welfare rights movement . . . has tried in a number of ways to establish a right to a basic minimum income. (68)

The concept of welfare as a privilege, however, has a significantly different meaning. It suggests that individuals receive benefits because of the community's generosity and willingness to provide them, not because poor people have a formal right to them. As Epstein states, "Welfare payments are never a matter of legal entitlements of the recipients, but only an expression of collective benevolence by the transferrers" (cited in Elster 1988:58). The distinction between welfare as a right and as a privilege may appear subtle; in fact, it has significantly shaped the extent to which aid has been provided to the poor throughout history.

A related question, with different political and social implications, concerns whether individuals have a formal right to work. That is, does the state have a positive duty to provide conditions of full employment for its citizens? Elster (1988) presents the central issue succinctly:

> Unemployment is endemic in capitalism. So is the demand for a right to work, as a remedy for that state of affairs. Ever since the *droit au travail* was the battle cry of the workers in the French Revolution of 1848, the claim has tended to surface whenever unemployment levels have been high. In the last ten or fifteen years, in particular, the proposal to create a legal right to work has been put forward and discussed in most Western countries. Conversely, the existence of an effective right to work is widely perceived as the major argument for the centrally planned economies of Eastern Europe. If mass unemployment is the Achilles heel of capitalism, the right to a job is the backbone of socialism. (53)

What is meant by the phrase "right to work"? In its most conservative form, it entails an obligation on the part of the state to enhance employment through such mechanisms as wage subsidies, unemployment taxes, stimulation of demand through government purchasing, business investment incentives, protection against foreign competition, assistance in the development of new firms or industries, and so on. Although these mechanisms may enhance employment, they tend to fall short of full employment. In its more radical form, the right to work entails substitution of public ownership for private ownership and the goal of full employment (Nickel 1978–1979).

Clearly, the concept of rights is central to any philosophical consideration of welfare. Not surprisingly, many competing perspectives are at play concerning the extent to which welfare is a right, as opposed to a privilege, and the extent to which individuals have a right to work. As Blau (1989) concludes, "There is no easy way of reconciling the differences among these views. But the concept of rights is a rich one that can help to illuminate the premises on which theories of the welfare state are based" (36).

IN PURSUIT OF THE COMMON GOOD AND THE PUBLIC INTEREST

From social work's unique vantage point, social welfare, in its many forms of services and benefits, is aimed ultimately at the enhancement of individuals' quality of life and that of the community. Social work's metier is its simultaneous concern about individual clients' well-being and amelioration of broad-based, deep-seated social problems that threaten the fabric and viability of the surrounding culture. It is this concern that gives rise to social work's enduring preoccupation with the role of the state and private sector in welfare, welfare rights, distributive justice, and so on.

This century-old preoccupation within social work, its most distinguishing attribute, has a philosophical anchor in the concepts of the *common good* and the *public interest*. Although these terms are often used interchangeably, they have different origins and meaning.

The concept of the common good emphasizes the communal and has its roots in ancient Greek political thought. The concept was revitalized during the Renaissance and, over time, played a central role in the political theory of civic republicanism. As Jennings, Callahan, and Wolf (1987) suggest, the common good incorporates a vision of society as a community whose members join in a shared pursuit of values and goals that they embrace in common, and who understand that the good of individuals is dependent on the good of the broader community: "The common good, therefore, refers to that which constitutes the well-being of the community— its safety, the integrity of its basic institutions and practices, the preservation of its core values. It also refers to the *telos* or end toward which the members of the community cooperatively strive— the 'good life,' human flourishing, and moral development" (6). Service by professionals that promotes the common good includes:

> the distinctive and critical perspective the various professions have to offer on basic human values, and on facets of the human good and the good life. It also includes the professions' contribution to what may be called civic discourse or public philosophy—that ongoing, pluralistic conversation in a democratic society about our shared goals, our common purposes, and the nature of the good life in a just social order. (6)

In contrast, the concept of the public interest emerged in the seventeenth and eighteenth centuries. At first it referred to national security and prosperity goals that enlightened monarchs should pursue in their economic and foreign policies. Over time it began to refer to the broad collective goal that any legitimate government should pursue and served as an intellectual foundation for the social philosophies of liberalism, utilitarianism, and democratic pluralism. Its principal assumption is that society is a rational alliance of primarily self-interested individuals whose collective good is constituted by the collection or aggregation of private interests (Jennings, Callahan, and Wolf 1987).

Thus, there is nothing inherently communal about the concept of the public interest. The public interest is promoted by enhancing individuals' pursuit of their own interests. Professionals' contribution to the public interest can be carried out by the delivery of high quality services to individual clients, strengthening the quality of the profession and its ranks, and so on.

Although the concepts of the common good and the public interest may seem to represent two views of the same phenomenon, in fact their respective implications often clash. In the end, they move us to consider very different aspects of professional service—one focusing primarily on the commonweal, the other on individual interests (whether clients' or professionals'). I would argue, in fact, that the tension between the public interest and common good views of social work signifies perhaps the most central debate in the profession today: What is the public purpose of social work?

By now it is well known that social workers are deeply divided about the public purpose of the profession (Reamer 1992). At one extreme, some argue that the profession's normative roots are in service to the poor and the least advantaged. Moreover, they hold that the profession's principal obligation, in addition to designing and offering assistance to the most vulnerable, is to seek structural change designed to prevent social problems such as poverty, crime, unemployment, disease, and so on.

At the other extreme are those whose professional center of gravity is located almost entirely in the realm of clinical services, in the form of counseling or psychotherapy, offered in a variety of settings, such as community mental health centers, family service agencies, and private practices. Ample data exist to demonstrate the significant rise in this segment of the social work profession (Gilbert 1983:23–26). For some social workers, social action and attention to structural change are not priorities. Rather, clinical services provided to individual clients are the principal focus.

What this split in the profession represents, described here only simplistically and in its extreme manifestations, is a division between social workers with a *common good* orientation and those with a *public interest* orientation. The former tend to view their primary, though perhaps not exclusive purpose as enhancement of the commonweal through efforts that may focus on individual well-being, community intervention, organizational change, legislative lobbying, and other forms of social work intervention. Social workers with a public interest orientation, in contrast, tend to view their primary, though perhaps not exclusive purpose as enhancement of individual functioning.

This double vision is not peculiar to social work. As Jennings, Callahan, and Wolf (1987) note, it is also characteristic of nearly every modern-day profession:

> Insofar as the professions attend to the public dimension of their ethical responsibilities at all, at present most tend to see their public duties as obligations to promote the public interest. This is not enough. Important as they are, activities such as contributing to the analysis of public policies and providing services to individuals in the aggregate do not exhaust the duties that the professions ought to discharge. The public duties of the professions extend beyond the realm of service to the public interest into the realm of service to the common good. (6)

It is not an overstatement to say that focus on this enduring tension between the common good and public interest orientations is essential to the future of social work. Embedded in it are core questions concerning the profession's principal aims and mission. This tension also incorporates a number of key philosophical issues, discussed above, concerning the nature of political society, the division of responsibility between the public and private sectors for the public's welfare, and contemporary applications of the "social contract." The evolution of this tension will have everything to do with the future character of social work and its place in the welfare arena.

CHAPTER TWO

ॐ

MORAL PHILOSOPHY

Mens sibi conscia recti.
A mind conscious of the right.

—VIRGIL

The subject of values and ethics has always had a central place in social work. As we established in the preceding chapter, social work is a self-consciously normative profession, with long-standing allegiance to a value-based mission. Although practitioners have disagreed over the years, sometimes vehemently, about which specific values should inform social work practice and in what way, one of the profession's principal attributes—which ultimately distinguishes it from other helping professions—is its persistent embrace of values and a distinctive ethical framework.

Social work's preoccupation with values and ethics has matured during its century-old history. What began as an abiding concern with the morality of the profession's original clients—"paupers"— has evolved into the present-day emphasis on the morality of practitioners and debate about the moral nature of the profession's aims. The meaning of values and ethics has shifted over time, from an early concern with the rectitude of paupers to moral norms and ethical standards for social workers themselves. Especially during the late nineteenth and early twentieth centuries—when friendly visiting and charity organization societies proliferated—moral paternalism was rampant, based on an assumption that social work's public mission is to enhance the morality of its clients to enable them to lead virtuous, wholesome, and gainful lives, independent of public or private coffers. A common aim was to help the hungry, homeless, jobless, and destitute (and, in some cases, Godless) to muster their internal resources to lead more productive lives. Those who strayed from life's straight and narrow path needed to be helped to return.

In contrast, during the settlement house movement, New Deal, War on Poverty, and Great Society eras, social workers placed much greater emphasis on the moral duties of a just society, that is, society's broad-based obligation to address problems of poverty, discrimination, and oppression. It was widely believed that social work's principal mission is to illuminate society's structural flaws and propose and implement programs and policies designed to promote a just order.

Especially since the early 1980s, social workers have broadened their interest in ethics to address the nature of ethical dilemmas in practice, ethical decision making and analysis, and ethical theory—in short, applied ethics. Although the vocabulary and methods of applied ethics do not yet pervade the profession, the subject of applied ethics began unquestionably to take hold in social work during the 1980s. Social work literature, course offerings in social work, conference presentations, and in-service training on the subject burgeoned during this period (Elliott 1984; Black et al. 1989; Reamer and Abramson 1982). The Council on Social Work Education modified its Curriculum Policy Statement to require content on applied ethics, and the eighteenth edition of the National Association of Social Workers' *Encyclopedia of Social Work*, published in 1987, included a chapter with substantial content on applied ethics (Reamer 1987).

The recent growth of interest in applied ethics among social workers parallels developments in nearly all the professions (Callahan and Bok 1980). Especially since the late 1970s, professions as diverse as medicine, law, journalism, nursing, business, engineering, accounting, law enforcement, and the military have turned significant attention toward applied ethics. In part this is a legacy of the 1960s and that era's preoccupation with the concept of rights—in the form, for example, of civil rights, welfare rights, patients' rights, and prisoners' rights. During that time the language of rights began to permeate the culture and led, ultimately, to heightened concern within the professions. Widespread publicity about scandals within the professions and among public officials also stimulated concern about ethics. Allegations and evidence of misconduct among well-known politicians, physicians, lawyers, clergy, athletes, and other public figures helped to alert professionals to the need to monitor conduct within their own houses more closely.

In addition, the introduction of remarkably sophisticated technology in a number of professions led to the creation of novel ethical dilemmas that had not existed previously. The invention of the artificial heart, for example, brought with it troublesome ethical questions about the limits of extraordinary health care and the allocation of limited resources. Similar questions were produced by such developments as the placement of a baboon's heart in an impaired infant, genetic engineering, and dialysis.

Also, now that most modern professions are at least in the vicinity of a century old, their practitioners seem more inclined to turn their attention to complex questions concerning their value base and professional ethics. During the earliest years of most professions' history, the tendency was to be preoccupied with the technical aspects of practice, in part to establish the profession's foundation of expertise and to justify its existence. Over time, as professions have firmly established themselves in the public's eye, professions have been more willing to raise self-critical questions about their basic values, moral aims, and ethical norms.

Like members of most professions, social workers now have a much more sophisticated understanding of the relevance of ethics to their day-to-day responsibilities (Reamer 1989; 1990). They have a more mature grasp of the ethical dilemmas that arise in social work practice and policy, and the influence of values on the profession's ultimate aims. They also have a greater appreciation of the value of ethical inquiry. As Emmet (1962) wrote some years ago with impressive insight and foresight:

> In these days when few of us think that we can look up the answers to moral problems at the back of the book, we may get further if we are prepared to take the risk of developing our powers of making moral judgments, rather than sit back and let these powers atrophy because of our uncertainties. . . . It would do no harm for social workers themselves to do more of it during their own training. Even if the result is to drive us back on to some moral principles or values for which we can give no further reasons, there will be a difference between

holding them in this way *after* a process of critical heart-
searching and just asserting them dogmatically. At any rate
we can learn . . . to see moral questions as problematic and
open ended, which means that they can be thought about and
discussed and also see there are reasonable ways of going
about this. (170, 171)

THE NATURE OF ETHICS

Ethics, or moral philosophy, is concerned with the nature of what
is morally right and wrong, good and bad. In general, ethical inquiry is divided into two branches: metaethics and normative ethics. Metaethics is concerned with the analysis of the meaning of
moral terms—such as right, wrong, good, bad, duty, and obligation—and of the methods used to support ethical claims and judgments. Thus, within metaethics we explore various arguments concerning what moral terms mean and the validity of their definitions.
For example, how should we define the term *duty*, and how do we
know whether someone has fulfilled his or her duty?

Normative ethics, in contrast, is concerned with the application
of moral concepts and principles to moral problems or ethical dilemmas. Thus, within normative ethics we might discuss individuals' right to privacy and the circumstances under which confidentiality should be broken. Or we might explore the most ethical way
to distribute scarce social service resources (this is a particularly
good example of the way in which ethical issues and issues of
political philosophy sometimes intersect). Normative ethics, then,
is more closely aligned with the kind of problem solving in which
social workers ordinarily engage, although metaethics certainly can
inform social workers' understanding and application of moral
criteria.

METAETHICS. Although social workers may not ordinarily use
formal philosophical language, they often engage in what amounts
to metaethical debate about the meaning of moral terminology and
concepts. For example, debate about the limits of clients' right to
self-determination often reduces to debate about what is meant by
the term *self-determination,* how it ought to be defined, and whether
self-determination exists objectively. Similarly, debate about the
boundaries of social workers' moral duty to assist people in need
often reduces to debate about what is meant by the term *duty,* how

it ought to be defined, and whether professional duty exists objectively. Metaethics, therefore, is not so much concerned with how to enhance self-determination or the carrying out of professional duty. Instead, metaethics is concerned with understanding what the concepts of self-determination and duty mean *in the first place,* and with whether or not these phenomena truly exist. One can imagine comparable metaethical speculation about other moral concepts related to social work, such as social justice, honesty, fairness, and paternalism. Metaethics is also concerned with the ways in which we derive ethical principles and guidelines related to these concepts.

Metaethics has two main schools of thought: *cognitivism* and *noncognitivism.* Cognitivists argue that it is possible to know, in fact, whether our beliefs about moral concepts are true or false. For cognitivists it is possible, at least in principle, to know what actually constitutes concepts such as justice and fairness. We may have some difficulty *determining* the truth or falsity of claims about moral concepts, but these claims *are* true or false. In contrast, noncognitivists reject this assertion and argue that claims about moral concepts do nothing more than express opinions or attitudes or give commands. For noncognitivists, a statement such as "It is never permissible to lie to a client" is not true or false; rather, it merely expresses a point of view.

Cognitivist theories can be classified further under the headings of *intuitionism* and *naturalism.* According to intuitionism, it is possible to know objectively what is meant by moral concepts such as justice and fairness, but these concepts cannot be reduced to measurable phenomena of the sort one might find in the natural sciences. From this point of view, moral concepts are nonnatural and indefinable and knowable only through intuition. The famous philosopher G. E. Moore, for example, argued that moral goodness is a simple, indefinable property that can be understood only by intuition. Similarly, the Oxford philosopher H. A. Prichard argued with respect to the moral term *ought* that judgments about what one morally ought to do in any given situation (e.g., tell the truth about clients' condition when completing insurance reimbursement forms, break the law to protect a client from an intrusive protective services investigation) are not analyzable or provable in any objective sense. For Prichard, no reason can be given for a person's ethical obligation to act one way or another. Rather, one's grasp of one's obligation is intuitive and immediate.

In contrast, naturalism assumes that moral concepts signify real qualities in the world that can be measured empirically using methods of natural science. Aristotle and Thomas Aquinas, for example, believed that goodness is an objective characteristic that can be measured by empirical, inductive methods. From this point of view, it is possible to use scientific methods to determine, for example, the fairest way to allocate scarce shelter beds to clients in need or the morality of a social worker's decision to violate a mandatory reporting law. Intuition is insufficient.

The attempt to identify the determinants of the objective rightness of moral claims has been referred to by Gewirth (1978a) as the "problem of the independent variable," which concerns "whether there are any objective independent variables that serve to determine the correctness or rightness of moral judgments" (5).

Most of the arguments philosophers have presented concerning the justification of moral judgments and principles have had difficulty standing up under sustained scrutiny. One common claim, for example, is that empirical observations of individuals' attitudes, behavior, or attributes cannot lead to normative conclusions or principles about morally right or wrong action; no logical connection exists between empirical or descriptive statements of fact and evaluative conclusions. This is what Hume referred to as the "is-ought" problem in philosophy, or what G. E. Moore dubbed the "naturalistic fallacy," where factual statements are mistaken for evaluative ones. That is, we can determine empirically whether certain behaviorally disordered clients benefit from strict, controlled treatment methods that rely occasionally on punishment; however, it is not clear that factual evidence concerning treatment effectiveness leads directly to a normative conclusion that such treatment methods *ought* to be used. As Searle (1969) observed:

> It is often said that one cannot derive an "ought" from an "is."
> The thesis, which comes from a famous passage in Hume's
> *Treatise,* while not as clear as it might be, is at least clear in
> broad outline: there is a class of statements of fact which is
> logically distinct from a class of statements of value. No set of
> statements of fact by themselves entails any statement of
> value. Put in more contemporary terminology, no set of *de-
> scriptive* statements can entail an *evaluative* statement with-
> out the addition of at least one evaluative premise. To believe
> otherwise is to commit what has been called the naturalistic
> fallacy. (120)

A common view often associated with intuitionism is known as the "moral point of view" (Baier 1965; Donagan 1977:218–21;

Frankena, 1973:113–14). The origin of the moral point of view can be traced to Adam Smith's argument that individuals are likely to reach agreement in their moral judgments only by assuming the position of an impartial spectator or of an "ideal observer" (Donagan 1977:218–21). An ideal observer is one who has such characteristics as being informed, impartial, fair, dispassionate, calm, willing to universalize, able to consider the good of everyone, and so on. Thus, a social worker who is in a position to decide the morality of, for example, breaching client confidentiality, terminating service, or allocating scarce resources would obtain as much information as possible about the nature and circumstances of the phenomenon being considered, take into account the various interests of all who may be affected by his or her decision, and, from an impartial position, weigh the various considerations against one another in order to determine the course of action that would result in the most favorable outcome.

In contrast to cognitivism, noncognitivism offers a radically different perspective on moral matters. According to noncognitivism, it is not possible to know, in fact, whether claims about moral duty or obligation, or about moral goodness or badness, are true or false. From this perspective, moral claims about clients' right to self-determination or social workers' obligation to tell the truth or obey the law merely express opinion or feeling, guide choices, or contain prescriptions for how people ought to act.

Although most noncognitivist theories were developed in the early twentieth century, their roots go back to such philosophical luminaries as Thomas Hobbes and David Hume. Noncognitivist *emotivists* argue that moral claims do no more than express how individuals feel about the issue they are addressing. Thus, when a social worker states, "It is wrong to lie to a client about her prognosis," she is only expressing her feeling about the morality of lying in this sort of circumstance; she is not making a factual statement about the moral issue. Noncognitivist *prescriptivists*, on the other hand, view such moral statements as mere expressions of a commandment or directive, in this case to not lie to a client.

NORMATIVE ETHICS. The ethical issues that have the most direct bearing on social work concern the application of moral concepts and principles to decisions about what is morally right or wrong, or good or bad, in professional practice. Moral philosophers have traditionally identified three central questions under which most, if not all, normative ethical issues can be subsumed (Gewirth 1978a:1–26). First, why should one be concerned with morality and ethics, in the sense of considering one's obligations to other individuals, especially when these obligations conflict with one's own interests? Second, whose interests, in addition to one's own, should we be concerned with, and in what manner should goods and resources be distributed among individuals? And third, what actions and resources are to be considered worthwhile, good, and desirable on their own account, and for what reasons? These three questions have been referred to as, respectively, the *authoritative, distributive,* and *substantive* questions of ethics.

THE AUTHORITATIVE QUESTION

Our decisions to intervene in clients' lives in certain ways tend to be influenced by several factors. We sometimes consider available evidence from research regarding the effectiveness of a particular treatment technique. Or, we may be influenced by a particular theory of human behavior, though there may be no empirical evidence to establish its validity. We may also be influenced by the apparent success of our experiences working with clients who have particular problems and by the experiences of our colleagues and supervisors. And, finally, we may be influenced by our values, our beliefs about what is morally right and wrong, or good and bad, in a particular situation.

The factors that tend to influence social workers' decisions about how to intervene in clients' lives can be generally classified as *technical, empirical,* and *ethical.* Technical factors relate to beliefs that certain methods of social work practice are appropriate for use with clients who present certain traits and problems. These beliefs are based on theories of social casework and policy and on experiences social workers have had over the years using a variety of social work approaches in various settings and with a number of different clients. They are based on what many social workers refer to as "practice wisdom." Very often these beliefs are shaped by the training one has received and by the method or methods of social work used by one's professional colleagues.

Empirical factors relate to science and to what is known from research about the effectiveness or likely consequences of specific social work approaches. For example, a practitioner's decision to use task-centered casework with a twelve-year-old child who is having difficulty completing school assignments may be based on a systematic review of the empirical evidence concerning the effectiveness of this method with children experiencing school problems. Or, a decision to reduce the caseloads of public aid workers may be influenced by research evidence that an inverse relationship exists between caseload size and client satisfaction with service.

Ethical factors relate to conclusions that are based on an analysis of what is morally right and wrong, or good and bad. For example, while empirical evidence may suggest that runaways who are briefly incarcerated tend to run away less than comparable runaways who are returned home, the argument that it would be fundamentally wrong, in a moral or ethical sense, to incarcerate a youth who is considered by law not to be responsible for his acts may be viewed by some as the critical reason for avoiding incarceration. That is, the ethical grounds may override the empirical factors.

The degree to which technical, empirical, and ethical factors should guide social workers' decisions about how to intervene in clients' lives has been the subject of extended debate (Vigilante 1974). Some argue that empirical evidence of the effectiveness of specific social work approaches cannot replace the intangible evidence one accumulates after years of practical experience working with clients. Others argue that guidelines based on a careful analysis of results of empirical research should be the principal guide to practice. Still others argue that to be guided ultimately by factors other than those based on beliefs about what is morally right or wrong, or about duty and obligation, is unacceptable.

Technical, empirical, and ethical factors should certainly be considered when one is faced with a decision about how to intervene. Surely our own professional experiences, the experiences of our colleagues, and theories of social work practice provide valuable information about the possible consequences of various social work strategies. Research, carefully designed and conducted, can provide valuable tests of various social work techniques. And, of course, questions should always be raised about the ethical aspects of various practice approaches. Ideally, the conclusions we reach based on research, professional experience, theories of social work practice, and ethical guidelines would be consistent with one another. We know from experience, however, that such consistency is frequently not achieved. Research findings may contradict what a previously untested theory of treatment has asserted. Ethical guidelines may conflict with traditional agency practices.

Technical, empirical, and ethical factors all have a place in our decisions as social workers. Ethical beliefs about what is right or wrong must serve, however, *in the final analysis,* as the primary justification of social work intervention. This is so for several reasons. First, decisions about what intervention would be most desirable in a given case necessarily reduce to questions about how to define the term *desirable.* Insofar as these questions entail further questions about the preferences of individual practitioners, they concern values. And, finally, insofar as questions of values ask what is right or wrong, or good or bad, they are ethical. For example, one social worker may argue that, based on her experience and review of relevant theories, the most desirable intervention for juvenile delinquents is the one that reduces recidivism rates to the greatest extent. Another worker may argue that the most desirable intervention is the one that results in the greatest degree of compensation for victims. Or, while one social worker may argue that, based on her experience, a dying patient should be informed of his or her impending death as soon as possible, another may argue that her experience suggests the wisdom in withholding such information until the patient specifically asks for it. Decisions about which worker's view has the greatest merit necessarily rest on questions of values, and hence on questions of ethics.

Certainly, empirical evidence can at times help us make such decisions. Research on the effectiveness of specific social work techniques can help resolve disagreements about the likely outcomes of certain interventions. Empirical evidence by itself, however, cannot be translated directly into decisions about the most appropriate treatment strategy. One major difficulty with basing decisions about intervention strategy on the results of empirical evidence is that a single set of empirical results can be interpreted differently by different people. As the "is-ought" problem implies, normative conclusions cannot be deduced directly and immediately from the empirical evidence itself. There is no logical connection between empirical, descriptive statements of fact and ethical judgments.

A related problem with the use of empirical evidence as the primary basis for making practical decisions relates to fundamental questions about the validity and reliability of data gathered in research. These questions, frequently debated by philosophers of science, concern such issues as the ability of researchers to construct accurate operational measures of the concepts studied, limits on the ability of researchers to make inferences about causal relationships among variables, and the effects of research procedures themselves that may bias empirical results (Heineman 1981; Mullen 1985; Peile 1988; Reamer 1979; Rosenthal and Rosnow 1969).

It is well known, for instance, that social work researchers have considerable difficulty operationalizing variables and concepts that are of primary concern to practitioners, such as mental health, ego strength, autonomy, and competence. It is difficult to obtain agreement among social workers about the most valid indicators of these concepts. As a result, it is frequently difficult to know whether research findings indicating that, for instance, casework is not effective are a consequence of the inability of researchers to accurately measure outcome or are solid evidence of the ineffectiveness of practitioners' efforts.

A serious limitation in social work research also results from researchers frequently being unable to control for extraneous variables when testing the effects of specific interventions. Random assignment of subjects to experimental and control groups is often not possible, and thus certain factors, such as historical events, contemporaneous events, and the effects of testing and maturation, are frequently not controlled for. As a result, social work researchers must frequently rely simply on correlations between specific interventions and measures of outcome. Our ability to make inferences about the causal relationships between social work efforts and outcome is thus quite limited.

It is clear, then, that technical factors, based on professional experience and theories of social work practice, and empirical factors, based on research, cannot by themselves justify practice decisions in social work. The very nature of our decisions requires us to address questions of values and ethics. This is not to say that nonethical considerations, such as economic constraints, empirical evidence, practice techniques, or political compromises, should not enter into professional judgments. Of course they should and frequently must. The inescapable conclusion, however, is that our professional decisions must be justified ultimately by statements (implicit or explicit) that a particular decision is ethically *right* or *wrong* for specific reasons and has consequences that are ethically *good* or *bad*. The very use of terms such as *right, wrong, good,* and *bad* to represent professional preferences and values leads us in the end to ethical concepts and ethical issues.

THE DISTRIBUTIVE QUESTION

The distributive question asks: Whose interests, in addition to our own, should we be concerned with and in what manner should goods and resources be distributed among individuals? As one might expect, philosophers have answered the first part of this question in a variety of ways. Their arguments have ranged from those asserting extreme forms of altruism, where an individual is concerned with everyone's interests other than his or her own, and those asserting extreme forms of egoism, where an individual is concerned with only his or her own interests. Between these extremes are arguments to the effect that individuals ought to be concerned with the interests of others, though not the interests of everyone. These arguments sometimes state that one should be concerned only or primarily with the interests of persons who lack certain skills or resources (for example, adequate housing or health care) or who belong to a certain community, religion, race, economic or social class, or to some other restricted group.

The debate regarding whose interests individuals ought to be concerned with is an important one for social workers to consider. The traditional mission of the profession has depended on assumptions about individuals' obligations to care for and give to one another, particularly in times of need. In the early years of the profession these assumptions were frequently based on religious beliefs about obligations to assist the wayward needy to learn Christian virtues. More recently, these assumptions about caring and giving have been based on beliefs that members of a democratic society incur fundamental obligations to aid those who have suffered the unfortunate consequences of a way of life organized around a system of free enterprise. It is these beliefs that have been the foundation for many contemporary social welfare programs for the poor, elderly, and disabled, food stamps, medical aid for the needy, disaster relief, federal subsidies and loan guarantees for failing corporations, services for the chronically ill, subsidized housing, mental health services, and many other publicly and privately financed programs.

We must consider, however, the extent to which we have in fact an ethical obligation to aid those in need and the extent to which such efforts, while perhaps desirable and commendable, are not morally required. The positions we take on this debate can indeed have extremely important consequences. If we assert that citizens of a democratic society have an obligation to aid those in need (which would, of course, first require a precise definition of what constitutes need), we would then organize ways to provide such aid. Decisions would be made about the extent to which government agencies would assume responsibility for providing aid, and these decisions would depend on assumptions about the place of the state in the lives of its citizens. If we deny that citizens of a democratic society have an obligation to aid those in need, however, social services and financial assistance would depend on the voluntary efforts and generosity of private citizens and services that can be purchased from private vendors under market conditions fostered by free enterprise.

POSITIVE AND NEGATIVE OBLIGATIONS. An important aspect of the general issue regarding the duty to aid concerns the choice social workers must frequently make between intervening in individuals' lives in order to provide assistance and alleviate suffering and avoiding intervention so as to respect individuals' apparent right to freedom from interference. These decisions often involve choices between what I will refer to as, respectively, *positive obligations* and *negative obligations*.

The distinction between positive and negative obligations is based in part on a distinction made by the philosopher Sir Isaiah Berlin (1969) in his classic discussion of positive and negative liberty. *Positive liberty* concerns the freedom to act as one wishes and the abilities and resources necessary for one to fulfill one's goals; *negative liberty* concerns freedom from coercion and interference. Negative liberty is perhaps best exemplified in John Stuart Mill's essay *On Liberty*, where he presents arguments against interference by the state in the lives of its citizens.

Over the years philosophers have debated about the proper balance between interference in the lives of individuals in order to provide services and alleviate suffering (in accord with positive liberty) and freedom from interference and coercion (in accord with negative liberty). As Berlin (1975) states:

> The freedom which consists in being one's own master, and the freedom which consists in not being prevented from choosing as I do by other men, may, on the face of it, seem concepts at no great logical distance from each other—no more than negative and positive ways of saying much the same thing. Yet the "positive" and "negative" notions of freedom historically developed in divergent directions not always by logically reputable steps, until, in the end, they came into direct conflict with each other. (149)

The distinction between positive and negative obligations is particularly important in cases where clients are involved in some form of self-destructive behavior, for example, substance abuse, abusive relationships, or suicidal activities. The debate concerning the obligation to prevent individuals from harming themselves is an ancient one. On one side are those who argue that the right to self-determination entails the right to engage in activities that may result in harm to oneself. Any interference on the part of others is viewed as unwarranted and wrong. Proponents of this point of view argue that it is permissible, for example, for a client to choose to continue living with an abusive spouse if he or she so wishes or for a troubled client to refuse counseling. Perhaps the strongest claim by adherents of this point of view is that it is even wrong to interfere with a client's informed, thoughtful choice to end his or her own life.

On the other side, of course, are those who argue that members of society have an obligation to protect one another from self-destructive behavior and that it is sometimes necessary to interfere with another individual's intentions for that person's own good.

The debate concerning the proper balance between a client's right to engage in apparently self-destructive behavior and a social worker's obligation to prevent harm centers on a concept that has long endured in the mainstream of social work practice: self-determination. The tension has been between those who believe in a client's right to set his or her own goals, and possibly make mistakes, and those who claim that at times clients can develop the ability and wherewithal to make informed choices only if they receive professional assistance. This conflict is illustrated vividly in the following passage by Biestek (1975):

> The principle of client self-determination is the practical recognition of the right and need of clients to freedom in making their own choices and decisions in the casework process. Caseworkers have a corresponding duty to respect that right, recognize that need, stimulate and help to activate that potential for self-direction by helping the client to see and use the available and appropriate resources of the community and of his own personality. The client's right to self-determination, however, is limited by the client's capacity for positive and constructive decision making, by the framework of civil and moral law, and by the function of the agency. (19)

Clearly, difficult decisions must on occasion be made by social workers either to strongly encourage or insist that clients avail themselves of specific professional services and courses of action or to avoid paternalism and respect a client's right to refuse assistance and, as Soyer (1963) aptly describes it, the client's "right to fail."

THE CONCEPT OF PATERNALISM. The concept of paternalism, though not the term itself, has been bandied about regularly since the time of Aristotle, who argued in his *Politics*—written in the fourth century B.C.—that some degree of paternalism is justifiable in a society in which certain elite individuals are clearly more informed and wiser than others. The classic commentary on paternalism, however, appeared in the nineteenth century in John Stuart Mill's essay *On Liberty*. Following the publication of this essay in 1859, Mill came to be regarded as the principal spokesperson for antipaternalism, especially with respect to the excesses of government intervention in private lives.

Since the publication of *On Liberty*, the nature of paternalism and its justification have been the subject of considerable debate. Concern with the problem of paternalism among contemporary philosophers was especially noteworthy during the 1960s, largely because of the widespread attention being paid then to issues of civil rights and civil liberties. Debate during those unsettling years about the rights of, for example, the mentally ill, prisoners, welfare recipients, and children gave rise to considerable philosophical controversy concerning the limits of government intervention and the rights of citizens under the care of the state. Professional practices that had previously been unchallenged were called into question. Is it permissible to sterilize a mildly retarded female adolescent "for her own good"? Is it permissible to require a ward of the state to accept a blood transfusion despite his protests? Do individuals committed to a state department of mental health have the right to the least restrictive alternative?

It is no accident that what is widely regarded as the seminal contemporary essay in the philosophical literature on paternalism appeared in the midst of national controversy about civil liberties. In his essay, "Paternalism," Gerald Dworkin (1971), a moral philosopher, defines *paternalism* as "interference with a person's liberty of action justified by reasons referring exclusively to the welfare, good, happiness, needs, interests, or values of the person being coerced" (108). For him, examples of paternalism include laws that justify civil commitment procedures on the basis of preventing the client from harming him- or herself, require members of certain religious sects to have compulsory blood transfusions, make suicide a criminal offense, require motorcyclists to wear safety helmets, and forbid persons from swimming at a public beach when life-guards are not on duty.

Dworkin's definition of paternalism is thus restricted to interferences with the actions of individuals that, to use Mill's term, are self-regarding. Philosophical discussions of paternalism since Dworkin's original formulation have expanded this definition to include interference with individuals' access to information, emotional condition, and so forth, in addition to actions per se. In her prominent essay on the justification of paternalism, the philosopher Carter (1977) defines a paternalistic act more broadly as "one in which the protection or promotion of a subject's welfare is the primary reason for attempted or successful coercive interference with an action or state of that person" (133). In a more detailed definition, Buchanan (1978), a philosopher concerned with medical ethics, describes paternalism as "interference with a person's freedom of action or freedom of information, or the deliberate dissemination of misinformation, where the alleged justification of interference or misinforming is that it is for the good of the person who is interfered with or misinformed" (372). Though Carter's and Buchanan's definitions of paternalism are more comprehensive than Dworkin's, all three contain the element of coercion or interference that is justified by references to the good of the individual who is being interfered with.

Paternalism can thus take a variety of forms in social work. In general, paternalistic actions can be placed in three categories: interference with an individual's intentions or actions; deliberate withholding of information; and deliberate dissemination of misinformation (Reamer 1983b). Interference with the intentions or actions of an individual can include, for instance, requiring that a client be institutionalized against his or her wishes, restraining a self-destructive client with force, or insisting that a client accept an offer of assistance or a particular service. Withholding information or providing misinformation can also occur under a variety of circumstances where it is believed that clients may harm themselves if they have access to truthful information, for example, withholding diagnostic information from a seriously ill client or failing to tell a troubled client that she can sign herself out of a residential program.

DISTRIBUTIVE JUSTICE. The second part of the distributive question, concerning the manner in which goods and resources should be distributed, has also been the subject of considerable debate among philosophers. As we observed in the chapter on political philosophy, it has been argued by some (Karl Marx, for example) that goods and resources should be distributed based on need. Others, such as David Hume and Jeremy Bentham, have argued that the greatest happiness will result from the most equal distribution of goods and resources. Still others have argued that a just distribution is based on dealing with people according to their merits. According to Aristotle, for example, the criterion of merit is virtue, and justice is achieved by distributing goods in accordance with the extent of one's virtue or goodness of character. Other criteria of merit cited by philosophers have included ability, social status, contribution, intelligence, and wealth.

Clearly, guidelines for distributing goods and resources are critical in a field such as social work. Practitioners must frequently make decisions about the distribution of services, financial aid to individuals, agencies, and communities, facilities, time, and other resources, and these decisions have important effects on individuals. According to what criteria should limited resources be distributed?

The distribution of scarce or limited resources in social work has generally been guided by four criteria: equality, need, compensation, and contribution. At times these criteria have been considered independently of one another, at times in combination. As I suggested in chapter 1, the idea of equality appears, at first glance, uncomplicated. Individuals with similar problems should have equal claim to services and resources such as counseling, nursing home beds, and financial assistance. The apparent simplicity of the principle of equality is, however, deceiving. Attempts to apply this principle to the actual distribution of services and resources have, in fact, been filled with difficulties.

To some, equality suggests that those who qualify to receive certain services or resources ought to receive them in equal shares. This interpretation of the idea of equality emphasizes the *outcome,* or the product, of a particular distribution; equal shares should be distributed to eligible recipients.

This interpretation differs from one that emphasizes specific *procedures* for distributing services and resources or, in particular, equality of opportunity. What is important here is not that services and resources be distributed equally, but that individuals (and communities, organizations, and so on) have equal opportunities to compete for them (often known as "first come, first served"). The emphasis here is on process rather than outcome.

Another interpretation of the principle of equality stresses the use of random selection, particularly when scarce services and resources cannot be distributed equally among eligible individuals, for example, in the case of shelter beds or public housing units. Thus, one possible application of the principle of equality involves equality of opportunity in the form of a lottery or random selection.

Limited services and resources are also distributed based on individual need. Instead of dividing up resources into equal pieces or allowing individuals to compete for them, either in the form of a lottery or according to "first come, first served," individuals are sometimes ranked according to their level or severity of need. Of course, what constitutes need is itself a complicated issue. Difficult decisions must be made concerning the relative importance of various needs and the relative intensity of individuals' suffering.

Perhaps the best-known contemporary statement concerning the obligation to aid those in need is found in John Rawls's (1971) *A Theory of Justice*. As I outlined in chapter 1, Rawls's theory assumes that individuals who are formulating a moral principle by which to be governed are in an "original position" of equality and that each individual is unaware of his or her own attributes and status that might produce some advantage or disadvantage. Under this "veil of ignorance" it is assumed that individuals will derive a moral framework, which Rawls calls the "difference principle," that ultimately protects the least advantaged.

An additional problem we encounter in our attempts to define need concerns the distinction between past and present need. Ordinarily we think about providing aid to individuals whose present needs seem to warrant assistance. But frequently social welfare policies take into consideration the needs of specific groups of individuals in past generations and their effect on present generations. This is particularly the case when past generations were deprived of needed services and resources because of discrimination. As a result, many contemporary social welfare policies are earmarked for members of specific ethnic or racial groups whose ancestors were denied services and resources that were made available to other citizens. Contemporary policies that include quotas for admitting minimum numbers of individuals of certain ethnic and racial groups to educational institutions, vocational training programs, and jobs are examples of attempts to distribute services and resources based not only on the needs of the current generation but on the needs and deprivations suffered by past generations as well (the principle of compensation).

The extent of our obligation to provide special or preferential treatment to individuals who descend from groups that have suffered discrimination in the past arouses considerable controversy. One side argues that while the consequences of past discrimination are unfortunate, the contemporary generation should not be held accountable for the injustices of its forbears. Providing preferential treatment to descendants of groups that were once unfairly treated at the expense of members of the contemporary generation results, it is often argued, in "reverse discrimination" which is equally unjust. The argument on the other side is that the current generation has an obligation to right the wrongs of past generations and that preferential treatment is necessary in order to restore some semblance of equality and equal opportunity among various ethnic and racial groups, both in the present and in the future.

The final principle that guides the distribution of services and resources is that of contribution. This principle, too, has been applied in many different ways, with many different intentions. Simply interpreted, this principle holds that services and resources should be distributed to individuals in proportion to the contribution they have made toward their production. In practice, the principle of contribution has guided the distribution of services and resources in various ways.

Perhaps the simplest example of distribution based on contribution is when clients exchange payment for specific services and resources, such as counseling, dental care, shelter, and child care. Individuals who contribute toward the support of these services receive them; individuals who choose not to pay for these services do not receive them, unless they are provided free of cost (in which case they are distributed according to some other principle, such as need). The principle of contribution thus involves a relatively simple exchange of fees for services which are provided almost immediately and depend on the ability of clients to pay.

Another version of this arrangement involves the exchange of fees for a service or resource that is to be provided in the future and that is prorated based on the amount of an individual's contribution prior to its delivery. Examples of welfare resources that are distributed in this manner are private pensions and insurance. Participants in these plans ordinarily contribute a fixed amount of money on a regular basis (for example, monthly or annually) to a fund; this money is then invested and in turn used to support individuals who contributed in prior years. In principle, a participant, or his or her beneficiaries, receives income years after the payments began and in proportion to the total amount contributed. Once again, resources from such funds are distributed only to those who have contributed to their support and growth.

The principle of contribution has also been applied in yet a third way, one that is particularly controversial. This application differs significantly from those based on fees for services or benefits provided immediately or in the future. Rather, it is based on the nonmonetary contribution of individuals in exchange for services and resources. That is, some have argued that individuals who have contributed a great deal to their communities—in the form of local leadership, philanthropy, and the like—have a greater claim on scarce resources (for example, a nursing home bed) than those who have contributed relatively little or have been a net drain or burden.

THE RELEVANCE OF MORAL DESERT. To some extent social workers' decisions about the allocation of limited resources are surely affected by their judgments about the extent to which individuals *deserve* assistance. Whether this is appropriate, of course, is debatable. Nevertheless, assumptions about moral desert have indeed been present and influential since the beginning of the profession.

In philosophical terms, much of the debate among social workers about the relevance of client desert has focused on the concepts of free will and determinism (Reamer 1983c). Social workers repeatedly make assumptions about the determinants of people's problems and shape interventions accordingly. For instance, some forms of mental retardation are, we may conclude, a result of certain chromosomal abnormalities and thus are amenable to only a limited range of treatments. Family discord, in contrast, may emerge as a result of, for example, personality quirks of family members, the strain of a sudden illness, financial catastrophe, or learning disabilities. Some might argue that poverty stems from structural problems in our economy that need to be addressed (for example, high unemployment or unfair tax structures), while others believe that poverty must be attacked by discouraging sloth. How we respond to these and other social problems—whether we focus our attention on environmental determinants or individual character—frequently depends on assumptions we make about the extent to which people's problems are the result of factors over which they have control (Perlman 1965). As Florence Hollis (1975) observed in an address delivered at a United Nations seminar on advanced study in social work: "The first question to be raised about these scientific principles is often the philosophical one of whether the assumptions of lawfulness in behaviour and of cause and effect relationships in behaviour does not mean that casework has become completely deterministic" (93).

The conclusions social workers reach about the causes of people's problems frequently lead to assumptions about the extent to which they deserve assistance. If we conclude that a person is chronically depressed because of a series of unforeseen, tragic events in his or her life, we may be more inclined to offer solace and support than if we decide that the individual's depression is a calculated, willful, protracted, and self-serving attempt to gain sympathy and attention. If we conclude that an individual has difficulty sustaining employment because of a congenital learning disability that that individual has persistently tried to overcome, we may be more willing to invest our professional time and energy than we would with someone who is fired from jobs repeatedly because he or she resents having to arrive for work at 8:30 A.M. every day.

These contrasting views concerning the determinants of human behavior represent one of the most enduring controversies in recorded history. Put simply, on one side are those who argue that human beings are willful actors who shape their own destinies and who independently make rational choices based on personal preferences and wishes. On the other side are those who claim that human behavior is largely or entirely determined by a series of antecedent events and factors, such that any given "choice" or behavior is a mere product of prior causes, be they psychological, environmental, mechanical, or physical (Frankfurt 1973).

The free will/determinism debate has ancient philosophical roots. Empedocles and Heraclitus, for example, are early sources of pre-Socratic thought on the meaning of determinism in nature and the idea of natural law. Ideas concerning determinism—especially the influence of divine will—were later given prominence in the fourth century B.C. by the Stoics, the Greek school of philosophy founded by Zeno.

The origins of modern-world debate about free will and determinism ordinarily are traced to the work of the eighteenth-century French astronomer and mathematician Pierre Simon de Laplace. Laplace's assertions about determinism in the world as we know it were heavily dependent on the scientific theory of particle mechanics, according to which a knowledge of the mechanical state of all particles at some particular time, together with a knowledge of all other forces acting in nature at that instant, would enable one to discover all future and past states of the world (Berofsky 1966). With this information, one could, in principle, discover not only all future and past mechanical states in the world, but all others as well, such as electromagnetic, chemical, and psychological states. As the philosopher Ernest Nagel (1970) has observed, "Determinism in its most general form appears to be the claim that for every set of characteristics which may occur at any time, there is some system that is deterministic in respect to those occurrences" (55).

The doctrine of determinism contains two essential ingredients: a belief in causal laws and the concept of predictability. According to determinism, then, problems such as crime, poverty, drug abuse, and mental illness can be traced to historical antecedents that have led progressively to the *victim's* current difficulties. Whatever ability people have to control their circumstances and to change is itself merely the outcome of prior causes. The philosopher John Hospers (1966) describes this view well in his essay, "What Means This Freedom?":

> The position, then, is this: if we *can* overcome the effects of early environment, the ability to do so is itself a product of the early environment. We did not give ourselves this ability; and if we lack it we cannot be blamed for not having it. Sometimes, to be sure, moral exhortation brings out an ability that is there but not being used, and in this lies its *occasional* utility; but very often its use is pointless, because the ability is not there. The only thing that can overcome a desire, as Spinoza said, is a stronger contrary desire; and many times there simply is no wherewithal for producing a stronger contrary desire. Those of us who do have the wherewithal are lucky. (40)

Proponents of the free will school of thought, on the other hand, deny that our thoughts, emotions, and behavior are always a function of prior causes over which we have little or no control. Adherents to this point of view generally fall short of claiming that no events are determined or that all events are truly random occurrences. Rather, they claim that some events follow from the exercise of free will or choice, that individuals do in fact have the capacity to behave independently of prior causes, though perhaps to varying degrees. As the ethicist Gerald Dworkin (1970) has noted:

The claim that we have free will is, then, the claim that for some actions at least the following is true: There is an alternative action (which may be simply refraining from the action to be performed) open to the agent. Put in the past tense after the agent has performed some action A: There was some alternative action which the agent could have performed other than the one which he in fact did. (6)

An alternative to extreme views of either free will or determinism, but which contains elements of both schools of thought, has become known in philosophical circles as the "mixed view" or "soft determinism." It is fair to say that currently the mixed view is the most prominent in circulation. It essentially entails three assumptions: (1) that the thesis of determinism is generally true, and that accordingly all human behavior—both voluntary and involuntary—is preceded and caused by antecedent conditions, such that no other behavior is possible; (2) that genuinely voluntary behavior is nonetheless possible to the extent that it is not coerced; and (3) that, in the absence of coercion, voluntary behavior is brought about by the decisions, choices, and preferences of individuals themselves (Taylor 1963).

Considerable evidence exists that the doctrine of soft determinism is prominent in social work. In general, both the profession's literature and its conventional wisdom derived from practice embrace the view that the problems under which clients labor are, to varying degrees, frequently the products of circumstances beyond their control, and that clients themselves are at times partly responsible for their difficulties and are—again, to varying degrees—capable of making thoughtful, rational, and voluntary decisions to alter the course of their lives. Florence Hollis (1975) has expressed this sentiment well:

> The casework position, I would think, would not be that of absolutism in either direction. We certainly do not take the libertarian stand that each action of man is completely free and unaffected by his previous character, life history, or current experience. On the other hand, neither do we believe that all choice, all behavior is the determined, necessary and inflexible result of previously existing physical or environmental causes. (106–7)

This position is based on what philosophers generally refer to as the compatibility argument, according to which the free will and determinist views are not, contrary to first impressions, necessarily mutually exclusive. Rather, they can be complementary. This is a view that has been espoused over the years by such noteworthy philosophers as Thomas Hobbes, David Hume, and John Stuart Mill (Ginet 1962).

Clearly, social workers are not consistent in their views on the issue. On the one hand are those individuals whose problems seem the result of circumstances well beyond their control. These are people who, we conclude, have not brought problems upon themselves. They are true victims. Infants who have been physically abused or neglected, people with congenital defects (such as physical impairment or Down Syndrome), and those who are diseased at birth are, by and large, regarded as individuals who were dealt an unfortunate hand at the very start of life. They have not behaved in ways that we consider to have invited the serious problems from which they suffer.

At the other extreme are people who, at least at times we are inclined to believe, have made voluntary decisions to lead their lives in ways that produce serious problems. Thus, able-bodied poor and unemployed who choose not to work merely because of their aversion to the task, drug abusers, and criminals are frequently viewed as people who have asked for their troubles. Able-bodied poor could work, drug abusers could abstain, and criminals could cease and desist if they really wanted to. They have simply exercised their free will to the contrary. A true determinist, of course, would argue that these people have "chosen" their problem-laden life-styles for a reason; they may suffer from a wide variety of intrapsychic maladies, economic obstacles, or political impediments that prevent them from behaving otherwise, though on the surface it appears that they have voluntarily chosen their current circumstances.

Between these two extremes, of course, are those who seem to straddle the free will/determinism fence. These are the people about whom social workers are most ambivalent. In their cases we tend to feel torn, caught between an intellectual understanding of the factors that may have brought about their distress and the frustration of feeling that they have themselves contributed voluntarily to the problem in a significant way, or have not done enough to remedy it.

We seem to understand a great deal about juvenile delinquents, for example. By now, a familiar litany of factors is cited to "explain" juvenile misbehavior: divorce, child abuse, inferior education, poor role models, drugs, and so on. Despite our intellectual understanding of the antecedents or determinants of delinquency, however, many social workers nonetheless are tempted to hold many of these youths responsible for their mischief. If they would only care enough about themselves, think about their behavior and others' feelings more carefully, and take a critical look at their own values, they could surely mend their ways. In the final analysis, we sometimes think the fault may be theirs. We sometimes think similarly about certain elderly people, whose forgetfulness, clumsiness, and poor hygiene annoy us; though their increasing frailty may "explain" their behavior, it is at times tempting to believe that these nuisances could be relieved considerably if these individuals would only try harder. The same holds for those who are experiencing a wide range of emotional difficulties, such as poor self-esteem, marital conflict, depression, loneliness, or some generalized form of anxiety.

Social workers' response to such people is, in large part, a function of their sense of these individuals' moral responsibility and desert. The concept of moral responsibility implies that individuals can, or ought to be, held accountable for their problems and misbehavior. Of course, to assert such a claim is to embrace, at least partially, the notion of free will. It would, after all, be irrational to argue that an individual whose problems are entirely due to factors beyond his or her control (hard-core determinism) is one who should, at the same time, be held accountable for them. To attribute fault or blame in such cases would fly in the face of logic as we know it. As David Hume (1739) observed in his eighteenth-century work, A Treatise of Human Nature: "Actions are by their very nature temporary and perishing; and where they proceed not from some cause in the characters and disposition of the person, who perform'd them, they infix not themselves upon him, and can neither redound to his honour, if good, nor infamy, if evil."

Yet, though some general consensus may exist that people whose circumstances are beyond their control should not be held responsible for these circumstances, the specific factors that determine whether an individual is truly a victim or not remain less clear.

Centuries ago, Aristotle argued that an individual is responsible only for those actions that are voluntary in nature. According to Aristotle, an action can fail to be voluntary in two principal ways: it can be the result of compulsion, or it can be carried out in ignorance (Feinberg 1970). Thus, if an oncoming and recklessly driven auto forces you off the road, and in doing so causes your passenger to be injured, you have been compelled—due to circumstances we would ordinarily consider beyond your control—to act as you did. We would not be likely to hold you morally responsible for your passenger's injuries. Further, if there were some concealed defect in your newly purchased living room chair, and a guest fell from it and harmed himself, common sense suggests you should not be held at fault.

A persistent problem, however, is that while there may be some general agreement that coercion and ignorance preclude the assignment of moral blame, we have had little success in social work reaching agreement about what, in fact, constitutes genuine coercion and ignorance. Take the problem of poverty, for example. Many social workers have at least a general predisposition to attribute the problem to such factors as poor education, racism and oppression, defects in Western capitalism, single-parent status, poor health and nutrition, and a host of related liabilities. But do social workers agree that these factors—acting independently or in concert—constitute coercion and ignorance in the strict sense? It is not hard for us to agree that a gun held to our back or an organic brain disease constitutes coercion (although in different forms). But what of factors that are, at least according to conventional wisdom, highly correlated with poverty? Is it reasonable to assert that these factors compel or coerce individuals into poverty? Further, what distinctions, if any, should we make between intraindividual factors (physiological or psychological), which can be coercive, and extraindividual factors?

Clearly, the degree to which we view poverty and other social problems as products of voluntary effort or coercion has profound implications for our response to them. As the philosopher J. J. C. Smart (1970) observed in his essay, "Free Will, Praise, and Blame":

> When, in nineteenth century England, the rich man brushed aside all consideration of his unsuccessful rivals in the battle for wealth and position, and looking at them as they starved in the gutter said to himself, "Well, they had the same opportunities as I had. If I took more advantage of them than they did, that is not my fault but theirs," he was most probably not only callous but (as I shall try to show) metaphysically confused. A man who said "Heredity and environment made me what I am and made them what they are" would be less likely to fall a prey to this sort of callousness and indifference. Metaphysical views about free will are therefore practically

important, and their importance is often in inverse proportion to their clarity. (197)

A final comment is in order on the concept of moral desert and its relevance to social work. Although social workers' beliefs about the victimization of clients frequently lead them to conclude that clients should not be held accountable for their actions (and therefore deserve assistance), on occasion practitioners' sentiments about clients' moral worth taint and dilute these convictions. Social workers' long-standing involvement with the poor illustrates this point. The profession has, generally speaking, been cognizant of and sympathetic to the reasons people are poor; we know that very few people are poor by choice. Nonetheless, in many professional social work circles at least a subtle contempt can be found for the poor, a feeling that, despite all we know about the social, economic, and psychological causes of poverty, many of the poor neither appreciate nor perhaps are worthy of our various services and ministrations. In some instances, our latent resentment of our clients casts a shadow on our intellectual understanding of their status as victim. The philosopher Harry Frankfurt (1973) commented on this problem in an essay on the subject of coercion and moral responsibility:

> We do on some occasions find it appropriate to make an adverse judgment concerning a person's submission to a threat, even though we recognise that he has genuinely been coerced and he is therefore not properly to be held morally responsible for his submission. This is because we think that the person, although he was in fact quite unable to control a desire, ought to have been able to control it. (79)

THE SUBSTANTIVE QUESTION

The third central question of moral philosophy asks what actions and resources are considered to be worthwhile, good, and desirable on their own account, and for what reasons. An important distinction is made here between actions and resources. When we raise ethical questions about actions—such as whether to breach client confidentiality or to withhold public assistance payments from individuals who have reported false information—we ordinarily ask whether the actions are right, wrong, or obligatory. We ask whether they ought or ought not to be done. When we raise ethical questions about resources—such as the value of social services, public assistance programs, a social worker's motives or intentions, or mental health facilities—we ask whether they are morally good or bad. Thus, when we make judgments about the morality of actions, we make judgments about moral obligation, or what philosophers refer to as *deontic* judgments. When we make ethical judgments about goods and resources, we make judgments about moral value, or what philosophers refer to as *aretaic* judgments.

WHAT IS GOOD? Philosophers have been preoccupied with this question for centuries. Many candidates have been suggested as things that are good for their own sakes, including life, truth, beauty, self-esteem, trust, happiness, knowledge, benevolence, freedom, peace, friendship, and so on. The conclusions social workers reach about what things are good certainly have important consequences. If we value trust, can we justify revealing information shared by a client in confidence? If we value knowledge, can we justify spending tax revenue on parades and carnivals rather than on educational programs for the disabled? If we value freedom and self-determination, can we justify interfering with a client who has decided, after considerable deliberation, to commit suicide?

Philosophers have frequently argued that judgments about what one ought to do (judgments of moral obligation) in particular cases are to be determined by judgments of value or judgments about the meaning or definition of *good*. Thus, if we accept that freedom is good, then we ought to act in ways that promote and enhance freedom—for example, by encouraging clients to select and purchase social services rather than assigning services to them unilaterally. Or, if we accept that truth is good, then we ought to act in ways that are consistent with this belief—for example, by providing candid assessments to clients who request reports about their progress.

A traditional difficulty encountered is, however, that actions suggested by these beliefs frequently conflict. For example, if we simultaneously value self-esteem and truth, it may be that reporting the truth to a client about his or her progress will result in diminished self-esteem. If we value equality and economic security, it may be that an equal distribution of community development funds among communities with different degrees of need will result in a lower degree of economic security than would result from an unequal distribution based on the severity of communities' need. Or, if we value the right to self-determination and the right to life itself, we encounter a difficult conflict of duty when a troubled client expresses his or her intention to commit suicide. In fact, ethical decisions in practice frequently do not involve choices between values that seem good and bad, but choices between values that, when considered independent of one another, seem good. These cases represent the greatest challenges for social workers concerned with ethical dilemmas.

CONFLICTS OF DUTY. One of the classic discussions of conflicts of duty is found in the opening passage of Plato's dialogue concerning civil disobedience, the *Crito*. In short, Socrates was condemned to death by the state for corrupting the youth of Athens with his teachings. He was accused, tried, and convicted in a manner considered by many to have been quite unjust. Friends offered to arrange a plan that would allow Socrates to escape from prison, a plan Socrates ultimately rejected. The story contains, however, a compelling description of Socrates' conflict of duty. Socrates provided arguments to show that he ought not to break state laws by escaping. First, he argued that we ought never to harm anyone and that escaping would harm the state since the state's laws would be violated. Second, if one remains living in a state when one could leave it, one tacitly agrees to respect its laws. But in Plato's *Apology*, Socrates is presented as saying that if the state spares his life on the condition that he cease teaching Athens' youth, he will not obey, because the god Apollo has assigned him to teach, and his teaching is necessary for the good of Athens. Thus, Socrates had to decide between his duty to obey the state, which would require him to cease teaching, and his duty to obey the god Apollo, which would require him to teach for the good of the state. His decision involved not only an appeal to values but a further decision about which values take precedence when they conflict.

The Oxford philosopher W. D. Ross (1930) has provided a useful distinction between what he refers to as *prima facie* duty and *actual* duty, in his classic discussion of conflicts of value and duty in his work *The Right and the Good*. A prima facie duty is an action we ought to perform, *other things being equal,* or independent of other ethical considerations (often known as the *ceteris paribus* provision). Thus, our inclination to simultaneously value self-determination and client well-being may lead to a conflict among prima facie duties if a client announces his or her plan to engage in some form of self-destructive behavior. This sort of conflict would require a social worker to identify his or her actual duty, that is, the product of an attempt to reconcile two or more conflicting prima facie duties.

Conflicts among prima facie duties frequently occur in social work, and decisions about one's actual duty in instances when they conflict represent perhaps the most compelling ethical challenges for practitioners. These are, in a phrase, the hard cases. These are the cases that require one to make difficult, frequently painful choices among options, none of which, oftentimes, seems entirely satisfying in the end. These are the cases in which one must decide, for example, whether information shared by a dangerous client in confidence should be disclosed to protect third parties, whether to blow the whistle on an impaired but valued colleague, or the extent to which one should interfere with a client who has carefully and thoughtfully decided to engage in self-destructive behavior. As Donagan (1977) has said in his *The Theory of Morality:* "It is possible, by breaking one moral prohibition, to entangle yourself in a situation in which, whatever you do, you must break another: that is, in which you are perplexed *secundum quid*" (152).

There have been, as one might expect, many opinions ventured about the ways in which individuals should reconcile conflicts among prima facie duties to determine one's actual duty. Ross, for instance, claims that prima facie duties stemming from such values as justice, fidelity, reparation, and gratitude are self-evident to all "thoughtful and well-educated people" who "have reached sufficient mental maturity and have given sufficient attention" to these duties. Concerning actions derived from prima facie duties, such as promoting the good of others, keeping promises, or telling the truth, Ross states: "The moral order expressed in these propositions is just as much part of the fundamental nature of the universe (and, we may add, of any possible universe in which there were moral agents at all) as is the spatial or numerical structure expressed in the axioms of geometry or arithmetic" (in Gewirth 1978b:982–83). In the end, however, Ross acknowledges that he does not provide a principle that resolves in an unambiguous manner conflicts among prima facie duties. Problems resolving differences of opinion remain.

A second point of view concerning guidelines for resolving conflicts among prima facie duties holds that an actual duty is that which results in the least harm. As Donagan (1977) observes:

What [common morality] provides depends on the fact that, although wrongness, or moral impermissibility, does not have degrees, impermissible wrongs are more or less grave. The explanation of this is simple. Any violation of the respect owed to human beings as rational is flatly and unconditionally forbidden; but the respect owed to human beings may be violated either more or less gravely. It is absolutely impermissible either to murder or to steal; but although murder is no more a wrong than stealing, it is a graver wrong. There is a parallel in criminal law, in which murder and stealing are equally felonies, but murder is a graver felony than stealing. In general, every wrong action impairs some human good, and the gravity of wrong actions varies with the human goods they impair. Although there is room for dispute in some cases as to whether or not this action is a graver wrong than that (for example, whether theft of one's reputation is worse than theft of one's purse), when they find themselves trapped . . . in a choice between these wrongs, not only do most moral agents have opinions about whether those wrongs are equally grave, and if they are not, about which is the graver; but also, if they adhere to the same moral tradition, their opinions on these questions largely agree. And, given that wrongs can differ in gravity, it quite obviously follows from the fundamental principle of morality that, when through some misdeed a man is confronted with a choice between wrongs, if one of them is less grave than the others, he is to choose it. This precept is a special application of a more general principle which I shall refer to as the principle of the least evil, and which was already proverbial in Cicero's time: namely, *minima de malis eligenda*—when you must choose between evils, choose the least. (152)

FOUNDATIONS OF ETHICAL THEORY. Contemporary philosophers have attempted to justify conclusions about morally right action in the face of conflicting duties in a variety of ways. Their theories generally represent two major schools of thought. First there are those who claim that certain kinds of action are inherently right or good, or right or good as a matter of principle. Adherents of this school of thought are generally referred to as *deontologists* (from the Greek *deontos*, or "of the obligatory"). For instance, a deontologist might argue that it is inherently wrong to lie to a client or to break a promise of confidentiality. Mainstream deontologists include philosophers such as H. A. Prichard, W. D. Ross, and Immanuel Kant. For Prichard and Ross, actions such as keeping one's promises, repaying debts, speaking the truth, and showing consideration for the feelings of others are inherently good and obligatory; this is so self-evident that no further reason can be given for its being obligatory (Gewirth, 1978b:991). For Kant, certain actions are morally right or obligatory if they are consistent with his *categorical imperative:* "Act only on that maxim through which you can at the same time will that it should become a universal law" (Kant [1790] 1928:19). That is, actions must be universalizable if they are to be morally right or obligatory, for example, breaking a promise or lying.

Adherents of the second school of thought argue that certain actions are to be performed not because they are intrinsically good, but because they are good by virtue of their consequences. Adherents of this school are generally referred to as *teleologists* (from the Greek *teleios*, or "brought to its end or purpose"). For instance, a teleologist might argue that in certain circumstances a social worker ought to lie to a client or break a promise of confidentiality if such an action would produce beneficial consequences. Teleologists sometimes criticize deontologists for practicing a naive form of what J. J. C. Smart (1971) refers to as "rule worship":

> Suppose that there is a rule R and that in 99 percent of cases the best possible results are obtained by acting in accordance with R. Then clearly R is a useful rule of thumb; if we have not time or are not impartial enough to assess the consequences of an action it is an extremely good bet that the thing to do is to act in accordance with R. But is it not monstrous to suppose that if we *have* worked out the consequences and if we have perfect faith in the impartiality of our calculations, and if we *know* that in this instance to break R will have better results than to keep it, we should nevertheless obey the rule? Is it not to erect R into a sort of idol if we keep it when breaking it will prevent, say, some avoidable misery? Is this not a form of superstitious rule-worship (easily explicable psychologically) and not the rational thought of a philosopher? (199)

Teleologists tend to be of two types, only one of which has significant relevance to social workers. *Egoism* is a form of teleology not typically found in social work, according to which the duty of each person is to maximize his or her own respective good. In contrast, *utilitarianism,* which holds that an action is right if it promotes the maximum good, has historically been the most popular teleological theory and has, at least implicitly, served as justification for many social workers' decisions.

Utilitarian theories have traditionally been of two kinds: (1) those that justify actions that tend to promote the greatest good in situations where one of several possible actions must be performed (*good-aggregative utilitarianism*) (Gewirth 1978b:995); and (2) theories, such as those proposed by Jeremy Bentham and John Stuart Mill, that justify actions that tend to promote the greatest good *for the greatest number,* considering not only the quantity of goods produced but also the number of people to whom the goods are distributed (*locus-aggregative utilitarianism*). The distinction between these two forms of utilitarianism is important when one considers, for example, whether to distribute a fixed amount of public assistance in a way that tends to produce the greatest aggregate satisfaction (which might entail dispensing relatively large sums to relatively few people) or produces the greatest satisfaction for the greatest number (which might entail dispensing smaller sums of money to a larger number of people). Similar dilemmas arise whenever decisions must be made concerning the distribution of limited resources, such as medical care, nursing home beds, or a social worker's time.

It is important as well to distinguish between *act* and *rule* utilitarianism. According to act utilitarianism, one determines the moral rightness or wrongness of an action by calculating its overall consequences in this one instance (the balance of benefits and harm). In contrast, under rule utilitarianism the moral rightness or wrongness of an action is determined by the consequences of acting according to a general rule or practice based on the one action. That is, a rule utilitarian would consider the consequences of the general observance of the practice. Thus, an act utilitarian might justify breaking a specific promise of confidentiality in order to protect a third party whom a specific client has threatened, while a rule utilitarian might argue that if such a practice were generally observed clients would have little faith in their social workers; ultimately, this would threaten the very mission of the profession and, therefore, is not an acceptable trade-off.

Utilitarian principles have traditionally been the most popular guides to social workers' ethical decisions. One reason utilitarianism has been so popular in the profession is that it appears to foster generalized benevolence; a principle that requires one to perform acts that result in the greatest good is, on the face of it, appealing to professionals whose primary mission is to provide aid to those in need. Utilitarianism also captures our intuition about what constitutes morally right action and, in its classic form, appears to provide useful guidelines for resolving ethical conflicts. Bentham's original presentation of utilitarianism in *An Introduction to the Principles of Morals and Legislation* ([1789] 1948) suggests that by examining the "intensity, duration, certainty, propinquity, fecundity, and purity" of the consequences of various actions, one could determine which acts ought to be engaged in: "actions are right in proportion as they tend to promote happiness; wrong as they tend to produce the reverse of happiness."

Despite its initial appeal, however, utilitarianism has a number of well-acknowledged limitations. One serious problem is the difficulty of assigning quantitative values to consequences of actions, particularly when the consequences are frequently qualitative in nature. It is difficult to identify all possible consequences in the first place, and equally difficult to agree on some method of quantification. In addition, it is difficult to make comparisons between individuals, since the consequences of an identical action (for example, the way in which we distribute scarce social services) may have a different meaning for different people.

A related problem concerns the kinds of consequences that should be considered when one is attempting to determine the rightness of particular acts (Mill [1863] 1957). Utilitarians have been inconsistent in their definitions of *good*, and it is not clear in many instances exactly what goods should be valued and pursued, and for what reasons. Bentham, for example, is known as a *hedonistic utilitarian* because of the value he placed on pleasure as opposed to pain. John Stuart Mill, however, argued that mere pleasure is not to be the sole criterion for evaluating consequences, as indicated by his well-known statement, it is "better to be Socrates dissatisfied than a fool satisfied." Socrates' state of mind might be less pleasurable than that of a fool, but, according to Mill, Socrates would be more content than a fool. For Mill there were "higher" and "lower" pleasures, though he was not too clear about the characteristics of these various pleasures. The philosopher G. E. Moore, on the other hand, believed that some states of mind, such as those of acquiring knowledge, had intrinsic value apart from the pleasure they produced. Philosophers who take this point of view are known as *ideal utilitarians* (Smart and Williams 1973).

Utilitarians have also been unclear about whether consequences expected to occur in the future should be considered in addition to more immediate consequences. Further, utilitarianism does not make clear the extent to which our goal should be the minimization of suffering, along with the maximization of good. The conventional view of utilitarianism suggests that each individual is responsible to do what he or she can to bring about the greatest good— *positive utilitarianism*. A close look at this prescription suggests, however, that one must ask whether this implies that our primary goal should only be the promotion of as much happiness and well-being as possible or, in contrast, what Sir Karl Popper (1966) refers to as the "minimization of suffering" and what J. J. C. Smart (in Smart and Williams, 1973:29–30) refers to as *negative utilitarianism:* "Even though we may not be attracted to negative utilitarianism as an ultimate principle, we may concede that the injunction 'worry about removing misery rather than about promoting happiness' has a good deal to recommend it as a subordinate rule of thumb. For in most cases we can do most for our fellow men by trying to remove their miseries."

Another limitation of utilitarianism, taken to its extreme, is the suggestion that social workers are obligated to help others *ad infinitum* and selflessly, allowing no time for nonaltruistic activities. As the philosopher Charles Fried (1978) has said in his *Right and Wrong:*

> For utilitarians there is always one right thing to do, and that is to promote in all possible ways at every moment the greatest happiness of the greatest number. To stop even for a moment or to rest content with a second best is a failure of duty. . . . If, as consequentialism holds, we were indeed equally morally responsible for an infinite radiation of concentric circles originating from the center point of some action, then while it might look as if we were enlarging the scope of human responsibility and thus the significance of personality, the enlargement would be greater than we could support. For to be responsible equally for every thing is to have the moral possibility of choice, of discretion, of creative concretization of one's free self wholly preempted by the potential radiations of all the infinite alternatives for choice. Total undifferentiated responsibility is the correlative of the morally overwhelming, undifferentiated plasma of happiness or pleasure. (13–14, 34–35)

Perhaps the most serious problem with utilitarianism is that technically it may permit subordination of the rights of a few individuals if a greater aggregation of good results. At least in principle, utilitarianism would justify trampling on the rights of oppressed groups and minorities (for example, by reducing welfare benefits or displacing low-income people for commercial development) if there would be some benefit to the majority. Clearly, such a framework runs counter to social work's deep-seated commitment to the least advantaged and oppressed. A compelling example of such thinking appears in Dostoevsky's (1914) classic, *Crime and Punishment*:

> Look here; on one side we have a stupid, senseless, worthless, spiteful, ailing, horrid old woman, not simply useless, but doing actual mischief, who has not an idea what she is living for herself, and who will die in a day or two in any case. . . . On the other side, fresh young lives thrown away for want of help, and by thousands, on every side. A hundred thousand good deeds could be done and helped, on that old woman's money which will be buried in a monastery! Hundreds, thousands perhaps, might be set on the right path; dozens of families saved from destitution, from ruin, from vice, from the lock hospitals—and all with her money. Kill her, take her money and with the help of it devote oneself to the service of humanity and the good of all. What do you think, would not one tiny crime be wiped out by thousands of good deeds? For one life thousands would be saved from corruption and decay. One death, and a hundred lives in exchange—it's simple arithmetic! (60–61)

THE DUTY TO AID

No one questions that social workers generally are committed to assisting people in need and to promoting good. In his *The Theory of Morality* Donagan (1977) refers to this as the *principle of beneficence:* "If a man respects other men as rational creatures, not only will he not injure them, he will necessarily also take satisfaction in their achieving the well-being they seek, and will further their efforts as far as he prudently can" (85).

But if one takes this commitment and utilitarian perspective to its extreme, it is hard to know what practical limits should be placed on social workers' duty to aid. Donagan (1977), for example, also argues that one's obligation to provide aid to those in need has limits. He claims that people have a duty to promote the well-being of others and that this duty derives from their character as "rational creatures, not from their desert" (85). This duty primarily includes contributing to the upbringing and education of children, especially orphans; helping those who have duties which, as a result of bereavement, injury, illness, or desertion, they can perform only with help; restoring to a condition of independence those who have been incapacitated by illness, accident, or injury; and caring for those who are crippled, deaf, or blind, or are chronically ill or senile. Donagan attaches, however, two important qualifications to his discussion of the duty to aid. First, no one is morally obliged to promote the well-being of others at disproportionate inconvenience to oneself: "One does not fail to respect another as a rational creature by declining to procure a good for him, if that good can be procured only by relinquishing an equal or greater good for oneself" (86). Second, one has the right to expect those in need to assume some responsibility for their own welfare: "Genuine benevolence, or willing the well-being of others, is willing that they live a decent human life, and so being prepared to help them in their efforts to do so; it is not an interminable bondage to alleviating the woes brought upon themselves by those who make little or no effort to live well" (209).

Charles Fried (1978) makes a similar claim in his *Right and Wrong:*

> The ... difficult problem, to which I have no satisfactory solution, is our duty to concrete persons who are the victims of unjust institutions. It seems insufficient to say that our duty is wholly discharged by working to change these institutions. And yet the duty we have to our fellow men is to contribute a *fair* share; it is not a duty to give over our whole lives. Can it be that we do wrong, violate our duty to contribute, when we refrain from a total sacrifice which is necessitated only by the plain violation of duty on the part of others? I cannot give an answer. I suggest that compassion and solidarity demand a great deal of us—and particularly if we are the (unwilling) beneficiaries of the unjust situation. But they do not demand everything. (130)

Moral philosophers make a useful distinction between actions that are considered obligatory and those that, while perhaps worthy of praise and to be encouraged, are not obligatory in the strict sense of the term. John Rawls (1971), for example, refers to obligatory actions as *natural duties:* the duty of helping another when he or she is in need or jeopardy, provided one can do so without unreasonable risk to oneself; the duty not to harm or injure another; and the duty not to cause unnecessary suffering. Other actions are considered commendable and praiseworthy, but not obligatory; these actions are called *supererogatory*. As Rawls (1971) says:

> These are acts of benevolence and mercy, of heroism and self-sacrifice. It is good to do these actions but it is not one's duty or obligation. Supererogatory acts are not required, though normally they would be were it not for the loss or risk involved for the agent himself. A person who does a supererogatory act does not invoke the exemption which the natural duties allow. For while we have a natural duty to bring about a great good, say, if we can do so relatively easily, we are released from this duty when the cost to ourselves is considerable. (114)

THE RELEVANCE OF ETHICS

In the early 1980s, at a time when the field of applied ethics—the application of moral theory and philosophy to ethical problems in the professions—was becoming institutionalized, Cheryl Noble (1982) wrote a provocative essay entitled "Ethics and Experts." In her discussion, Noble challenged the assumption that applied ethicists have contributed significantly to the resolution of debates about abortion, capital punishment, euthanasia, genetic engineering, warfare, and reverse discrimination. She concluded that applied ethics is of limited value because ethicists too often get caught up in the analysis of abstractions that are far removed from pressing real-world problems.

Although some of Noble's assertions express traces of truth, by now we know she was essentially mistaken. While some analysts have strayed too far in the direction of intellectual gymnastics that have little bearing on modern-day problems, to date the net result of applied ethics—despite its limitations—has indeed been significant. Although ethicists have not produced definitive guidelines to resolve enduring issues related to every complex dilemma, and should not be expected to do so, their assessments have undoubtedly done much to illuminate critical issues and to suggest practical options and alternatives. One need only look at the emerging literature on issues such as organ allocation, fetal research, psychosurgery, drug screening, frozen embryos, and termination of life support. Our thinking about these phenomena is becoming increasingly mature and insightful, and this is partly due to the work of ethicists. (Certainly others, such as theologians and policy analysts, have contributed much as well.)

Noble *was* right to suggest, however, that ethics has been over-sold somewhat. In a sense, ethicists have shot themselves in the foot whenever they have suggested to impressionable audiences that ethicists are capable of producing all-purpose or one-stop the-ories that can resolve complicated, seemingly intractable problems. They have invited disappointment by heightening expectations for the arrival of a messianic ethical theory.

Fortunately, most ethicists are past that sort of hubris, and their goals are more modest. As Macklin (1988) has concluded in her comments about medical ethics, "Rarely does bioethics offer 'one right answer' to a moral dilemma. Seldom can a philosopher arrive on the scene and make unequivocal pronouncements about the right thing to do. Yet, despite the fact that it has no magic wand, bioethics is still useful and can go a long way toward 'resolving the issues,' once that phrase is properly understood" (52).

In this respect, attempts to produce grand ethical theory have had the unfortunate consequence of producing moral skeptics and relativists. Too many have been sold a bill of goods about the clarity and efficacy of ethical theory. As Baier (1988) astutely observes:

> The obvious trouble with our contemporary attempts to use moral theory to guide action is the lack of agreement on which theory we are to apply. The standard undergraduate course in, say, medical ethics, or business ethics, acquaints the stu-dents with a variety of theories, and shows the difference in the guidance they give. We, in effect, give courses in compar-ative ethical theory, and like courses in comparative religion, their usual effect in the student is loss of faith in *any* of the alternatives presented. We produce relativists and moral skep-tics, persons who have been convinced by our teaching that whatever they do in some difficult situation, some moral the-ory will condone it, another will condemn it. The usual, and the sensible, reaction to this confrontation with a variety of conflicting theories, all apparently having some plausibility and respectable credentials, is to turn to a guide that speaks more univocally, to turn from morality to self-interest, or mere convenience. (26)

What, then, can we expect ethics to offer social workers? Several things. First, ethical inquiry can greatly enhance our understanding of the moral issues related to social work. Policies related to phenomena such as confidentiality, self-determination, paternalism, truth telling, allocating scarce resources, and whistle blowing, for example, require more than consideration of relevant intervention strategies. Although it is essential that we take into account available technical knowledge concerning casework and social welfare policy, we must also examine issues of rights, duties, and justice. In order to grapple adequately with such complex issues, it is helpful to enumerate the various moral duties and rights involved in practice and the ways in which they compete with each other. One should also ask what constitutes a duty and a right in the first place, and these are traditional questions of ethics. As Singer (1988) argues, it is important to have "some understanding of the nature of ethics and the meaning of moral concepts. Those who do not understand the terms they are using are more likely to create confusion than to dispel it, and it is only too easy to become confused about the concepts used in ethics" (153).

It is particularly useful for practitioners to have at least a rudimentary grasp of ethical theories, speculation about their validity and value, and possible connections to social work. It is true, for example, that deontological and utilitarian theories come up short when it comes to providing clear guidance in a number of ethical controversies. Careful consideration of these two classic perspectives—along with others that focus on rights, duties, and virtue— can produce a series of conflicting conclusions. Also, in some instances, these contrasting views may lead to the same outcome, although based on different conceptual premises and theoretical assumptions. What, then, one might reasonably ask, is the point? It is that these theoretical schools of thought contain elements many people find compelling or intuitively appealing, and one must consider their implications, their merits and demerits. The final outcome may be that reasonable people will disagree, but the process of debate and scrutiny of these perspectives is likely to produce the kind of thoughtful judgment that is always more valuable than simplistic conclusions reached without the benefit of careful, sustained reflection and discourse. Moreover, such thorough analysis often leads to appropriate and principled shifts in opinion. As Macklin (1988) claims:

> As long as the debate between Kantians and utilitarians continues to rage and as long as the Western political and philosophical tradition continues to embrace both the respect-for-

persons principle and the principle of beneficence, there can be no possible resolution of dilemmas traceable to those competing theoretical approaches. But the inability to make a final determination of which theoretical approach is ultimately "right" does not rule out the prospect for making sound moral judgments in practical contexts, based on one or the other theoretical perspective.

The choice between utilitarian ethics and a deontological moral system rooted in rights and duties is not a choice between one moral and one immoral alternative. Rather, it rests on a commitment to one moral viewpoint instead of another, where both are capable of providing good reasons for acting. Both perspectives stand in opposition to egoistic or selfish approaches, or to a philosophy whose precepts are grounded in privileges of power, wealth, or the authority of technical experts. (66–67)

It is helpful to remember that in the final analysis the Darwinian forces of the intellectual marketplace will determine which theoretical perspectives are most helpful and persuasive. Pushing competing points of view to their respective limits, in dialectical fashion, helps to reveal the strengths and weaknesses of a position, and eventually helps the fittest arguments survive. Narveson (1988) makes the point nicely:

If some ethical theory would prove to be genuinely indeterminate at some point where determination is needed, then there is nothing to say except that it is a fatal objection to that theory as it stands. It would have to be supplemented, patched up, or discarded. If, for example, it could be established that the whole idea of cardinal utility is in principle incoherent, then that is a blow from which utilitarianism, as usually understood, could not recover. The point here is that we must not identify the whole enterprise of moral philosophy with any particular theory within it. But why should there not be progress? Old theories will fall into disuse or simply die from fatal conceptual diseases; new theories will replace them. So it goes. None of this has any tendency to establish that the enterprise is unfounded or that we can never expect any definite results. (104)

Nickel (1988) offers a particularly useful framework for assessing the value of applied ethics. According to the "strong" version of applied ethics, some particular ethical theory is considered to be true, well founded, authoritative, and it is possible in principle to settle policy issues by deriving a prescription from that theory (139–48). Thus, someone who accepts Rawls's theory of justice would use it to determine the most ethical way to distribute scarce social service resources. One would draw on Rawls's concepts related to the veil of ignorance, original position, difference principle, and the least advantaged to determine the most ethical strategy.

As I noted earlier, however, few embrace the "strong" version of applied ethics. As Ayer (in Singer 1988:149) observed several decades ago, "It is silly, as well as presumptuous, for any one type of philosopher to pose as the champion of virtue. And it is also one reason why many people find moral philosophy an unsatisfactory subject."

Instead, most contemporary ethicists prefer what Nickel calls the "weak" version of applied ethics, where ethical concepts and theory are used mainly to illuminate policy issues and their moral features. According to the weak version, it is helpful to survey available concepts and theories (and to formulate new ones) to try to shed light on compelling issues and to consider them from various, and often competing, perspectives. Weak applied ethics does not assume that any one theory is completely adequate. As Nickel (1988) concludes:

> I am open-minded about the future prospects of moral theorizing, but I doubt that we have much moral theory in hand that can be offered with confidence as a guide to policy in hard cases. As guides to policy, I am much more comfortable with middle-level moral principles that are widely accepted than with grand principles such as the principle of utility or Rawls's difference principle. (148)

ETHICS AND VIRTUE

Even if we embrace the more realistic "weak" version of applied ethics, it is important to acknowledge that no amount of cognitively oriented discussion of ethics can substitute for an innate sensitivity to matters of justice, right and wrong, and duty and obligation. At some point we must deal with the moral fiber of professionals themselves, not just with their intellectual grasp of an intriguing collection of ethical theories and concepts. As Jonsen (1984) astutely argues, ethics guidelines "are not the modern substitute for the Decalogue. They are, rather, a shorthand moral education. They set out the concise definitions and the relevant distinctions that prepare the already well-disposed person to make the shrewd judgment that this or that instance is a typical case of this or that sort, and then decide how to act" (4).

We are, after all, seeking a certain form of virtue here, one that is informed by reason. Virtue certainly can be taught, but probably not so well in university classrooms or agency conference rooms. Most of us got whatever virtue we now possess long before we walked into those settings, and it is this deep-seated virtue that is essential if we are to respond effectively to ethical dilemmas in social work. It is one thing to engage in a depersonalized, stripped-down, yet intellectually sophisticated discussion of complex moral matters related to social work. It is quite another to take seriously the question, "Why be moral in the first place?" As C. S. Lewis (1947) observed some years ago:

It still remains true that no justification of virtue will enable a man to be virtuous. Without the aid of trained emotions the intellect is powerless against the animal organism. I had sooner play cards against a man who was quite skeptical about ethics, but bred to believe that "a gentleman does not cheat," than against an irreproachable moral philosopher who had been brought up among sharpers. (3–4)

Motive is relevant. We must move beyond the sterile analysis of theory and concept (while continuing to incorporate both) to focus on why people do or do not care about doing what is ethically right. For this to happen, we need to broaden our lens to include issues of commitment and caring to complement our concern with grand ethical guidelines and principles, and to include what Kass (1990) has described as the " 'small morals' that are the bedrock of ordinary experience and the matrix of all interpersonal relations" (8). Kass goes on to conclude: "Perhaps in ethics, the true route begins with practice, with deeds and doers, and moves only secondarily to reflection on practice. Indeed, even the propensity to *care* about moral matters requires a certain *moral disposition,* acquired in practice, before the age of reflection arrives. As Aristotle points out, he who has 'the that' can easily get 'the why.' "

❧

CHAPTER THREE

LOGIC

Careful and correct use of language is a powerful aid to straight thinking, for putting into words precisely what we mean necessitates getting our own minds quite clear on what we mean.

—WILLIAM IAN BEARDMORE BEVERIDGE

Some years ago, when I worked in the forensic unit of a psychiatric hospital, I attended a staff meeting to discuss the progress of one of the patients. This twenty-seven-year-old man was hospitalized after being found "not guilty by reason of insanity" on an arson charge. Following his criminal court trial, he was placed in the custody of the state's forensic unit. He had a history of psychiatric hospitalizations and, over the years, had been arrested for a variety of offenses, including sexual assault, robbery, and arson.

The patient's current hospitalization had just passed the six-month point. At the staff meeting, attended by the unit's administrator, psychiatrist, chief of nursing, activities coordinator, and two social workers, the patient's progress and record were reviewed. The discussion focused on the staff's efforts to work with the patient on his impulsive and occasionally explosive behavior. One of the social workers recommended that the staff continue the intensive, one-on-one therapy that had been provided during the preceding two months. When the unit administrator asked why, the social worker responded, "Because ever since we started the therapy, there have been far fewer explosive incidents. It's clearly working."

The staff psychiatrist looked in the patient's record and noted that she had changed the patient's neuroleptic medication at about the time the intensive therapy started. It was her impression that the new medication accounted primarily for the significant behavioral change.

This brief interchange illustrates a logical pitfall frequently encountered in practice. Social workers routinely introduce interventions designed to bring about change in a client's life, a family, community, or organization. Following the introduction of the intervention, the social worker may observe change, whether positive or negative. A child's hyperactivity may diminish following the introduction of a behavioral treatment program. A family's conflict may exacerbate following hospitalization of one of its members. A community's unemployment rate may drop following a large-scale vocational training program. Morale in a social service agency may improve following implementation of a new set of personnel guidelines recommended by a management consultant.

Given social workers' interest in effecting change, we are tempted to believe that our interventions are responsible for the outcomes we witness. As I saw in the forensic unit staff meeting, however, such beliefs can be fraught with logical error. When we make claims about the effectiveness of interventions, we make claims about causality. Too often, however, our claims fail to meet the canons of ordinary logic. The forensic patient's behavioral change may have been the result of the new medication or a number of other factors, not the social worker's therapeutic efforts. Changes in a community's unemployment rate may be a function of a dip in regional interest rates banks charge to businesses rather than a result of a local vocational training program. Just because an intervention precedes an outcome does not necessarily mean the intervention accounts for the change. It may, but it may not. To assume that it does may be to commit the fallacy of *post hoc, ergo propter hoc* ("after this; therefore, because of this").

In addition to the variety of intervention, interpersonal, and other change-agent skills social workers must master, they must also learn a range of cognitive skills to enable them to reason logically about practice. Adherence to the canons of deductive and inductive logic strengthen social workers' ability to intervene effectively and to persuade others of the value of their efforts. Departure from these canons—in the form of logical fallacies—can seriously undermine social workers' efficacy and credibility.

THE RUDIMENTS OF LOGIC

Put simply, logic is the study of the methods and principles used to distinguish good or correct reasoning from bad or incorrect reasoning (Cohen and Nagel 1934; Suppes 1957; Smullyan 1962; Salmon 1963; Harre 1970; Ingle 1976; Kahane 1990). Social workers' effectiveness depends on their ability to present compelling arguments and reasonable inferences in light of available evidence (Siegel and Reamer 1988; Gambrill 1990; Gibbs 1991). We present arguments about the need for increased social welfare spending based on evidence concerning poverty trends. We present further arguments concerning the need for new substance abuse treatment programs based on the results of program evaluations. We present still other arguments concerning the need for psychiatric hospitalization based on evidence drawn from interviews with a client. In each instance, social workers offer conclusions that are allegedly supported by the available evidence. Logical analysis helps us to examine the relationship between such conclusions and the evidence offered to support them.

In the study of logic, an argument consists of one statement that is the conclusion and one or more statements of supporting evidence. The statements of evidence are known as "premises." For example, the social worker who attended the forensic unit staff meeting seemed to offer the following argument:

1. If the patient's behavior improved following my intervention, my intervention caused the improved behavior.
2. The patient's behavior improved following my intervention.
3. Therefore, the intervention caused the change in the patient's behavior.

This is the typical form of an argument. The first two statements are the premises, and the third statement is the conclusion.

When we offer an argument, we are saying that the premises present evidence for the conclusion. This can occur in two ways. First, we are claiming that the premises contain statements of fact.

Second, we are claiming that these facts provide the evidence needed for the conclusion. For example, if the second premise above is false (i.e., the social worker really did not provide intensive, one-on-one therapy), clearly it does not provide evidence for the conclusion. This is so obvious it is hardly worth saying. But there is a second, more complicated way in which a premise may not offer evidence for a conclusion. Even if the premises are true (that is, they accurately state the relevant facts), they may not lead *logically* to the conclusion. Apart from the accuracy of any factual statements contained in the premises of an argument, the premises must be related logically to the conclusion. Hence, when we assert that the premises of an argument support the conclusion, we are not saying that the premises are true; rather, we are saying that *if* the premises are true, there would be good evidence for the conclusion.

It is possible, then, to have a logically correct argument that contains one or more false premises, and a logically incorrect or fallacious argument that contains true premises. These are the kinds of situations social workers need to avoid. Some examples may help to clarify this. Consider, for instance, a social worker who is director of an emergency shelter and soup kitchen. At a meeting with her board of directors, where she is providing an overview of the program's clientele, she essentially says the following:

1. Increased housing costs lead to increased demand on emergency shelters.
2. Local housing costs have increased significantly within the past twelve months.
3. Therefore, increases during the past year in the demands for our shelter beds are the result of increased housing costs during this period.

Although the *form* of this argument is logically correct, it happens that the second premise was not true. In this particular community, housing costs had increased significantly for the first three months of the year, but then declined steadily during the next nine months. Housing experts agreed that the increase in demand for local shelter beds was the result primarily of cuts in the county's welfare (general relief) benefits and increased deinstitutionalization by the nearby state psychiatric hospital. The director's mistaken conclusion could lead to misplaced efforts on her part to address the increasing demand for her shelter's services. Her time might be spent more productively organizing advocacy efforts designed to reinstate previous levels of welfare benefits, and working with officials at the state hospital to enhance their discharge planning procedures and policies.

A logically *incorrect* or fallacious argument that contains true premises also can be problematic. For example, at a meeting with a family caring for a dying mother, a hospice social worker essentially presented the following argument:

1. Many families in your situation need some respite relief.
2. Our agency provides respite services.
3. Therefore, our agency should provide your family with respite services.

No doubt, the two premises are true. The conclusion, however, does not follow logically from these premises. *If* this family needs some respite relief (it may not), it is not necessarily the case that the social worker's agency is the most appropriate service provider. The agency's fees may be too high, the family's insurance coverage may not reimburse for services provided by this particular agency, other agencies may offer more skilled services, and so on. The true premises do not lead logically to the argument's conclusion.

It is important to distinguish between two major types of arguments social workers make: deductive and inductive. A deductive argument is one where the conclusion *must* be true if all of the premises are true. In addition, all the information in the conclusion is already contained (at least implicitly) in the premises. For example:

1. Every victim of sexual abuse has emotional scars.
2. All of this agency's clients are victims of sexual abuse.
3. Therefore, every client of this agency has emotional scars.

With this form of argument, the only way the conclusion can be false is for one or both of the premises to be false. If both premises are true, the conclusion must be true.

This is not necessarily the case, however, with an inductive argument. With an inductive argument, it is quite possible for a premise to be true and the conclusion to be false. With an inductive argument, if all the premises are true, the conclusion is *probably* true but not necessarily true. Some time in the future we might find an exception. For example:

1. Every past client of this agency has had emotional scars.
2. Therefore, every current client of this agency has emotional scars.

With this form of an inductive argument, the premise lends some weight to the conclusion, but it does not necessarily lead to it. In this respect, inductive arguments are much weaker (and more common in social work) than deductive arguments.

MORE ON DEDUCTION

Deductive forms of argument are either valid or invalid. An invalid form of deductive argument is called a "fallacy." Shortly I will have more to say about common fallacies in social work. First, though, it will be useful to review commonly accepted forms of deductive arguments. Many deductive arguments rely on what are known as *conditional* (or *hypothetical*) statements. This is a statement composed of two component statements joined by the conjunction "if . . . then . . ." Here are several examples:

1. If my client attempted to commit suicide, then he needs counseling.
2. If an AFDC client is paying more than 30 percent of her income for housing, then she needs an increase in benefits.
3. If larger numbers of pregnant women abuse alcohol, then there will be an increase in children born with fetal alcohol syndrome.

In each of these examples, the part of the statement that is introduced by "if" is known as the *antecedent,* and the part that follows the "then" is known as the *consequent.* In example 1 above, "my client attempted suicide" is the antecedent, and "he needs counseling" is the consequent. A conditional statement has a standard form, which is:

If p, then q.

An equivalent form of this conditional statement looks like this:

If not q, then not p.

This particular type of statement is known in logic as a *contrapositive.* The contrapositive of example 1 above would be:

1. If my client does not need counseling, then he did not attempt to commit suicide.

It is important to understand the form of conditional statements in order to distinguish valid and invalid (or fallacious) arguments. Valid arguments take two basic forms. The first is known as "affirming the antecedent" (or *"modus ponens"*). When we affirm the antecedent, we have a first premise that is a conditional statement ("If my client attempted to commit suicide, then he needs counseling"), and a second premise that affirms or asserts the antecedent of this conditional ("My client attempted to commit suicide"). The conclusion of the argument is the consequent of the first premise ("Therefore, he needs counseling"). This valid form of argument is represented as follows:

If p, then q.
p.
Therefore, q.

A second valid form of deductive argument is called "denying the consequent" (or *"modus tollens"*). With this form of argument, the first premise is a conditional statement ("If larger numbers of pregnant women abuse alcohol, there will be an increase in children born with fetal alcohol syndrome"), and the second premise is the denial of the consequent of that conditional ("There has not been an increase in children born with fetal alcohol syndrome"). The conclusion, therefore, is that larger numbers of pregnant women have not abused alcohol. The form of "denying the consequent" is:

If p, then q.
Not q.
Therefore, not p.

Two invalid forms of argument exist, both of which I have observed often in social work. The first is known as the fallacy of "affirming the consequent." With this form (which, unfortunately, bears close resemblance to the valid form of affirming the antecedent), the second premise asserts the consequent of the first premise and the conclusion is the antecedent of the first premise. This invalid form looks like this:

If p, then q.
q.
Therefore, p.

Or as a concrete example:

1. If my client attempted to commit suicide, then he needs counseling.
2. My client needs counseling.
3. Therefore, my client attempted to commit suicide.

Clearly, my client may need counseling for reasons having nothing to do with suicide. Another common example of "affirming the consequent" in social work looks like this:

1. If I continue to provide long-term residential care for emotionally disturbed adolescents on my caseload, this will cause their mental health to improve.
2. The mental health of the emotionally disturbed adolescents on my caseload has improved.
3. Therefore, the long-term residential treatment I provided to these youths caused their mental health to improve.

Again, it is clear that this is not a valid argument, since improved mental health also may be the result of a variety of other factors in these youths' lives, such as changes in family relationships, developmental or maturational changes, and so on. As we noted earlier, just because social workers' interventions temporally precede changes in clients' lives, it is not necessarily the case that the interventions caused the change (although we certainly hope that is the case).

The second invalid form of argument is known as the fallacy of "denying the antecedent." This form of argument is similar to the valid form of argument of denying the consequent. Consider the following example:

1. If the poverty rate in our community is increasing, we will need to implement a vocational training program.
2. The poverty rate in our community is not increasing.
3. Therefore, we do not need to implement a vocational training program.

Obviously, there may be very good reasons for implementing a vocational training program in this community, even though the poverty rate currently is not increasing. The existing poverty rate and unemployment rate in the community may be high. The median level of education among adults may be low. Thus, there may be a variety of compelling reasons to design a comprehensive vocational training program in an effort to enhance community residents' employability. That the poverty rate is not going up may not be very significant.

With this fallacy, the second premise denies the antecedent of the first premise ("The poverty rate in our community is not increasing") and the conclusion denies the consequent of the first premise ("Therefore, we do not need to implement a vocational training program"). Invalid arguments that entail the fallacy of denying the antecedent take the form of:

If p, then q.
Not p.
Therefore, not q.

It is also important to realize that when we make arguments about social work practice, we cannot assume that true conclusions are accompanied by true premises. With the fallacies of affirming the consequent and denying the antecedent, we can have a conclusion that is true when the premises are not.

VALID ARGUMENTS IN SOCIAL WORK

Because social workers often offer arguments in an effort to persuade others of the merits of their points of view (for example, with respect to the need for increased services or funding), it is important to examine common forms of valid arguments. One such form of valid argument that is often effective is known in logic as *reductio ad absurdum*. Sometimes this argument form is used to establish a positive conclusion, and sometimes to refute someone else's thesis.

For example, suppose we want to argue that under certain circumstances government should be able to coerce its citizens (for example, in the form of taxing citizens to pay for welfare programs). According to the argument form of *reductio ad absurdum*, we begin by assuming that this claim is false (i.e., we assume that government should *not* be able to coerce its citizens under any circumstances). On the basis of this assumption, we deduce a conclusion that we know to be false (in this case, for example, everyone believes government should be able to use coercion to prevent certain of its citizens from randomly murdering others, so the conclusion would assert that government should *not* be able to use coercion to prevent this). Since a false conclusion follows from our assumption of a false premise by a valid deductive argument, the assumption must have been false. The basic structure of this argument form goes like this:

To prove: *p*.
Assume: Not *p*. Deduce: A false statement.
Conclude: Therefore, not *p* is false; therefore, *p*.

A classic example from Plato's *Republic* will help to illustrate the *reductio ad absurdum* (Salmon 1963:31). In Plato's dialogues, Socrates typically asks a question and then proceeds to refute the answers given by showing that they lead to unacceptable ("absurd") conclusions. Consider this excerpt:

Well said, Cephalus, I replied; but as concerning justice, what is it?—to speak the truth and pay your debts—no more than this? And even to this are there not exceptions? Suppose that a friend when in his right mind has deposited arms with me and he asks for them when he is not in his right mind, ought I to give them back to him? No one would say that I ought or that I should be right in doing so, any more than they would say that I ought always to speak the truth to one who is in his condition.
You are quite right, he replied.
But then, I said, speaking the truth and paying your debts is not a correct definition of justice.

The structure of this argument is typical for the *reductio ad absurdum:*

To prove: Speaking the truth and paying debts is not a correct definition of justice.
Assume: Speaking the truth and paying debts is a correct definition of justice.
Deduce: It is just to give weapons to a madman. But this is absurd.
Conclude: Therefore, speaking the truth and paying debts is not a correct definition of justice.

THE RELEVANCE OF SYLLOGISMS

Analysis of the validity of arguments frequently entails what logicians call *categorical syllogisms* and *categorical statements*. A categorical syllogism (or simply a "syllogism") is a deductive argument in which a conclusion is inferred from premises composed entirely of categorical statements. There are four forms of categorical statements, illustrated by the following examples:

a. All welfare clients are lazy.
b. Some welfare clients are lazy.
c. No welfare clients are lazy.
d. Some welfare clients are not lazy.

Each of these forms of statements has a name. Forms *a* and *b* are *affirmative,* and forms *c* and *d* are *negative.* Also, forms *a* and *c* are *universal* and forms *b* and *d* are *particular.* Any statement in the form of "All X are Y" (e.g., All welfare clients are lazy) is known as *universal affirmative.* Any statement in the form of "Some X are Y" (e.g., Some welfare clients are lazy) is known as *particular affirmative.* Any statement in the form of "No X are Y" (e.g., No welfare clients are lazy) is known as *universal negative.* And any statement in the form of "Some X are not Y" (e.g., Some welfare clients are not lazy) is known as *particular negative.*

Also, each categorical statement contains two terms, a *subject* term and a *predicate* term. In the above examples, each X (welfare clients) stands for the subject term, and each Y (lazy) stands for the predicate term.

In social work, as in any field, we need to be concerned about the validity of syllogisms, or the arguments practitioners make. The validity of a syllogism depends on its form or the way in which it is structured.

If we think of a syllogism as having two premises and one conclusion (All X are Y; All Y are Z; Therefore, all X are Z), we see that while each statement contains two terms—a subject term and a predicate term—the complete syllogism contains only three different terms, e.g., X, Y, and Z. One of these terms (Y) occurs once in each premise and is known as the "middle term." Each of the other two terms (X and Z) occurs once in the conclusion and once in a premise, and are known as "end terms." Consider this syllogism:

All suicidal clients are troubled people.
All troubled people need counseling.
Therefore, all suicidal people need counseling.

Here, "troubled people" occurs once in each premise and, therefore, is the middle term. "Suicidal clients" occurs once in a premise and once in the conclusion and, therefore, is an end term. "Counseling" occurs once in the conclusion and once in a premise and, therefore, also is an end term.

Not surprisingly, logicians have constructed rules for determining whether a particular syllogism is valid. These rules are based on a concept known as *distribution*. When a given term occurs in statements contained in a syllogism (such as "troubled people") it may be distributed or undistributed. Whether a term is distributed or not (as it appears in any given statement) depends on the type of statement it occurs in and whether it is the subject term or the predicate term in the statement.

A term is distributed in a categorical statement if that statement says something about each and every member of the class designated by that term. For example, the statement "All suicidal clients are troubled people" says something about every suicidal client (i.e., that each is troubled), but it does not say anything about every troubled person. Thus, with this type of categorical statement (universal affirmative), the subject term (suicidal clients) is distributed and the predicate term (troubled people) is undistributed.

As we shall see below when we discuss common fallacies in social work, it is important to note that this form of statement says something about the general *class* referred to by its predicate term (in this case, troubled people). "All suicidal clients are troubled people" says that the class of troubled people includes suicidal clients. Of course, it is one thing to make such a statement about a class and quite another to make a statement about each member of that class. Some things that are true of a class as a collection may not be true of its individual members (a group of clients in a residential program may be assertive, although not every member of the group may be assertive individually), and some things that are true of the members of a class as individuals may not be true of the class as a collection (a number of individual social workers may be highly skilled professionals who have difficulty managing a group practice together).

The distribution of terms in categorical statements differs depending on whether the statement is universal affirmative, particular affirmative, universal negative, or particular negative. In contrast to the form of universal affirmative that we just reviewed, in universal negative statements (e.g., "No clients with eating disorders have high self-esteem") both terms are distributed. This statement says that every client with an eating disorder is someone without high self-esteem and that every person with high self-esteem is not a client with an eating disorder. Considered collectively, this statement says that the two classes—clients with eating disorders and people with high self-esteem—are mutually exclusive.

In contrast, with particular affirmative statements ("Some clients with eating disorders have high self-esteem") both terms are undistributed; that is, the statement says nothing about every subject term (every client with an eating disorder) or about every predicate term (every person with high self-esteem). Finally, with particular negative statements ("Some clients with eating disorders do not have high self-esteem") the subject term (clients with eating disorders) is undistributed, although the predicate term (people with high self-esteem) is considered to be distributed. This takes some explaining. According to logicians, the predicate term here essentially says, "There is at least one client with an eating disorder who does not have high self-esteem, and every person who has high self-esteem is distinct from that person." Although this may seem odd, for logicians such a predicate term is distributed, since collectively this statement says that the class of clients with eating disorders is not entirely included within the class of people with high self-esteem.

Before we review the rules for testing the validity of syllogisms, we can summarize the way in which terms are distributed for each of the four types of categorical statements:

Universal Affirmative statements (All X are Y): The subject term (X) is distributed and the predicate term (Y) is undistributed.

Particular Affirmative statements (Some X are Y): The subject term (X) is undistributed and the predicate term (Y) is undistributed.

Universal Negative statements (No X are Y): The subject term (X) is distributed and the predicate term (Y) is distributed.

Particular negative statements (Some X are not Y): The subject term (X) is undistributed and the predicate term (Y) is distributed.

According to the canons of logic, the three rules for testing the validity of a syllogism are:

  I. The middle term must be distributed exactly once.
 II. No end term may be distributed only once.

III. The number of negative premises must equal the number
of negative conclusions.

Any syllogism that satisfies all three of these rules is valid. Any
syllogism that violates one or more of these rules is invalid. Let us
examine fairly simple valid and invalid arguments that a social
worker might offer. First, consider this one:

1. All individuals with an M.S.W. degree attended social work
   school.
2. Some social service workers did not attend social work
   school.
3. Therefore, some social service workers are not individuals
   with an M.S.W. degree.

In this syllogism, the first premise is universal affirmative; its
subject (all individuals with an M.S.W. degree) is distributed and
its predicate (attendance at social work school) is undistributed.
The second premise is particular negative; its subject (social service workers) is undistributed and its predicate (attendance at social work school) is distributed. Rule I is satisfied because the
middle term (attendance at social work school) is distributed once
(in the second premise). Rule II is satisfied because no end term is
distributed only once; one end term (individuals with an M.S.W.
degree) is distributed in both of its occurrences, and the other end
term (social service workers) is undistributed in both of its occurrences. Rule III is satisfied because there is one negative premise
(Some social service workers did not attend social work school) and
one negative conclusion (Some social service workers are not individuals with an M.S.W. degree).

Consider this argument:

1. All AFDC recipients are low-income families.
2. Some low-income families are dishonest.
3. Therefore, some AFDC recipients are dishonest.

This is the sort of argument that is sometimes offered (or implied)
by critics of public welfare programs and that may seem persuasive
to a naive, uncritical, or impressionable audience. But clearly the
argument is fallacious. With this syllogism we see that Rule I is
violated because the middle term (low-income families) is not distributed in either occurrence. In addition, Rule II is violated because while one end term (AFDC recipients) is distributed in the
premises it is not distributed in the conclusion. Rule III is satisfied

because the syllogism contains no negative premises and no negative conclusions.

Consider this third example:

1. All homeowners need health care.
2. No homeless people are homeowners.
3. Therefore, no homeless people need health care.

With this syllogism, Rule I is violated because the middle term (homeowners) is distributed twice. Rule II also is violated because one end term (health care) is distributed in the conclusion but not in the premises. Rule III is satisfied because there is one negative premise (No homeless people are homeowners) and one negative conclusion (No homeless people need health care).

Seasoned social workers know, of course, that arguments offered in day-to-day practice rarely are this simple and straightforward. Arguments concerning real-life problems of mental illness, poverty, delinquency, aging, health care, and so on, often are very complex and contain a large number of premises, some of which may be only implicit or scrambled, that lead up to a conclusion. To determine the validity of more complex arguments offered in social work contexts requires identifying the premises and conclusion, translating the premises and conclusion into categorical statements, and, if necessary, supplying missing premises. For instance, imagine someone who argues as follows:

Many people argue that work release programs for incarcerated criminals that require menial labor are worthless because they do not provide realistic job training. They believe that a valuable program is one which provides work experience in an actual work site, not menial labor such as cleaning up litter, painting park benches, and so on. But this is wrong. The most important ingredient in any work release program is an opportunity for restitution—paying the community back for one's criminal behavior. Menial labor provides this kind of opportunity. Therefore, work release programs should require menial labor.

If we convert this argument into categorical statements, we have something like the following:

1. All worthwhile work release programs for incarcerated criminals provide opportunities for restitution.

2. All work release programs that require menial labor provide opportunities for restitution.
3. Therefore, all worthwhile work release programs for incarcerated criminals are programs that require menial labor.

Most social workers will intuitively sense that something is wrong with this argument, although to naive or uncritical listeners this line of reasoning may seem persuasive. The argument seems to miss the point that while work release programs that require menial labor may provide opportunities for restitution, so do programs that provide more realistic job training. More formally, we can say that this argument is invalid because it does not satisfy the three rules we reviewed earlier. Rule I is violated because the middle term (opportunities for restitution) is not distributed once. Rule II is violated because there is one end term (work release programs that require menial labor) that is distributed only once. Rule III need not concern us since we have already encountered at least one rule violation and there are no negative premises or conclusions.

Social workers often encounter complicated and confusing arguments, and it can be difficult to sort them out in a way that enables easy identification of logical flaws. In fact, complicated or convoluted arguments sometimes are successful for this very reason; it may seem just too difficult to pinpoint the logical problem.

LOGICAL FALLACIES IN SOCIAL WORK

A wide variety of logical fallacies are committed in social work practice (Siegel and Reamer 1988; Gambrill 1990; Gibbs 1991), and it will be helpful to review them systematically. Familiarity with these fallacies—that is, arguments that are psychologically persuasive but whose conclusions are not implied by their premises—can help social workers recognize them and thus avoid committing them. While some of these fallacies stem from attempts at logical deduction (deducing a conclusion from a set of premises), many occur in the context of *inductive* arguments. Inductive arguments are those that provide conclusions whose content goes beyond that of their premises. With inductive arguments, we cannot be certain that the conclusions will always be true if the premises are true, although we may be able to say that they are probably true. Although inductive arguments sometimes are necessary in social work, they can also get us into trouble. As we shall see, this may occur when social workers use evidence from past experiences to predict (or induce information about) future events.

Many kinds of fallacies exist. Aristotle, for example, identified thirteen types of fallacies in his book *Sophistical Refutations*. Over the centuries, however, philosophers have discovered and labeled dozens more. In fact, in 1970 David Hackett Fischer listed 112 different fallacies in his book *Historian's Fallacies*, although we will review only those that are particularly relevant to social work.

Fallacies germane to social work practice can be divided into several major categories: (1) fallacies of deductive reasoning; (2) fallacies that concern causation and correlated events; (3) fallacies of relevance; and (4) fallacies of imprecision.

FALLACIES OF DEDUCTIVE REASONING. As we have already seen, some of the more common fallacies involve attempts to present conclusions based on premises. These include the fallacy of *affirming the consequent, denying the antecedent, the fallacy of division,* and *the fallacy of composition*. We have already reviewed the fallacies of affirming the consequent and denying the antecedent, so we need not cover all this ground again. To recap briefly, these two fallacies are committed when we are dealing with conditional ("if . . . then . . .") statements. The two valid forms of argument are affirming the antecedent (*modus ponens*) and denying the consequent (*modus tollens*). The fallacies of affirming the consequent and denying the antecedent essentially get things backward.

The fallacy of division and the fallacy of composition are rather different. Instead of involving conditional statements of the form "If *p*, then *q*," they are relevant to the categorical syllogisms we just discussed. These two fallacies involve what logicians call *collective* and *distributive* statements. The fallacy of division occurs when someone concludes (distributively) that every member of a group (or class) has a certain attribute from the premise that the group (collectively) has that attribute. For example:

The Jones family is quite dysfunctional.
Therefore, every member of the Jones family is dysfunctional.

We know from experience that families social workers consider dysfunctional often include individual members who are well functioning. It would be a mistake to conclude that the label attached to the family applies to each of its members outside the context of the family as well.

The converse fallacy is the fallacy of composition. This fallacy occurs when someone concludes (collectively) that a group has an attribute because (distributively) every member of that group has that attribute. For example:

Each social worker at the Cross Country Family Service Agency is very well organized.
Therefore, the Cross Country Family Service Agency is very well organized.

It may well be that each social worker at the agency is well organized. All of us, however, can probably recall dealing with agencies that were disorganized despite individual staff members' ability to be organized. Just because each member of a basketball team is talented does not mean that the individuals work well together to produce a talented team.

FALLACIES THAT CONCERN CAUSATION AND CORRELATED EVENTS. Social workers often make comments that imply causation. This is not surprising, given that social workers are in the business of designing and implementing interventions to bring about outcomes. The nature of social work invites assumptions and statements about causation, for example, concerning the effectiveness of counseling, group work, family services, employment training programs, residential care, community organizing, organizational change, or staff development.

Unfortunately, the frequent opportunities for social workers to make observations about causation tend to lead to occasional fallacious claims. Among the most common is the fallacy of *post hoc, ergo propter hoc* ("After this, therefore because of this"). This is the fallacy of assuming, when one event follows another, that the first event must have caused the second. For example, consider the oft-cited story about a group of people who were frightened by an eclipse of the sun. The local witch doctor beat his drum and, lo and behold, the eclipse went away. His people concluded that the drum beating caused the eclipse to disappear. Obviously, parallels exist in social work. A depressed client was hospitalized and during the six months following discharge reported considerable improvement in his mental health. The social worker may assume that the hospitalization was the causal determinant, when we know full well that other events in the client's life may have something (or every-thing) to do with his mood change. Without adequate controls (a strict single-subject design or a controlled clinical experiment test-ing the effectiveness of the counseling), it is not possible to know that the social worker's intervention accounted for the client's change.

Recently, I served on the governor's staff in Rhode Island to help design a program to expand the supply of affordable housing for low-income people in the state. Housing costs in the area had increased rapidly, and many low-income people were unable to afford housing or were spending an extraordinary portion of their monthly income for it. Many experts believed that increased hous-ing costs were a result, in large part, of an inadequate supply of rental units on the market. We assumed that if we could expand the supply of housing units, rents would stabilize (consistent with elementary laws of supply and demand). I worked with a number of people for nearly a year to obtain public funds to help subsidize the cost of constructing and rehabilitating housing units.

We were successful in getting the program started, and before long the number of affordable housing units available in the local market increased significantly. Shortly after the appearance of these units, housing prices in the area stabilized and, in some areas, declined. Some of my colleagues were quick to assume that our affordable housing program was the cause. I suspect the program was a determining factor; however, there also seemed to be other factors at work. For example, the unemployment rate in the state began to increase at about the time the affordable housing program started. Because fewer people were working, the wages and income that had partly fueled the recent housing-cost increases declined, and this phenomenon, most agreed, helped to put the brakes on escalating housing costs. Also, interest rates began to increase and this, too, dampened the demand for housing. The declining local economy also led to a number of foreclosures in the condominium market, which led to the conversion of some condominiums to rental units. This further added to the supply of units on the rental market, which probably contributed to the stabilization of housing costs.

Other factors may have been involved as well. The main point is that while it was tempting to believe that our ambitious affordable housing program was the principal cause of the change in the housing climate, it appears that many other factors may also have been involved. This is important to acknowledge, since a full under-standing of causal determinants in one instance may influence how we design interventions when similar circumstances arise in the future. History provides important lessons, so our grasp of historical events must be accurate.

A close cousin of the fallacy of *post hoc, ergo propter hoc* is known as *cum hoc, ergo propter hoc* ("With this, therefore because of this"). The mistaken assumption here is that changes we see *during the course* of an intervention are a result of the intervention. Again, this may be true, but often it is not. As with the *post hoc* fallacy, other causal determinants may be involved. If a child becomes less hyperactive during the course of a social worker's counseling, the social worker may be tempted to assume that the counseling is the reason. That may be, but it is also possible that influential changes are occurring in the child's family, diet, school activities, or friendships. Any or all of these factors may be affecting the child's behavior as well. It is also quite possible that the child's behavior is changing simply because of normal maturation.

Some years ago I read a newspaper account of a well-publicized study of the relationship between children's television-watching habits and aggressive behavior. The study's authors found that the number of hours children watched television correlated significantly with their tendency to engage in aggressive behavior. That is, the greater the number of hours a child watched television, the more aggressive was the child's behavior. A cursory reading of the newspaper article probably suggested to many that the television watching itself was the primary cause of the children's aggressive behavior, and that an effective way to reduce aggressive behavior is to reduce television watching.

This may, in fact, be an effective intervention. Social workers who have experience with aggressive children, however, know that the television watching itself may not be the primary problem, although it may be part of it. Children who watch television excessively may be children who are not supervised by parents conscientiously, who do not get much physical exercise, and who do not have ample opportunity to develop social skills by playing with other children. Simply pulling the plug on the television may not do the trick. A reduction in television watching also may need to be accompanied by working with the parents to help them supervise children more effectively, create opportunities for physical exercise, and encourage constructive play with other children. These are the phenomena that may be linked with the children's aggressive behavior. Again, without strict controls, it is difficult to identify the primary determinants of the children's aggressive behavior. The least we can do, however, is to avoid assuming that a *correlate* of a behavior (or any other phenomenon of interest to social workers) is the *cause* of it.

FALLACIES OF RELEVANCE. A number of other fallacies are encountered in social work that have one common trait: their premises are logically irrelevant (in the logical sense, though perhaps not the psychological sense) to their conclusions. For instance, the fallacy of *argumentum ad baculum* ("appeal to force") occurs when one appeals to force or the threat of force to gain acceptance of a conclusion. An antiabortion activist who threatens the administrator of a counseling agency that she will use her political connections to have United Way funding terminated if the agency does not acknowledge that abortion is morally wrong is an example. Any effort to connect a desired outcome with the threat of force engages in this fallacy, since logically these considerations have nothing to do with the substantive request.

Another common fallacy is the familiar *argumentum ad hominem* ("argument directed to the 'man'"). One form of *argumentum ad hominem* occurs when one attacks a person who is presenting an argument rather than attacking the logic of the argument itself. Legislators may dismiss the arguments of an aggressive, troublesome welfare rights activist because they dislike his or her personality. A social work administrator may discount the opinion of a division director because he or she finds the director abrasive.

A second common form of *argumentum ad hominem* has more to do with assumptions about an adversary's personal or professional circumstances than with deliberate attempts to attack the individual. For example, imagine that a social worker is trying to persuade a city council member to support a grant request that would provide funds for a private agency to offer a job training program for welfare recipients. The social worker might try to convince the council member that such a program is likely to produce satisfied clients who ultimately may be loyal supporters and voters. To the extent that the social worker emphasizes the benefits of a successful program for the council member's political career, rather than the actual merits of the program, the social worker commits the fallacy of *argumentum ad hominem*. That is, the social worker is appealing more to the special circumstances of the council member than to the evidence concerning the likely effectiveness of the program.

The fallacy of *argumentum ad ignorantiam* ("argument from

ignorance") occurs when an individual argues that something is true because no one has ever been able to prove it is not, or that something is not true because no one has ever been able to prove that it is. But in these instances, we may be saying more about our limited ability to prove claims to be true or false than about their *actual* truth or falsity. Many myths in social work are perpetuated in this way.

Take, for example, the widespread belief that welfare benefits consistently produce dependency. For a variety of reasons, this myth persists, partly because social welfare experts have not produced sufficient evidence to prove that welfare benefits do not consistently produce dependency. Just because sufficient evidence has not been produced to challenge the myth does not mean the myth is true.

Similarly, some people argue that family planning clinics located in high schools will encourage sexual activity, and ultimately will increase, rather than prevent, teenage pregnancy. Arguments sometimes are offered that because no evidence exists that such family planning clinics are effective, these clinics must be encouraging rather than discouraging teenage pregnancy.

Another fallacy involves attempts to get a conclusion accepted by appealing to sentiment rather than to the facts involved. This is known as the fallacy of *argumentum ad misericordiam* ("appeal to pity"). While sentiment may certainly deserve a place of consideration whenever matters involve human beings, sometimes we are moved to excess. Take, for instance, the case of a social worker who recently was convicted of sexual molestation of a fourteen-year-old female client. During his criminal court trial, he argued that he should be acquitted because, as a youth, he too was subjected to sexual abuse and has had difficulty recovering from this trauma. This social worker described himself as a victim of circumstances beyond his control. He seemed unwilling to accept responsibility for his actions, preferring instead to appeal to the jury's sense of pity. While it may have been important for the jury and judge to have an understanding of factors in the social worker's background that may help to explain his misconduct, pure appeal to pity seems to deny the facts.

This type of fallacy can be grouped broadly under the fallacy generally known as *argumentum ad populum,* where one makes an emotional appeal (rather than a factual one) "to the people" or "to the gallery." More narrowly, *argumentum ad populum* may be defined as an attempt to gain approval for a conclusion by arousing the emotions of the masses rather than by persuasion with relevant facts. This is a common strategy in the social welfare arena. Politicians may try to generate support for their programs and policies by stirring emotional reactions to opposing positions.

Consider, for example, the case where a local family service agency proposed development of a group home for the retarded in a residential neighborhood. The professional staff spent months seeking a site, raising public and private funds to support the facility, designing the program, recruiting staff, and soliciting local community support.

Much to their surprise, a number of local residents and their city councilman actively opposed the group home. The councilman, in particular, spoke about the risk the group home residents would pose to neighbors, especially children. He scheduled a number of neighborhood meetings to discuss the proposal and to warn residents about the problems he anticipated. The councilman's efforts clearly were designed to scuttle the project. His appeal to the "people" relied to a great extent on emotion rather than facts concerning the successful operation of group homes for the mentally retarded in many other communities. Social workers have encountered similar displays of *argumentum ad populum* in debates about welfare rights, family planning programs, homelessness shelters, and deinstitutionalization of a variety of populations.

Social workers sometimes encounter special problems when so-called experts are relied on to support a point of view. Whether it is in the form of testimony before a legislative subcommittee, testimony in court, consultation on a challenging clinical case, or claims that appear in a government report, social workers may be presented as experts whose special training justifies this title. Certainly, in many instances this is warranted.

Occasions arise, however, when the appeal to such expertise may be inappropriate and may constitute the fallacy of *argumentum ad verecundiam* ("appeal to authority"). A social worker who has considerable training in the area of substance abuse treatment may not be a voice of authority in a court case involving child abuse. A social worker who is an expert with respect to home-based services for the elderly may cross the boundary of professional responsibility if she presents herself to a newspaper reporter as an expert on juvenile delinquency. Although social workers' training and knowledge may warrant a claim of expertise in some areas, these attributes may not warrant the claim in all areas. By way of comparison, a physician who is trained in psychiatry is not an expert on obstetrical matters, although obstetrics is a subspecialty within the physician's broad field of medicine.

It is also not unusual in social work to find circular arguments presented to support a conclusion. This form of argumentation is known as *petitio principii* ("begging the question"). For example, consider an instance where a group of administrators opposes the distribution of information about contraception to residents in a group home for troubled girls. They argue that information about sex and pregnancy must be handled responsibly and that responsible handling of this information requires a considerable measure of maturity. They argue, further, that the very placement of these girls in the group home demonstrates their lack of maturity. This argument begs the question about whether the girls can be taught to handle responsibly information related to sex and pregnancy.

Similarly, one can imagine a case where a social worker argues that long-term treatment is necessary for the social work agency's emotionally disturbed clients, since long-term treatment is called for when clients have especially complex problems. The social worker then argues that the long average length-of-stay of the agency's clients constitutes evidence of the complexity of their problems.

A final fallacy of relevance in social work is committed when an argument that claims to support a particular conclusion is instead more closely related to a different conclusion. When committed intentionally, this fallacy of *ignoratio elenchi* ("irrelevant conclusion") is committed when an individual is trying to mislead an audience into accepting one conclusion by seducing the audience to accept a more obvious and appealing conclusion. For example, at a recent legislative hearing on a bill that would enhance housing benefits for AFDC recipients, a state legislator argued that because everyone in the legislature is opposed to creating dependency among welfare recipients, they should oppose this program that would increase aid. While it may be true that the legislators are opposed to encouraging dependency, the legislator's argument does not address whether the specific benefits contained in the pending bill would actually encourage dependency. The broad conclusion he reached concerning the legislators' views about dependency is not relevant to the AFDC benefits proposal in the way he suggests.

Similarly, an antiabortion activist might try to convince staff of the governor's office that the governor should veto legislation that would allow state funding of abortions for medically indigent women. The activist might argue that because no one wants to murder innocent people, the governor should veto the legislation. The activist's argument fails to acknowledge the enduring debate about whether abortion constitutes murder.

FALLACIES OF IMPRECISION. The final group of fallacies concerns instances where arguments use terms or numbers imprecisely. This sort of ambiguity can be deceptively misleading, particularly when someone uses it intentionally as camouflage.

A common fallacy of imprecision occurs when someone uses a word that has more than one literal meaning. If two different senses of the word are necessary for an argument to be plausible, one commits the fallacy of *equivocation* (also known as the *synonymic* fallacy). Consider the following argument:

1. Crimes should be punished with severe sentences.
2. The high unemployment rate in this community is a crime.
3. Therefore, the high unemployment rate in this community should be punished with a severe sentence.

Clearly, this argument is puerile. The nonsensical conclusion results from the term *crime* being used equivocally.

Unfortunately, not all fallacies of equivocation in social work are this trivial. Some arguments that commit this fallacy sound so reasonable that they may result in counterproductive interventions or actions contrary to the profession's values. Consider, for instance, an argument that was presented to a community mental health center director by a spokesperson for a local group that opposed a group home for the area:

> I am here to speak for a group of people who are upset about your proposal. Now, we are not a bunch of crazy, paranoid people who think that you are out to get us. We're very ordinary people, with ordinary children, who want a nice, safe community with only these kinds of normal people in it. Things are fine here just as they are. We don't want them disturbed. We don't like the idea that you want to march in here and tell us who our neighbors are going to be. That's not the normal way of doing things around here. We have the right to decide whether we want a group home here. It's not right for you to make that decision for us. If you were concerned about our safety, you wouldn't handle things this way.

Although this train of thought is rather convoluted, there appears to be an implicit argument:

1. Ordinary people want to live in a safe community with only normal people in it.
2. Your agency's strategy for this group home is not normal.
3. Therefore, your agency is not interested in the safety of our community.

Although this argument has a number of problems, one of them is that the meaning of the term *normal* shifts throughout the passage. In the beginning, *normal* seems to be associated with mental health or the absence of mental illness. Later on, the term refers to the usual way proposals allegedly are reviewed in this community. Thus, in one place *normal* means *healthy* and in another it means *typical*.

A similar problem can occur with the fallacy of *amphiboly*, when someone constructs a sentence poorly or punctuates improperly. If a social worker says, "Sue has not been depressed for more than three weeks," it is not clear whether Sue has not been depressed at any time for longer than a three-week period or whether she has not been depressed within the past three weeks. If a social worker writes in a client's record, "The client reported that he will not use drugs when he has custody of his child," it is not clear whether the client said he will not use drugs at any time, including when he has custody of his child, or will use them only when he does not have custody of his child. Clearly, imprecision in language can create significant problems.

Several other fallacies of imprecision occur when numbers or statistics are used improperly. For example, it is not unusual for a social worker to generalize information obtained from one setting to another, even though the second setting may differ significantly from the first. This is generally known as the "fallacy of biased statistics."

A former colleague of mine used to be the associate director of a respite program for families of Alzheimer's patients. The program, located in a rural community, provided respite care so that each week family caretakers could have some time for themselves and some relief from the burden of constant care giving. The staff had successfully recruited families interested in receiving respite care for several hours each week and a talented group of respite workers.

After helping to administer this program for two years, my former colleague was offered an attractive job to start and direct a respite program in a large city nearby. After several months on the new job, however, my former colleague called me in distress. She was having difficulty recruiting families to participate in the program, even though she used the same recruitment methods used in her former program. No matter what she tried, she said, families seemed reluctant to sign up for the respite services.

After some discussion, it became clear that my former colleague had assumed that residents of this large city would desire respite services as much as her former clients from the rural community. It turned out, however, that the urban families were much less willing to rely on strangers to care for their family members. My former colleague's impression was that families in the rural community, in general, were more trusting of respite workers recruited and referred by the program. In a nutshell, she made the mistake of assuming that "data" from one setting could be generalized to another.

This fallacy of biased statistics can also occur in psychotherapy. A clinical social worker may observe one set of behaviors in the office that may not be representative of behaviors that occur at home or elsewhere. For instance, a colleague of mine was working with a single mother whose child was having behavioral problems. A local pediatrician had diagnosed the child as having attention deficit hyperactivity disorder. This child had difficulty following directions and sitting still for sustained periods of time.

The social worker spent several weeks helping the mother to master a variety of behavioral techniques to use with the child, including various forms of positive reinforcement. During sessions in the office, the social worker observed the mother using the techniques very effectively. The mother praised the child skillfully when he engaged in appropriate behavior and established clear consequences for inappropriate behavior. The social worker also had the mother keep a record of the child's appropriate and inappropriate behaviors at home.

After a number of weeks the mother was distressed that her child's behavior at home had not improved. After some discussion, it appeared that the mother's interventions at home differed from what the social worker observed in the office. As a result, the social worker had to spend considerable time with the mother refining her home-based behavior management techniques. It was a mistake, then, for the social worker to assume that the "data" she observed in the office could be generalized to the home.

Another fallacy of imprecision occurs when percentages are

equated inappropriately. For instance, at a recent press conference, a state public welfare administrator said the following:

I am pleased to be able to report that we are beginning to close the gap between rich and poor. During the past fiscal year, the income of the average AFDC recipient increased by 8.5 percent, while the income for the average corporation president, as reported by the Bureau of Labor Statistics, increased only 5.2 percent.

The message is misleading, however. If the income of the average AFDC recipient was $8,000, the increase was $680, but the increase for a corporation president earning the average salary of $225,000 was $11,700! This is not exactly closing the gap, despite the difference in the percentage increase.

Speaking of problems with percentages, some social welfare practitioners have a troubling tendency to commit the fallacy of "confusing a proposition with its converse." A classic illustration involves assumptions people sometimes make about the characteristics of individuals who live below the official poverty line. Many members of the general public (and, I have discovered, even some social workers) believe that the majority of people living in poverty in the United States are black. This is not true. In the United States, many more white people than black people are living below the poverty line. It *is* true that the percentage of black people who live below the poverty line is greater than the percentage of white people who do so. But this is not to say that most people who live below the poverty line are black. More specifically, while it might be true to say that "the majority of black single mothers with four or more children live below the poverty line," it does not follow that "the majority of people who live below the poverty line are black single mothers with four or more children."

Two other fallacies of imprecision occur when social workers draw comparisons between two groups of people or sets of figures. In the first, known as the "error of the first kind" (or "Type I error"), social workers assume that a difference between groups exists when no true difference exists. Imagine that a social worker compares two different approaches for treatment of an eating disorder. One group of randomly assigned clients in a residential program receives psychotropic medication and a second group of randomly assigned clients receives traditional counseling. At the conclusion of the treatment, the first group gained an average of 12 pounds and the second group gained an average of 10.5 pounds. Not surprisingly, the social worker concludes that the psychotropic medication is a more effective intervention. It is possible, however, that she is wrong. Depending on the dispersion of weight gains in the two groups, this average difference may be the result of chance factors. Statisticians have established widely accepted criteria for determining the likelihood that the result occurred by chance, given the data obtained from the clients.

The reverse fallacy also can occur. With the "error of the second kind" (or "Type II error"), a social worker concludes that no real difference exists between two groups when in fact a significant difference does exist. Suppose a social worker compares two groups of juvenile offenders, one group randomly assigned to a community-based program and the other randomly assigned to the local training school. At the end of a two-year follow-up period, no difference is evident between the recidivism, or rearrest rates of the two groups. Youths in both groups were rearrested an average of 2.5 times.

As a result, the social worker may conclude that no difference exists between these two interventions. Each is equally effective (or ineffective). This conclusion may not be warranted, however. It is possible that one of the interventions is actually superior, but, because of chance factors, the true difference was concealed. In a number of instances, failure to control for initial differences between the two groups may account for the error in the results (owing to a flaw in the random assignment or matching techniques, for example).

LOGIC AND LANGUAGE

We can see from this review of logical fallacies that using language carefully and understanding how language is used in order to determine the validity of arguments is an important element of social work. The way we define terms and use them to advance arguments has important bearing on our ability to carry out our professional mission. Language is central to our work, and thus we must understand its various functions. Logicians typically distinguish among three different uses of language. The first—and most obvious—is to *inform*. When a social worker makes an entry in a case record, the primary purpose is to convey information about a client's circumstances and the social worker's intervention. Social workers agree that they must keep track of this information in order to enhance the quality and continuity of care.

Similarly, when a social worker presents testimony in court concerning a child who allegedly has been abused, the primary purpose is to offer information. This information will then be used to determine whether the child was in fact abused and to influence the judge's handling of the child and alleged perpetrator. Hence, the informative function of language serves to present specific knowledge in the form of propositions or arguments on a given topic. In social work this may take the form of entries in case records, consultations with colleagues and supervisors, letters to outside agencies, testimony in court or before public officials, research reports, and so on.

A second function of language is to *express*. When we use language for its expressive function, we are less concerned with presentation of information or knowledge, and more concerned with the expression of feelings, emotions, and attitudes. When a clinical social worker discusses with a client her feelings about the termination of their long-standing professional relationship, her purpose is chiefly expressive. She is not primarily interested in conveying information and knowledge; rather, she wants to convey her emotions. The language the social worker uses in this instance differs from the language one ordinarily would find in a case record. Similarly, when a social worker counsels a client who has just been raped, a principal function of her use of language may be expressive, to convey her feelings about what has just happened to the client.

A third function of language is to attempt to influence people's behavior and actions. In these instances our intention is to *direct;* we intend for something specific to happen as a result of our communication. We are not simply conveying information or expressing feelings, emotions, or attitudes. When the director of a hospital social service department issues a memo telling staff that they need to review their case records before an upcoming accreditation site visit, he is directing them toward an action. He is not primarily conveying information or knowledge, nor is he chiefly expressing his emotions, feelings, and attitudes. The same directive function of language applies when a probation officer informs a client that he must meet him on Tuesday morning at 11:00 A.M.

Of course, much of the time our communications serve more than one function. When an administrator of a social service agency convenes her staff to encourage them to increase their involvement in social justice activities, she may simultaneously provide them with information about local social problems, express her emotions about the need for social workers' involvement in social justice, and direct them (subtly or otherwise) to engage in these activities. When a protective service worker confronts a pregnant client about her substance abuse, she may be simultaneously informing her about the consequences for the fetus of continued substance abuse, expressing her feelings about her client's behavior, and directing the client toward a specific course of action.

Sometimes the distinctions among the various language functions are clear. It is rather easy to distinguish a stirring, passionate speech concerning social work's social justice mission from a bland research report summarizing the results of a new treatment strategy for bulimia. It is also easy to distinguish between an entry in a case record and a court order requiring a client to seek substance abuse treatment.

In other instances, however, the distinctions are more subtle, and this is where social workers' antennae need to be raised. An opponent of increased welfare benefits may present what sounds like neutral, balanced, and objective testimony before a legislative subcommittee. It may take a seasoned practitioner to detect logical flaws in the argument that stem from subtle but influential expressive or directive messages embedded in the presentation.

A similar problem can occur whenever an individual attempts to create the illusion that his or her principal purpose is to convey objective information when, in reality, the information is biased, presented selectively, and laced with subtle expressive or directive messages. This can occur especially when individuals use what are known as *emotive words*. If the opponent of increased welfare benefits uses in his testimony the term *bureaucrat* rather than *program administrator,* he may subtly influence his audience because of the emotive meaning the term *bureaucrat* often has. To many, this term conjures up images of the apathetic official who is inefficient, unproductive, authoritative, and hostile to his task. Similarly, use of the term *abortionist* rather than *Planned Parenthood physician* during discussion of proposed family planning legislation may be manipulatively influential.

Thus, if we are interested in resolving disagreements, we must be clear about how language is used. If we are disputing the truth of specific information, certain rules concerning the truth or falsity of facts apply. If our attitudes differ, however, the ground rules necessarily differ. I know how to address a disagreement over whether AFDC recipients have been able to keep pace with increases in the cost of living or whether long-term psychotherapy is more effective than short-term psychotherapy for treatment of depressed adolescents. But a disagreement over feelings and emotions concerning the morality of abortion moves us into an entirely different field of play. In these instances we must acknowledge that our disagreement may not be over facts (although there may be some room for dispute here, with respect to when life begins) but over our beliefs about what is moral and immoral. Disputes about matters of attitude are fundamentally different from disputes about matters of fact.

If we are going to be careful in our use of language, we must pay particular attention to the ways in which we define the terms we use. This is especially important in social work practice, given the special terminology and jargon used in the profession.

THE ROLE OF DEFINITIONS

Definitions have several different purposes. One is to increase our vocabulary and our ability to communicate about what we experience. Hence, we periodically introduce new terms and definitions in social work to describe new phenomena or new ways of viewing or interpreting existing phenomena. Some years ago, for example, Laura Epstein and William Reid introduced the term *task-centered treatment* to refer to a specific strategy of intervention with troubled clients. Their definition of this term included details concerning length of treatment, intervention techniques, recording methods, and outcome measures. The introduction of this new term provided a shorthand method for communicating about this complex intervention approach. A definition given to a new term when it is first introduced is sometimes called a *stipulative* definition. New terms appearing in the American Psychiatric Association's widely used *Diagnostic and Statistical Manual of Mental Disorders* have stipulative definitions, although there may not be complete consensus about them.

A second function of definitions is to eliminate ambiguity. Obviously, this is very important in social work since the specific meaning of terms may not be entirely clear. A term may have more than one meaning, which may, in turn, lead to confusion about how one should act; we encountered this problem before in our discussion of the fallacy of equivocation.

Take, for example, confusion about the term *domestic violence*. Many programs claim to address this important problem. Yet, their definitions of what constitutes abuse vary considerably. This can create confusion for clients, staff, referral sources, foundations that fund social service programs, and others who are involved in some way with the phenomenon of domestic violence. Definitional clarity would help. Similar problems occur with terms such as *mental illness, poverty, psychotic, disabled, delinquent,* and even *social worker.* Definitions that are designed to eliminate ambiguity surrounding existing terms, by providing sufficient detail to clarify meaning, are known as *lexical* definitions.

In those specific cases where our concern is not so much with respect to the meaning of a term, but rather with its relevance or application to a given case, we are dealing with what are known as *precising* definitions. For example, people may not disagree with the definition of *child abuse* used by a particular state child welfare agency, but some disagreement may arise about whether the definition fits a particular case that has come to the agency's attention. Clarification of the formal definition for application to this particular case constitutes a precising definition.

Although individuals may genuinely disagree about the meaning of a particular term, disputes often result because people simply have failed to define their terms precisely. Precise definition can go a long way toward resolving professional disagreements. A classic illustration of the need to clarify terms appears in William James's *Pragmatism:*

> Some years ago, being with a camping party in the mountains, I returned from a solitary ramble to find everyone engaged in a ferocious metaphysical dispute. The *corpus* of the dispute was a squirrel—a live squirrel supposed to be clinging to one side of a tree-trunk; while over against the tree's opposite side a human being was imagined to stand. This human witness tries to get sight of the squirrel by moving rapidly round the tree, but no matter how fast he goes, the squirrel moves as fast in the opposite direction, and always keeps the tree between himself and the man, so that never a glimpse of him is caught. The resultant metaphysical problem is this: *Does the man go round the squirrel or not?* He goes round the tree, sure enough, and the squirrel is on the tree; but does he go round the squirrel? In the unlimited leisure of the wilderness, discussion had been worn threadbare. Everyone had taken sides, and was obstinate; and the numbers on both sides were even. Each side, when I appeared, therefore appealed to me to make it a majority. Mindful of the scholastic

adage that whenever you meet a contradiction you must make a distinction, I immediately sought and found one, as follows: "Which party is right," I said, "depends on what you *practically mean* by 'going round' the squirrel. If you mean passing from the north of him to the east, then to the south, then to the west, and then to the north of him again, obviously the man does go round him, for he occupies these successive positions. But if on the contrary you mean being first in front of him, then on the right of him, then behind him, then on his left, and finally in front again, it is quite obvious that the man fails to go round him, for by the compensating movements the squirrel makes, he keeps his belly turned towards the man all the time, and his back turned away. Make the distinction, and there is no occasion for any further dispute. You are both right and wrong according as you conceive the verb 'go around' in one practical fashion or the other."

Although one or two of the hotter disputants called my speech a shuffling evasion, saying they wanted no quibbling or scholastic hair-splitting, but meant just plain honest English "round," the majority seemed to think that the distinction had assuaged the dispute. (cited in Copi 1986:133)

In other instances definitions enhance our theoretical understanding of a concept relevant to social work. Over the years, for example, a great deal of confusion has arisen among clinicians about the definition of the term *borderline*. Various attempts to define this term constitute more than an effort to enhance professionals' vocabulary and eliminate ambiguity, although the latter certainly is part of what we are trying to accomplish. Primarily, attempts to define this puzzling term represent an effort to clarify this concept theoretically. What exactly *is* borderline personality disorder? What does it mean to say that a client has this diagnosis? What does this concept entail, theoretically? What we are dealing with here is more than superficial ambiguity. Rather, we are struggling to come up with a *theoretical* definition to help us understand and clarify a theoretical construct.

Finally, definitions also may have an emotive function. That is, our definitions may carry with them significant messages intended to move or stir the listener. If we define *poor* as "the condition of being without sufficient resources to meet basic needs, such as food, clothing, shelter, and health care," we may evoke a very different response than that obtained by a definition such as "a condition of impoverishment brought about by insufficient effort to earn income." Abortion defined as "termination of a pregnancy" is quite different from the definition "deliberate murder of a human fetus." Definitions whose purpose is to influence emotions, feelings, or attitudes are generally known as *persuasive* definitions.

In their analysis of definitions, logicians also make a useful distinction between the *extension* and *intension* of a word. Consider, for example, the word *delinquent*. The extension (or *denotation*) of the word refers to the group or class of all objects (in this case people) to which the word correctly applies. In contrast, the intension (or *connotation*) of the word refers to the specific properties or attributes a thing must have in order to be an extension of that word. Hence, while the extension of *delinquent* is the class of all people considered to be delinquent, the intension consists of whatever criteria we use to determine who is and is not delinquent. These might include whether someone is a minor, has engaged in one or more specific behaviors (such as robbery, auto theft, assault, drug sales), has been arrested by the police, and has been adjudicated in a juvenile court.

Of course, reasonable people can disagree about the particular attributes that should determine the intension of the word. Some social workers, for example, might not require that a youth be arrested and adjudicated in court for the youth to be labeled a delinquent. Instead, they might be satisfied with a youth's mere admission that he or she has engaged in one or more illegal activities. Other social workers might insist, however, on arrest and adjudication as necessary conditions for the label *delinquent*.

This is an important point. All of us are aware of significant disagreements among social workers with respect to the meaning of terms or, specifically, the attributes people, communities, or organizations must have before a label can be properly applied to them. Social workers may disagree about what certain terms really entail, terms such as *borderline client, low-income community,* or *poorly administered agency.* Actually, these debates concern differences of opinion about the *intension* of these terms. Because the criteria or attributes social workers ultimately settle on have a profound effect on clients, these debates over the meanings of terms have important and practical significance. Labels often influence the way in which social workers assess and intervene.

Thus, social workers must carefully consider how they go about defining terms used in the profession. In some instances the word being defined (the *definiendum*) has been in circulation for some time, and few disagree on how to define it (with the *definiens*). For example, most social workers seem to agree on the definition of *runaway youth*. Professionals generally agree that this term refers to minors who leave their home. There may be some confusion around the margin (for example, whether this term should include youths who are thrown out of their homes), but, by and large, practitioners agree on the *definiens*.

This is not the case, however, with a term such as *borderline*. Social workers disagree considerably about the class of people to whom this term applies (its *extension*) and the specific attributes that determine the things to which the term applies (its *intension*). Some may rely on the definition in the American Psychiatric Association's *Diagnostic and Statistical Manual of Mental Disorders*. Others find this definition too limiting and prefer more expansive descriptions of the psychodynamic features of clients who manifest certain behavioral and emotional traits. Still others have difficulty articulating exactly what constitutes a "borderline client" but claim to be able to point one out ("I know one when I see one"). This way of indicating the extensional meaning of a term is known as *ostensive definition*.

LOGIC AND PRACTICE

Effective social work relies to a great extent on the effective use of language. Through language, practitioners and clients communicate what they understand about their respective worlds and lives, and these communications shape interventions and outcomes. I suspect that clear, precise language that conforms to the canons of logic is more likely to be credible and helpful than language that is ambiguous, confusing, and laden with fallacy.

Given the pace of contemporary social work and its rush of events, the precision our communications warrant is easily lost. It is too easy to be facile and glib with jargon and to have distressingly low expectations of the quality of argumentation social workers engage in. As we have seen, unclear and illogical communication can lead to mistaken conclusions about clients' problems and to harmful interventions (or to tragic failure to intervene). In the end, our failure to be precise is counterproductive and undermines a fundamental mission of social work: to communicate cogently and persuasively about problems in living and social justice.

ɛ/ɕ

EPISTEMOLOGY

It is a mark of the educated man and a proof
of his culture that in every subject he looks for
only so much precision as its nature permits.

—ARISTOTLE

As the social work profession has matured, social workers have increasingly turned their attention toward research and the creation of knowledge designed to further social work's mission, whatever it is deemed to be. Following the lead provided by allied disciplines, such as sociology and psychology, social work training programs have introduced ever more ambitious courses and content related to social work research and evaluation. Undergraduate and graduate programs that in the early twentieth century were devoted almost exclusively to training related to social work practice, administration, and policy now allocate significant portions of their curricula to content on social work research, program evaluation, clinical evaluation, statistics, and data analysis. Literature grounded in research and empiricism has also become more evident in social work's books and journals.

Although the profession exhibits considerable support for a "scientific" approach to social work and to the development of the profession's knowledge base, considerable debate exists about the ways in which social work's embrace of "science" has evolved. This debate simmered in the profession until the early 1980s; since then, however, it has come to a full boil. What began as a series of rather polite exchanges among a relatively small group of social work scholars has developed (some would say degenerated) into an occasionally overheated and divisive controversy about the nature, creation, and control of social work knowledge.

THE NATURE OF THE DEBATE

Evidence of a "scientific" approach to social work can be found as early as the late nineteenth century, during the heyday of the charity organization societies. Many practitioners during this era believed that scientific philanthropy offered the best hope for understanding pauperism and that the scientific method could be used for systematic study and treatment of individual cases (Reid 1987; Zimbalist 1977). In the early twentieth century, the classic works of Virginia Robinson, Florence Hollis, Gordon Hamilton, and Edith Abbott helped to shape social workers' thinking about the scientific study of social work practice (Orcutt 1990).

Perhaps the best-known benchmark during the early twentieth century was the publication of Mary Richmond's *Social Diagnosis* (1917), which described social diagnosis as a consequence of scientific problem solving. The early twentieth century social survey movement also represents one of the era's most ambitious efforts to bring the benefits of scientific methods to bear on social problems.

Despite these and other early efforts by social workers, for a number of decades the profession depended heavily on research talent and concepts cultivated in allied social science disciplines. For the first eighty years of professional social work education, students typically were assigned research texts written for sociology and psychology students. With the exception of Polansky's (1960) edited collection of articles about research written exclusively for social workers, little else was available. Not until the late 1970s and early 1980s did we begin to see the emergence of a critical mass of social work research texts (for example, Bloom and Fischer 1982; Grinnell 1981; Jayaratne and Levy 1979; Reid and Smith 1981).

Over time, the social work profession has developed a cadre of practitioners and scholars who have applied a wide range of research tools and methodological techniques to questions related to clinical practice, social welfare administration, policy, and community development. By now the profession has ample precedents of survey research, secondary analysis of data, single-case or single-subject designs, and experimental research. Although research-based knowledge in the profession remains somewhat fragmented and inconsistent, the fund of social work knowledge has unquestionably grown enormously as practitioners and scholars have made increased use of research tools (Schuerman 1987).

Not all the profession's members regard these developments as progress, however. While many applaud social work's efforts to generate its own scientifically determined knowledge base and research methods, others decry what they view as a regrettable and dangerous preoccupation with traditional—some would say discredited—science and empiricism.

Seminal commentary on the nature of social work research began with Gordon's 1965 essay in *Social Work* on the differences between knowledge and values in the profession. Several years later, in what has turned out to be a prescient set of observations, Gyarfas (1969) argued that the growth of interest in social work research on issues of "social structure" and "macro issues" was leading to a neglect of core social work issues related to clinical process, and individual client growth, change, and development.

Although the subsequent decade saw a smattering of publications exploring the nature and purpose of social work research (for example, Austin 1976; Briar 1979, 1980; Fanshel 1980; Kirk, Osmalov, and Fischer 1976; Maas 1977; Polansky 1971), in 1981 Heineman Pieper* launched what turned out to be the first salvo in a protracted, spirited, and sometimes vitriolic debate about the merits of social work research.

Heineman Pieper's major thesis was that social work scholars were embracing an antiquated research model that philosophers of science and social scientists from other disciplines were abandoning. This archaic research model, according to Heineman Pieper, rests on a naive assumption that core practice-related concepts can be defined by empirical or quantitative measures. Thus, she argues, social work researchers have restricted inappropriately the scope and nature of the questions studied in the profession: "In a misguided attempt to be scientific, social work has adopted an outmoded, overly restrictive paradigm of research. Methodological rather than substantive requirements determine the subject matter to be studied. As a result, important questions and valuable data go unresearched" (Heineman 1981:371).

* Heineman Pieper's first major article was published under the surname Heineman (1981). All references to this author will be to Heineman Pieper.

Heineman Pieper's principal target is "logical empiricism" (commonly known as "logical positivism"), the philosophical school of thought that emerged in Vienna in the 1920s. According to logical empiricism, researchers should seek "objective" scientific methodology to measure phenomena, emphasizing observable properties of material things that can be subjected to experimental methods.

This perspective rests on several key assumptions. In principle, a single, tangible reality can be reduced to its component parts, which can then be studied independently. The researcher (or observer) can be separated from that which is observed, and what is true at one time may, under appropriate circumstances, also be true at another time and place. Further, logical empiricism assumes linear causality, that is, independent (or causal) variables are correlated in a linear fashion with dependent (or outcome) variables. Finally, this paradigm assumes that the results of sound research are independent of investigators' values and biases (Lincoln and Guba 1985:28). For Heineman Pieper, social work researchers' preoccupation with features of logical empiricism (for example, experimental design, quantitative measurement, and analysis) has meant that alternative methods of inquiry—including qualitative single-case studies, ethnomethodology, and historical research—have been shunned.

THE PHILOSOPHICAL CONTEXT

Before examining the social work debate in depth, it is important to understand the philosophical context that surrounds it. The debate among social workers about the nature and methods of social work research is an extension of long-standing controversy about *epistemology*, or the theory of knowledge (the Greek word *episteme* means "knowledge").

Epistemologists attempt to answer such questions as "What can be known?" and "Are there reliable ways to determine what is true?" Epistemological theories are generally divided into two groups, depending on whether they stress the function of reason (the *rationalist* theories) or sense experience (the *empiricist* theories). Many rationalist theories maintain that we cannot attain any certainty by means of our senses. Thus, empirical measurement cannot provide us with certain knowledge about such phenomena as depression, self-esteem, or ego strength. According to rationalism, what we can know are "mental objects," and these are known by reason and not by the senses.

Perhaps the best exemplar of rationalism is Plato. According to Plato, what can be known are unalterable features of the world, or what Plato referred to as "Ideas" or "Forms." Consider, for example, the concept of depression. What does it mean to say that Mr. X and Ms. Y are depressed? Although Mr. X and Ms. Y are two distinct individuals, they appear to have something in common that enables us to use the same term—*depressed*—to refer to them both. Because these two people share something in common, we are able to classify them together. The common attribute is designated by the term *depression*.

Using such general terms, of course, helps to facilitate communication in social work. Terms such as *poor, disabled, delinquent, enmeshed,* and *addicted* help social workers express opinions and exchange information efficiently, although one must always be concerned about the possibility of inappropriate labeling. When we use such terms we are essentially making a claim about our knowledge, that is, that we "know" that a particular individual is poor, or disabled, or depressed, and so on. But how do we know this? Clearly, we need to do more than simply point to Mr. X and Ms. Y in order to demonstrate our knowledge of what depression is. This approach would be tautological. Instead, we need to demonstrate our knowledge of the general concept of depression.

A famous illustration of Plato's point appears in his dialogue *Euthyphro,* which presents a conversation between Socrates and the priest Euthyphro (Stroll and Popkin 1979:32). The priest tells Socrates that he is going to the courthouse to accuse his own father of murder. When Socrates asks Euthyphro why he is bringing the case to court, Euthyphro responds that this is the holy thing to do. Socrates then asks Euthyphro what is holiness. Euthyphro replies that holiness is doing what he is doing when he brings his father's case to court. Socrates points out that this is not a particularly useful definition of the concept since it only provides an example of holiness. To know whether a particular act is, in fact, holy, one must first know the meaning of the general concept "holiness."

The question that remains, of course, is how one acquires such knowledge. For Plato, sense experience does not and cannot provide us with adequate knowledge of general concepts. We can use our senses to ask people questions about how often they feel "blue" (or how much income they earn, the crimes they have committed, or the illegal substances they use), but these data will not tell us what depression *is* (or what poverty or delinquency or addiction is). At best, from this point of view, we can describe individuals' attributes based on their responses to questions. But that is all.

Plato distinguished between two basic types of information: *visible* information and *intelligible* information. Visible information is obtained when we see certain stimuli that lead us to certain conclusions. When we see a man slumped in a chair crying and frowning, we may be inclined to conclude that he is sad. When we see a woman dressed in tattered clothes, pacing the sidewalk, and asking for money, we may be inclined to conclude that she is poor. When we see a man standing in the middle of a busy intersection uttering obscenities and burning his clothes, we may be inclined to conclude that he is mentally disturbed.

But Plato argued that such conclusions based on sensory data may be mistaken. We can never be completely sure that any particular set of behaviors or attributes that we have observed really constitutes the phenomenon we think it constitutes. We can only have an opinion that this is the case. On the basis of visible information alone, one does not *know* the general concept or Platonic Ideas; one does not know what these phenomena are *really* like. We know only how they seem to us. Thus, Plato argued, we cannot obtain knowledge only through visible information.

Conversely, Plato maintained, *intelligible* information can constitute knowledge. To convey this point Plato had Socrates relate the famous "Allegory of the Cave" (Stroll and Popkin 1979:36). In this allegory, the normal human condition is compared to that of living all the time in a cave, where one can only see shadows cast on a wall by objects that are out of sight and a light source that is not visible. If we were in this position our entire lives—from the moment of birth—presumably we would assume that the shadows constituted the real world. We would not realize that other objects existed in the world or that the ones cast on the cave's wall reflected others we had never seen. Our beliefs about reality would not reflect reality.

But Plato asks us to consider what would happen if we were suddenly released from the cave and had an opportunity to see the real objects that cast the shadows. Only at this point—once we are free of the distorted lens through which we view the world—would we be in a position to know the real world as it truly exists. This, according to Plato, is the kind of transformation that is necessary in order for humans to attain true knowledge, or the Platonic Ideas.

But how can such a transformation occur? For Plato it is important for us to realize that visible information is, by definition, limited and unable to provide us with complete or genuine knowledge about the world, that visible information is subject to differing interpretations.

To demonstrate this, Plato pointed out that if one looks at one's fourth finger, it is hard to know objectively whether it is big or little. The fourth finger is bigger than the fifth one and smaller than the third. One cannot answer the question without knowing what is really meant by the terms *big* and *little* (Stroll and Popkin 1979).

For Plato, efforts to understand the essential nature of such concepts require the use of reason rather than the senses, particularly reason grounded in basic principles of mathematics. This is because arithmetic and mathematics help one to learn with ideas alone, and not with the "shadows" created by objects that are not visible. Such training presumably will free one from dependence on sensory experience and stimuli and enable one to grasp pure concepts.

Nearly two thousand years after Plato, the seventeenth-century French philosopher René Descartes offered another major formulation of the rationalist thesis. Concerned about the rampant skepticism that seemed to surround him, Descartes set out to determine what portion of knowledge was reliable and certain. In his famous works *Discourse on Method, Meditations,* and *The Principles of Philosophy,* Descartes developed his answer to the question, "What can be known?" Using what is known as the Cartesian "Method of Doubt," Descartes maintained, along with Plato, that sometimes we are deceived by our senses. An object in water may appear different when it is out of water. Food we eat when we are congested may taste different from food eaten when we have a clear nose. An object seen when the sun shines brightly may appear different when viewed at dusk. Hence, our senses may be deceptive or unreliable. Our belief that a client is depressed, inebriated, or delusional based on our visual observation may be unreliable if our perception is distorted somehow by illness, clinical bias, or some other influence.

THE EMERGENCE OF EMPIRICISM

Empiricism as we know it today developed in opposition to mainstream rationalism. Empiricists argue that while sense information may not be entirely certain, these data are important and ought to be collected and considered.

A particularly important chapter in the history of the empirical movement began in England early in the seventeenth century, in part as a result of major scientific discoveries by such luminaries as Robert Boyle, Robert Hooke, and Sir Isaac Newton. The scientists of the Royal Society argued that while it may be impossible to discover the true nature of worldly phenomena, using sense data we can generate compelling hypotheses about what occurs in the world.

The keynote statement of the time on empirical theory was made by the seventeenth-century political philosopher John Locke. In his *Essay Concerning Human Understanding*, Locke dismissed many of the rationalists' assertions and attempted to distinguish between what can be known and what cannot be known given the capacities that humans possess. He hoped to help humans identify those areas of knowledge worth pursuing and those whose pursuit would be futile.

The empiricist tradition was developed further in the eighteenth century by George Berkeley, in his works *The Principles of Human Knowledge* and the *Three Dialogues Between Hylas and Philonous*, Immanuel Kant, in his *Critique of Pure Reason*, and, most notably, by David Hume, particularly in his *Enquiry Concerning Human Understanding*. Hume proposed a number of basic empiricist principles, some of which continue to have currency. Hume proposed development of a "science of man," which would involve the application of Newton's experimental method to the whole area of human mental phenomena.

An offshoot of empiricism was nineteenth-century positivism, founded by Auguste Comte. Comte argued in his *Cours de Philosophie Positive* that the empirical methods that had worked so well in the natural sciences should be applied to the new social science, sociology. An emphasis on the practical application of the scientific method was also strengthened by the philosophy of pragmatism endorsed by William James, Charles Peirce, John Dewey, and George Herbert Mead—a philosophy that was remarkably consistent with the ideological orientation of such social work notables as Jane Addams, Grace and Edith Abbott, and Sophonisba Breckinridge (Orcutt 1990).

The so-called Vienna Positivists—Moritz Schlick, Rudolf Carnap, Friedrich Waismann, and Otto Neurath—ultimately developed a form of positivism that influenced much of twentieth-century thought about the role of empiricism in the social sciences (although noteworthy criticisms of this view have been penned by philosophers such as Karl Popper, Herbert Simon, Imre Lakatos, Paul Feyerabend, Thomas Kuhn, Stephen Toulmin, Willard Van Ormond Quine, William Wimsatt, Michael Polanyi, and Ian Mitroff). It is the legacy of this positivism—logical positivism—that has triggered so much intense debate in social work, particularly with respect to its tenet that a proposition is meaningful if and only if it can be empirically verified with sensory observation and experience.

SOCIAL WORK AND POSITIVISM

During most of its history, social work—along with the mainstream social science disciplines—has embraced the positivist tradition. For decades enthusiastic attempts were made to apply the scientific method and its principles to investigation of social phenomena related to enduring social work concerns, such as poverty, mental health, health care, aging, child welfare, criminal justice, and community organizing (Zimbalist 1977). Empirical studies abound in the form of case studies, controlled experiments, single-subject designs, program evaluations, and social surveys (Orcutt 1990). Course work on research methods almost invariably was organized around the traditional topics of hypothesis testing, theory construction, experimental design, sampling, measurement, reliability, validity, and data analysis.

By the early 1980s, however, a small group of critics began to question the appropriateness of this hypothetico-deductive model for social work. Beginning especially with Heineman Pieper's controversial critique, a number of social work scholars and practitioners began to chip away at the positivist foundation that had been erected in social work. Without question, this assault fomented controversy that ranks among the most spirited the profession of social work has seen.

For Heineman Pieper and other critics, logical positivism is fundamentally flawed because our empirical observations are fallible, and data gatherers may influence that which they observe and the interpretation of these phenomena. By now ample evidence suggests that researchers' expectations, client apprehension, and other "demand characteristics" of the research context may distort data (Orne 1969; Rosenthal and Rosnow 1969). Empiricists also find it difficult to operationalize abstract concepts encountered in social work (such as ego strength, self-esteem, homeostasis) and frequently have trouble documenting causal relationships among variables. True experimentation, including random assignment to experimental and control groups, and pretests and posttests, is rare in social work, either because a sufficient number of research subjects are not available or because withholding an intervention from some clients would be unethical.

In addition, some important research questions simply do not lend themselves to experimentation. For example, no one would ever propose that we randomly assign children to abusive and nonabusive settings to investigate the causal effects of abuse. In short, social work contexts and circumstances often are such that research principles and designs would need to be compromised in order to carry out any inquiry whatsoever. As Heineman Pieper (Heineman 1981) has observed: "Like physics, genetics, and mathematics, social work and the other behavioral sciences must accept that reality cannot be perceived either directly or in its full complexity and, therefore, that science represents our best efforts at solving important problems for which there can be no guaranteed or permanent solutions" (391).

Heineman Pieper's indictment of conventional social work research triggered a vigorous controversy, laced with a form of rancor that has rarely found its way into social work literature. Schuerman (1982), for instance, challenges Heineman Pieper's claim that the views of social work researchers are derived from logical empiricism:

> Social work research uses a wide variety of methodologies with varying intellectual roots. It is a gross oversimplification to assert that the principles used by social work researchers are derived from logical empiricism, although they may be consistent in some respects. Most of these principles have roots that far predate the Vienna circle. The principle of parsimony in conceptualization and theorizing was explicated by Ockham in the fourteenth century. The idea of experimentation, that is, manipulating things to see what will happen, is at least as old as mankind. The use of experimentation to establish general laws was advocated by Francis Bacon in the sixteenth century. The use of contrast groups to deal with variability of subjects' responses to experimental conditions was anticipated by Boylston in the investigation of small-

pox vaccine in the early eighteenth century and was given a statistical underpinning in the late nineteenth century. (144–145)

Geismar (1982) also took issue quickly with Heineman Pieper's assertions about the hold logical empiricism has on social work researchers:

> I have read with interest Martha Brunswick Heineman's criticism of research approaches giving primacy to methodological rather than substantive requirements. . . . I wondered, however, why Heineman zeroed in on logical empiricism as the culprit for the kind of research ritualism she was describing. . . .
>
> The fact is that such empiricist excesses as absurd reductionism or phenomenal absolutism are not the stuff that social work research is presently made of, nor do social work researchers as a group affirm these days that explanation and prediction are synonymous. . . .
>
> This reader was particularly puzzled by Heineman's statement that social work research is characterized by "discrete canons of scientific acceptability, which are used to evaluate service models and research findings" (371) embodied in the work of two writers. She must surely be aware of the fact that social work research, whether it be in the form of "how to do it" writings or substantive inquiries, covers a wide spectrum of approaches. These range from the narrowly behavioristic to the qualitiative-comparative. None of these has a monopoly on the social work research market or can claim to best represent the research enterprise.
>
> Heineman's attack on logical empiricism is less a critique of social work research than it is a game of putting up and shooting down straw men. Her "alternatives," which include the views that a good theory is a better explanation rather than the only correct one or that electronic data-gathering devices can introduce different data biases, represent widely accepted mainstream thinking among social science and social work researchers. To depict the author's alternatives as the antithesis to an orthodox, obsolete philosophy (where does one find it nowadays?) does little to further the movement toward more effective models of social work research. (311–12)

Heineman Pieper's (Pieper 1982) replies both to Schuerman and Geismar were confident and stern. She maintained that Schuerman's critical remarks were "groundless" and that his:

> objections either continue to avoid the issues raised in the article or hit hard at straw men. For example, he reads the article to say that I am against clarity of meaning, definitions based on sensory experience, consensual validation, and replication. These sentiments are expressed nowhere, and, in fact, I am all for these scientific shibboleths as ideals or Platonic forms. However, as the article says, in the real world these research ideals are problematic in that there is no possibility of an unambiguous, unchallenging definition of, say, an observable or a sensory experience and thus no possibility that following Schuerman's particular definition of observable or his criteria for adequate replication will guarantee anything except probable agreement with those researchers who happen to see the world and define things the way he does. The question that arises is, Why should Schuerman's particular definitions or criteria control what other social work researchers can do? This is the main issue raised by the paper—namely, why the social work profession allows certain researchers to use discredited scientific criteria to proscribe or restrict research questions, data, or methods which other social work researchers believe will significantly enhance the knowledge base and clinical tools of social work. Unfortunately, Schuerman never addresses this central issue or even acknowledges that it was raised. (147)

And in reply to Geismar, Heineman Pieper (1982) focused especially on the difficulty that social work researchers with a nonpositivist orientation have entering the inner circle that controls access to research funds, publication outlets, faculty tenure, and other research-relevant employment:

> Since Geismar indulges in unsupported impressions, I would like to add one or two of my own. In my experience, social workers who submit articles to the leading journals for publication, try to get dissertations approved, or apply for research grants, jobs, or tenure do not, in fact, find the field of social work hospitable to research methodologies or interests which are not consonant with the assumptions of logical empiricism. On the contrary, a perusal of dissertation abstracts and the

articles selected for publication in research journals indicates not only the continued hegemony of positivist assumptions and prescriptions but also a distressing absence of critical and analytic discussion of the foundations of social work research. (312)

The exchange between Heineman Pieper and Schuerman prompted Gyarfas (1983)—now some fourteen years after her original expression of concern about this general issue—to comment both on the process and the content of their disagreement about the role of positivism in social work research:

> It is both exciting and sad to read the exchange between Martha Brunswick Heineman (now Martha Heineman Pieper) and John R. Schuerman about the state of research in social work. Exciting because an important controversy that has shaped social work development has found its way into print; sad because, in a way, the dialogue epitomizes the troubles that beset social work. Both writers represent their points of view aptly, but neither really "hears" the other. . . .
> Now that the controversy between behaviorists and nonbehaviorists has begun to surface, it would be nice if the protagonists allowed themselves to listen and learn from each other. In short, behaviorally oriented researchers could help nonbehaviorists learn to define their concepts in observable measurable terms, while the latter could teach the former something about the multiplicity of variables that must be accounted for in valid social work research. Both could profit from the exchange of information. (150)

The most ambitious response to Heineman Pieper's article (Heineman 1981) was Hudson's (1982) essay, "Scientific Imperatives in Social Work Research and Practice." Hudson's stated purpose was to examine Heineman Pieper's "very serious accusations, indictments, or concerns" about logical empiricism and "to set forth, in this author's opinion, a sounder view of the use of scientific imperatives in the conduct of social work research and practice" (246). Hudson's thesis was presented boldly: "Heineman has set forth a number of fallacious conclusions which she arrived at through the use of faulty logic, misinformation, and a basic failure to understand the fundamental tenets of scientific thought and behavior" (246–47).

Hudson questioned the accuracy of Heineman Pieper's assertion that social work has embraced logical empiricism as a model of science. Instead, Hudson maintained, the large number of social work researchers with whom he has had contact have not expressed the conviction that their knowledge of the world is certain and unchangeable; seemed to reject the use of propositional logic that is not grounded by real-world referents; and have not advocated the pursuit of some ultimate Platonic truth: "In short, I do not see a long train of social work researchers following dutifully behind the logical empiricism villain" (248).

Hudson's remarks, in turn, prompted a succinct critique from Holland (1983), who accused Hudson of asserting a view that "would appear to rule out most of what human beings consider important in life—love, courage, hope, faith, commitment, and so forth" (337). Holland took Hudson to task for his "ambiguities, oversimplifications, and gratuitous sarcasm" (337), concluding:

> By insisting that any experiences that cannot be operationalized, observed, and measured are meaningless, Hudson's extreme position would seem to the casual observer to eviscerate not only most of what the profession of social work deals with, but also much of what humanity has deemed most important. (338)

Hudson (1983) refuted Holland's contention that he, Hudson, argued for exclusive use of direct observation in social work research: "Nowhere in my article did I assert or imply such a thing. Holland seems to have read something that was not even there. Indeed, I did not, do not, and will not advocate such an absurd position" (339).*

A second major debate—comparably impolite—about the role of empiricism in social work was stimulated by Fischer's (1981) essay in *Social Work*, published the same year as Heineman Pieper's original article (Heineman 1981), "The Social Work Revolution." In this equally seminal article, Fischer presented a position quite contrary to Heineman's, arguing that the profession needed to

---

* For additional debate on and discussion of issues raised by Heineman Pieper concerning the role of empiricism in social work, see Ruckdeschel and Farris (1981, 1982), Geismar and Wood (1982), Karger (1983), Haworth (1984), Imre (1984), Mullen (1985), Ruckdeschel (1985), Brekke (1986), Epstein (1986), Goldstein (1986), Rodwell (1987), Weick (1987), Peile (1988), Zimmerman (1989), Beckerman (1990), Berlin (1990), DeRoos (1990), Hartman (1990), Meyer (1990), Scott (1990), Videka-Sherman, Reid, and Toseland (1990), Wood (1990), and the "Letters to the Editor" section of *Social Work Research and Abstracts* 22:2 (1986), 2.

move away from practice strategies that had not been validated empirically. Fischer maintained that until the time at which he was then writing, most social workers interested in direct practice had been guided by a "rather loosely structured superordinate model" (199) consisting largely of widely held theoretical understandings that, for the most part, were not empirically based. Drawing on Kuhn's (1962) popular discussion of the nature of scientific revolutions, Fischer concluded that social work was experiencing a paradigm shift, where:

> In essence, the practice of social work appears to be moving away from the use of vaguely defined, unvalidated, and haphazardly or uncritically derived knowledge for practice. In its most salient characteristics, the paradigm shift appears to involve a movement toward more systematic, rational, empirically oriented development and use of knowledge for practice. For want of a better phrase, this could be termed a movement toward *scientifically based practice* in social work. (200)

Fischer's conclusion was based on what he believed was evidence of increased development of research tools used to generate knowledge about practice, integration between research and practice, and availability of a wide range of intervention procedures of demonstrated effectiveness. For Fischer, this was a laudable trend that would supplant social workers' tendency to select practice approaches based on faith, comfort with familiar interventions, the charisma of certain theoreticians or respected practitioners, or consensus among "experts" or colleagues. These latter approaches, according to Fischer, tended to ignore use of "systematic, rigorous, rational criteria of selection. They generally precluded critical analysis of available approaches, such as analysis of research to determine the availability of evidence of the effectiveness of each approach" (200).

Fischer looked forward to a "new breed of social worker" (205) who would be a *scientific practitioner*. Such a practitioner is one who (1) systematically monitors and evaluates the progress he or she makes with each case; (2) grounds his or her practice to the extent possible in empirically based knowledge, particularly making use of the numerous interventive techniques already available that have evidence of effectiveness, and using those without such evidence only with due caution; and (3) has the skills and attitudes—the commitment—to keep learning and searching for new and more effective approaches to intervention.

Gordon (1983) then took Fischer to task in his *Social Work* essay, "Social Work Revolution or Evolution?" In a frontal assault on Fischer's contention about the Kuhnian-type revolution taking place in social work, Gordon accused Fischer of dealing with the issue "carelessly, selectively using Kuhn in a misleading manner and revealing a bias unbecoming a scholar" (181). Gordon argues that Kuhn's criteria for a scientific revolution cannot be extended to social work, and that Fischer misread Kuhn's definition of a paradigm shift. He also criticizes Fischer's conclusion that Bartlett's *The Common Base of Social Work Practice* was not empirically based: "Certainly, Fischer must know the difference between empirical and quantitative, and thus, one must conclude he is deliberately promoting a cause rather than adopting a scholarly approach" (182). Gordon's principal claim was that Fischer's view of the role of measurement and research in social work is far too narrow and that his advocacy of "rank empiricism" only "perpetuates the gap between research and practice that he and others have lamented but not narrowed" (182, 183).

At this point Fischer and Gordon took off their intellectual gloves in their highly visible altercation in the pages of *Social Work*. Fischer (1984) summarily rejected Gordon's critique and accused him of writing a "disjointed" document consisting mainly of a:

> plethora of periphrastic platitudes, a gallimaufry of obfuscations and misunderstood quotes taken out of context, a hodgepodge of inconsistencies and non sequiturs, a mishmash of outdated conceptions, a grab bag of unsupported speculations, and a hugger-mugger of self-serving self-references. (71)

Fischer further chastised the "curmudgeonly Gordon" (71) for misunderstanding the nature of empiricism and empirically based practice. Fischer reiterates his view that:

> empirically based practice refers to practice that is grounded *in* research, not grounded *by* research. Empirically based practice refers to attempting to validate what we do and attempting to use practice techniques and methods that have been shown to be effective whenever they are available. Empirically based practice refers also to carefully monitoring and evaluating what we do to avoid any potential harm to our clients, as well as to enable us to enhance programs that are having positive effects. (72)

Gordon (1984) was somewhat more restrained in his reply, although he claimed to have "successfully unveiled the real Fischer" who engages in "verbal abuse, name-calling, and general lashing-out to redefine the issues in a way that attempts to put his ideas in a better light" (74). Gordon defended his commitment to empirical research, and claimed that Fischer simply misunderstood the important distinction between "empirical" and "empiricism."

THE RELEVANCE OF POSITIVISM

Fortunately, out of this unpleasant fray has come a much clearer understanding of the strengths and limitations of positivism as it pertains to social work research. While a superficial reading of the various antagonists' positions suggests they are poles apart, a closer reading suggests considerable common ground. One obvious conclusion is that virtually no social work scholars defend or advocate for extreme versions of the positivist perspective. Clearly, some scholars are far more sympathetic than others to the potential contributions of empirical and quantitative methods, yet it is difficult to find anyone who argues that all social work research should be reduced to narrowly construed empiricism. Further, most social work scholars recognize the value of qualitative, nonempirical inquiry, although some may disagree on exactly which methods and techniques are valid. Hence, the heart of the debate seems to concern the extent to which nonempirical methods and approaches are valid and a useful supplement to sound empirical methods, and the extent to which empirical methods are able to capture what is important about social work practice.

As a result of the protracted debate, some consensus has emerged concerning the strengths and limits of positivism. Empirical measurement offers the opportunity to systematically monitor and evaluate social work intervention, and test practice-relevant hypotheses. It offers the possibility (though not a guarantee) of consistency, reliability, and replication that may be difficult to achieve with nonempirical inquiry.

Yet, empirical methods have their notorious limitations, related primarily to problems of (1) concept formation and measurement, (2) research design, (3) relevance, and (4) dehumanization.

CONCEPT FORMATION AND MEASUREMENT. Two significant problems have emerged in social workers' efforts to conduct empirical research. The first concerns researchers' ability to identify conceptually the variables most relevant to practice phenomena. For decades, for example, social work and other mental health researchers have tried to identify factors that influence "successful" clinical treatment. Despite these ambitious and partially fruitful efforts, however, researchers continue to struggle to identify those factors that can be studied more closely. When we deal with phenomena as complex and mysterious as human relationships, we have considerable difficulty identifying in the first place the concepts that may warrant empirical investigation. Many social workers believe that hard-to-identify traits affect what occurs between social worker and client; despite endless speculation, no one agrees on which attributes matter most (Covey 1982; Witkin 1991).

Social workers are equally frustrated in their efforts to explore the causes of complex social problems such as poverty, criminal behavior, mental illness, and child abuse. We may have some superficial understanding of factors that lead to these troublesome phenomena, but social work researchers are far from agreeing on what variables are relevant and ought to be studied. Some focus on intrapsychic dynamics, such as defense mechanisms and self-esteem. Others lean more heavily toward environmental variables that may be germane, such as family dynamics, unemployment, and public policies. Social workers view the practice world through various lenses, and hence many disagree about what ought to be measured in empirical studies.

One practical consequence of our limited understanding of complicated social problems and interventions is that our empirical inquiry often is based on and generates rather simplistic research models or frameworks. Although we may have an intellectual understanding of the need to investigate etiological and intervention factors as they occur in their complex, multivariate contexts, our research methods may force us to focus only on artificially segmented portions. This sort of "context stripping" (Mishler 1979; Wood 1990:377) ultimately sanitizes and dilutes the quality of our inquiry. Enormously complex phenomena, such as domestic violence, depression, and addiction, may be reduced to vaporous, primitive analyses because of our inability to know what to measure (Ruckdeschel and Farris 1981; Witkin 1991). Hence, much of what occurs in social work practice is indeterminate (Maas 1968; Pieper 1985; Beckerman 1990). As Epstein (1986) notes:

Yet even if quasi-experimental and single-subject designs were consistently employed to test therapeutic social work information, the results would probably still be weak and remain indeterminate. The therapeutic social work intervention is an extremely complex proposition, depending on the concurrence of many separate truths for its own power. . . . The indeterminacy of practice is the core of social work's immaturity. It is a long-standing trait of the field and does not appear to be close to resolution through the solution of the problems that obstruct the production of reliable, replicable information. (154, 155)

Like all scientists, social work researchers suffer from what Simon (1957) referred to as "bounded rationality." That is, human beings are not as omniscient, rational, and consistently logical as we might like to be. Inevitably, our decisions and ability to grasp the world around us are affected by a variety of nonrational and nonlogical factors. Social workers have a limited ability to identify and understand the implications of the many variables that are related to practice (DeRoos 1990). As a result, our research tends to be flawed. As Simon (1957) observed: "The capacity of the human mind for formulating and solving complex problems is very small compared with the size of the problems whose solution is required for objectively rational behavior in the real world—or even for a reasonable approximation to such objective rationality" (198–99).

In certain instances, of course, social work researchers have a reasonable understanding of the relevant variables. Not all studies entail enormously complex and elusive factors. Investigations of the effects of parents' reinforcement of a child's "appropriate" behavior may be fairly straightforward. Needs assessments or client-satisfaction surveys may not pose such daunting challenges with respect to identifying relevant variables.But even here, social workers may encounter significant measurement problems. And even when researchers concur on *what* to study, a variety of methodological obstacles may prevent accurate measurement.

One problem concerns social workers' ability to measure precisely. We may *know* that in any given project it is important to measure such concepts as trust, poverty, hope, self-esteem, addiction, or aggression. It can be extremely difficult, however, to produce sensitive and valid operational definitions and empirical indicators of these concepts (often known as the problem of face validity). Although we may be able to construct reasonably reliable self-report or other instruments for recording feelings, attitudes, and behaviors related to these phenomena, much of what social workers measure still must be considered "soft" and elusive (Brennan 1973; Holland 1983; Imre 1982, 1984).

Social workers who collect empirical data—whether in the form of interviews, questionnaires, or observation—also face unique circumstances that may bias the results. These "demand characteristics" of social research (Orne 1969) may distort the accuracy or affect the validity of data collected from human subjects. Social work clients may have understandable incentives to provide socially desirable responses to interview or survey questions, their apprehension about being surveyed or evaluated may affect their responses, and researchers' own expectations, biases, and values can affect clients' responses as well as researchers' interpretation of them (Allen-Meares and Lane 1990; Berlin 1990; Imre 1984; Pieper 1985; Reamer 1979; Riecken 1962; Rodwell 1987; Rosenberg 1969; Rosenthal and Rosnow 1969; Sudman and Bradburn 1974; Williams 1964). As Heisenberg (1958) noted in his classic statement in *Physics and Philosophy,* under some circumstances researchers' efforts to measure may affect the phenomena they attempt to measure, thus preventing truly accurate measurement. This physics-based observation provides a useful analogy for social workers. As Bronowski (1973, cited in Beckerman 1990:401) notes:

> One aim of the physical sciences has been to give an exact picture of the material world. One achievement of physics in the twentieth century has been to prove that aim is unattainable. . . . It turns out that . . . errors cannot be taken out of observations.

DESIGN. A considerable portion of empirical social work research is devoted to analysis of cause-effect relationships, particularly related to treatment or intervention effectiveness. These *explanatory* studies, however, often are compromised because of design limitations. These limitations usually pertain to problems of internal validity and external validity.

Internal validity ordinarily is defined as the extent to which changes in a dependent (or outcome) variable are attributable to changes in one or more independent (or causal) variables. Key to explanatory studies is the ability to control for extraneous factors that might account for change in the dependent variable apart from the intervention. Ideally, these extraneous factors—which may include the effects of maturation, contemporaneous events, historical events, and measurement—are best controlled for by using a classic experimental design. Such designs include random assignment of eligible clients to experimental and control groups, followed by the collection of baseline or pretest data, the introduction of the intervention to clients in the experimental group, and follow-up or post-test data collection. There is widespread consensus that, in principle, this strategy is the most effective way to control for extraneous factors. Under this arrangement, differences in outcome between the experimental and control groups are attributable only to the intervention. Without a control group, it is difficult to know what would have happened to clients without any intervention. Without random assignment to an experimental and control group—that is, if intact groups are used for experimental and control groups—differences in outcome may be due to initial differences between the groups.

While the classic experimental design may work well in laboratory settings, social work researchers often encounter difficulty implementing it. As I noted earlier, several obstacles stand in the way. First, social work agencies often are not in a position to place clients in experimental and control groups. This may be because the number of clients needed to fill these two groups may be insufficient or because it would be unethical to withhold the intervention from any clients who otherwise might be eligible for a control group. Although a practical way around this problem may be found in some instances (for example, an agency with limited resources may place waiting-list clients in a control group for a period not to exceed the time they would ordinarily spend on the waiting list), ethical considerations often preclude use of control groups.

Second, social work agencies often are not in a position to randomly assign clients to experimental and control groups. Because of logistical constraints, a social work researcher may need to settle for a comparison of two intact groups of clients, for example, groups of clients from two different residential programs, or groups of clients who received two different interventions.

Third, social work researchers often face timing problems. Researchers' timetables for data collection and intervention may not coincide with those of agency staff and clients. An agency may be willing to accommodate a researcher's data collection only some weeks after an intervention has begun; as a result, the design may produce only a partial glimpse of what actually occurs in the program.

These design constraints typically mean that a social work researcher has difficulty ruling out a variety of plausible alternative explanations for a study's results. As a consequence, social work studies that set out to identify causal relationships among variables often need to settle for the mere identification of various correlations among variables. Given that the variables involved in social work practice phenomena typically do not emerge in a clean linear fashion, the research designs we often end up using seem unable to capture the complex interactions and relationships that occur. As Gyarfas (1983) concludes:

> In recent years, the tendency to limit social work practice and research to one-dimensional experimental designs . . . has had the effect of devaluing a rich body of social work knowledge, thereby impoverishing the profession as a whole. Concepts that should have been refined and tested in complicated, sophisticated research designs have been thrown out like the proverbial baby in the bath water because we lacked the research technology at the time to examine them rigorously. (150)

External validity, on the other hand, refers to the extent to which results of a study can be generalized to other contexts. Here, too, social work researchers often encounter limitations. For practical reasons, research samples may be small or nonrepresentative, limiting the results' generalizability. Although it is ideal to design studies based on probability samples (for example, simple random or stratified random samples), social workers often must settle for nonprobability samples (for example, accidental, purposive, quota, snowball). Master lists of clients or potential research subjects often are not available, thereby precluding the use of probability samples.

Rodwell (1987) has summarized succinctly the various design limitations that accompany much empirical research:

> The logical positivist and empiricist roots are questioned on several grounds. (1) Controlled experiments have little resemblance to actual practice. (2) No observation is free from bias. The practitioner is not neutral, and clients' perceptions are often useful for understanding both the problem and the treatment process. (3) No techniques of control can change

the fact that problems are messy, complex, and interactive. Reducing them to simple variables or sets of variables moves the practitioner away from, rather than closer to, desired solutions. (4) Situational knowledge seems more productive than do universal laws. Client uniqueness cannot be accounted for in a single reality. Generalization is less important than is understanding the individual. (5) No statistical technique or research design can obviate the need for, or replace the informed judgment of, the researcher. (6) No value-free observation or data exist. The recognition of bias has greater value than has attempted objectivity in creating a forum for understanding. (237)

The regrettable result of these various limitations is that a significant portion of empirical social work research is seriously flawed. Unfortunately, however, consumers of empirical research, and often the researchers themselves, fail to acknowledge adequately that these limitations exist (Vigilante 1974; Karger 1983; Schuerman 1987; Witkin 1991). As Guzzetta (1980:8, cited in Karger 1983:201) concludes: "Despite the fact that social work does not readily lend itself to empirical, scientific, experimental studies, the strong desire to believe that it does has led us to accept any research that purports to be scientific."

RELEVANCE. Much empirical social work research also has seemed of limited relevance to practitioners. Because many—although certainly not all—research designs and measurement instruments seem unable to tap adequately into core social work concepts, practitioners often complain that research results are of marginal value. As Brennan (1973, cited in Karger 1983:201) observes, quantitative methodology cannot adequately examine the interpersonal, social, and cultural dimensions that social workers must consider in practice; these factors are "too elusive, unpredictable and multi-faceted to be captured by social science theory and methodology. . . . Many theories, hypotheses, or generalizations that hold under artificially . . . controlled experimental conditions . . . fall apart . . . when applied to . . . confounding situations which social workers encounter in professional practice." As a result, social work researchers often tend to focus on that which they seem to be able to measure, which may be of relatively limited value and relevance to practitioners (Allen-Meares and Lane 1990; Beckerman 1978; Pieper 1985; Siegel 1984; Wood 1990). This tendency can result in what have become known as Type III or Type IV errors (Dunn and Mitroff 1981; Ratcliffe 1983; Weick 1987): either solving the wrong problem or solving a problem not worth solving, perhaps because researchers are blinded by the methodology available to them. As Schon (1983) noted in his novel study of professionals:

> In the varied topography of professional practice, there is a high, hard ground where practitioners can make effective use of research-based theory and technique, and there is a swampy lowland where situations are confusing "messes" incapable of technical solution. The difficulty is that the problems of the high ground, however great their technical interest, are often relatively unimportant to clients or to the larger society, while in the swamp are the problems of greatest human concern. (42)

Clinical practitioners also may have difficulty applying to their individual cases the results of research based on aggregate or grouped data. The lack of fit between the so-called idiographic (case specific) needs of practitioners and the nomothetic (aggregate) nature of much research data can be particularly frustrating for practitioners who want to be able to translate empirical findings into practice-relevant guidelines (Beckerman 1978; Gyarfas 1969; Scott 1990). As Wood (1990) argues, "experimental group-comparison research reports on group aggregates, but practitioners deal with clients who are each, in Erikson's term, 'a universe of one' and who may or may not be like the clients who responded to the experimental intervention" (377).

Researchers also sometimes dwell on results that are statistically significant but that may lack substantive significance. This has become especially problematic as the use of bivariate and multivariate statistical procedures has proliferated throughout social work. Lengthy and complex discussions of empirical findings may emphasize statistically significant results based on what are actually tiny correlations with little practical meaning. Practitioners who are able to follow the technical analysis often end up scratching their heads wondering what relevance such trivial statistically significant results might have to their pressing day-to-day concerns. As Pieper (1985) maintains, a frequent "problem with the present approach to statistical analysis is that a blind adherence to rules is being substituted for a thoughtful examination of assumptions and an ongoing assessment of the substantive value of our research guidelines" (7).

DEHUMANIZATION. A final problem concerns allegations that empirical methods sometimes reduce clients to mere manipulable pawns in the researcher's hands. Use of control groups, reversal designs where interventions are withdrawn, deception, and subtle coercion may lead to dehumanization of the very people social workers seek to help (Gyarfas 1969; Imre 1982, 1984). Saleeby (1979, cited in Karger 1983:201) argues, for example, that: "Practice articulated from the experimental paradigm . . . [assumes] . . . that any degree of manipulation, deception, and control is fair if done in the service of socially acceptable or human ends. But the problem is that the method itself . . . may have within . . . [it] . . . the seeds of dehumanization."

Some also have argued that researchers' preoccupation with scientific method and technical analyses has diluted, although not entirely supplanted, social workers' concern with enduring value issues that have buttressed the profession's conceptual foundation. This argument maintains that attempts to reduce social work phenomena to quantifiable variables distracts practitioners' attention from key value-based issues concerned with concepts such as justice, equality, altruism, and so on (Reamer 1990:23–27). Weick (1987) makes the point succinctly:

> In examining the development of the profession, two interrelated but distinct strands of influence appear. The legacy of humanism gave to social work its wisdom about the worth of individuals and fostered a commitment to the importance of values in the practice of social work. At the same time, the fledgling profession was influenced by the concepts and methods of the natural sciences, which emphasized knowledge as it was gained from the observation and measurement of quantifiable phenomena. In a way that is characteristic of later trends, social work accepted a difficult duality by embracing the importance of both knowledge and values in the teaching and practice of social work.
>
> The balance between these two elements was, however, an unequal one. As social work struggled to develop a coherent practice, it became increasingly aligned with the social sciences, whose orientation was shaped by a nineteenth-century physical science model. . . . As a result there is an inherent disparity at the foundation of social work. The knowledge developed under the rubric of classical science has overshadowed and in many ways usurped the domain of values. Values

have become subordinated to knowledge as evidenced by the ubiquitous maxim of "knowledge-guided practice." (218–19)

Clearly, problems related to concept formation and measurement, design, relevance, and dehumanization limit somewhat the value of positivism in social work. The picture that empirical methods provide us of the practice domain tends to be incomplete, due to a combination of primitive measures, flawed designs, and other sources of "noise" or error. Although we may fantasize that the phenomena that concern us in social work occur as orderly, precise "clocks," in fact they are much more like amorphous, disorderly, unpredictable, and elusive "clouds" (Popper 1965).

TOWARD A MODEL OF KNOWLEDGE

The decade of the eighties saw especially vigorous debate about the role of positivism in social work research. During those years, a number of thoughtful alternatives emerged in response to the widely acknowledged limitations of positivism. It is important to note that while many social work scholars have been critical of positivism, few have advocated discarding all of its elements. Rather, most proposed alternatives emphasize the need to go beyond positivism while continuing to incorporate its useful features.

Consensus seems to be emerging that the most viable model of social work research must contain a number of key elements, including a variety of qualitative and quantitative methodologies and multiple data sources. These elements appear in different forms in alternative, though somewhat overlapping, research models known variously as a qualitative approach (sometimes known as a normative approach), naturalistic approach, heuristic approach, and hermeneutical approach.

Clearly, a *qualitative approach* to social work research may have a useful role, including ethnography, ethnomethodology, participant observation, naturalistic research, field research, and phenomenological research. In contrast to a conventional empirical approach—which is likely to emphasize objectivity, prediction, causation, determinism, experimentation, quantification, observational detachment, and an aim for certainty—a qualitative approach is more likely to focus on subjective interpretation (which can, in principle, be studied objectively), explanation, close involvement with research subjects, process, values, insight, intuition, symbols, relativism, and faith (Peile 1988).

Qualitative methods are particularly useful as a way to understand how clients interpret their life circumstances and behave in their natural environments (Haworth 1984; Ruckdeschel 1985) and how social workers conduct their work (Scott 1990). As Feinstein (1967, cited in Scott 1990:565) notes, every practitioner possesses rich qualitative knowledge which may not be transformed easily into quantifiable measures:

> A clinician performs an experiment every time he treats a patient . . . yet we had never been taught before to give our ordinary clinical treatment the scientific "respect" accorded to a laboratory experiment. . . . We had been taught to call it "art," and to consign its intellectual aspects to some mystic realm of intuition that was "unworthy" of scientific attention because it was used for the practical everyday work of clinical care.

What has become known as the *naturalistic approach* to social work research builds upon the principal assumptions of the qualitative approach (Denzin 1971; Lincoln and Guba 1985; Lofland 1974; Rodwell 1987; Willems and Raush 1969). According to naturalism, inquiry is based on several key axioms (Lincoln and Guba 1985; Rodwell 1987):

1. *The nature of reality.* There is no single reality. Rather, multiple realities exist that can be understood from varying perspectives. These diverging realities make prediction and control unlikely, although some level of understanding is possible.
2. *The relationship between observer and observed.* The researcher and the subject interact and influence each other. The "demand characteristics" (Orne 1969) of the research context are such that research subjects are influenced by cues transmitted by researchers, and researchers are influenced by cues conveyed by their subjects.
3. *The limits of generalizability.* The principal goal of inquiry is to generate idiographic knowledge that pertains to the individual case.
4. *The limits of causal connections.* Straightforward, asymmetrical, and linear causal relationships are virtually non-

existent. As Meyer (1990) notes with respect to clinical social work: "The data in cases never really add up linearly; they only interact and become more complex and 'curvy' " (398). Given the complexity of causal connections among entities social workers study (for example, clients, interventions, organizations, communities, demographic trends), it is difficult to distinguish causes from effects.

5. *The relevance of values.* Values are central to research. Values influence the initial choice of a problem to investigate, the methodology and theoretical framework used to conduct the inquiry, and the analysis and interpretation of results.

According to naturalism, this set of principles requires that research be conducted in natural, not artificial, contexts. Thus, methodology involving observation of clients in their ordinary living environments and social settings would be preferred to controlled laboratory experiments. Data may be based on intuition and feelings in addition to more traditional language-based sources. Data may be collected through qualitative means, such as observation, reading, listening, and speaking. Whenever possible, data sources may be consulted for their interpretation of findings. Also, researchers will be careful to offer conclusions tentatively.

The naturalistic framework is consistent with Simon's (1957) conclusions about "bounded rationality." Simon argues that nonlogical, but not irrational, factors are essential to human inquiry and problem solving. He argues further that human beings' efforts to understand and negotiate their environment depend on a subjective approach to an incomplete picture of the objective world. Our actions are based on this relatively simplified understanding of objective reality.

In light of constraints related to limited time and understanding, human beings must accept that they are unable to "maximize" their choices consistently, that is, selecting that alternative that maximizes or leads to the maximization of the desired goal. Instead, our decisions must be guided by what Simon calls "satisficing," where our choices result in an outcome that is "good enough." The rules we follow for problem solving under these less-than-ideal-but-realistic circumstances are called *heuristics*. Although we might prefer precise algorithms for decision making, we must be content with heuristics, roughly equivalent to "rules of thumb," that provide us with reasonable guides (DeRoos 1990; Mullen 1985; Simon 1957).

According to Wimsatt (1981), heuristics have three major properties: (1) they do not guarantee a correct solution; (2) the time, effort, and computational complexity involved in producing solutions are significantly less than for an algorithmic procedure; and (3) failures and errors that result from using heuristics are systematic (DeRoos 1990). Given our "bounded rationality," it is difficult in social work research to simultaneously maximize generality, precision, and realism; ordinarily, each of these attributes will be achieved only at the expense of at least one of the others (Levins 1966).

As with naturalism, the heuristic approach assumes that controlled experiments often produce artificial or unrealistic results; researchers are not neutral observers; subjects' perceptions and interpretation are valuable sources of information; efforts to reduce complex social work phenomena to simplistic causal models are of limited value; it is more worthwhile to pursue situational knowledge than universal laws; informed judgment needs to supplement statistical analysis; and values are an essential component of any inquiry and ought to be acknowledged as such (Mullen 1985; Pieper 1985; Simon 1966). The heuristic approach challenges what its proponents see as restrictive research standards that limit the value of much social work inquiry. According to the heuristic formulation, social work research that is grounded in empiricism, quantification, objectivity, and prediction is blind to the world as it really exists.

A common, critical thread in the naturalistic and heuristic approaches is the emphasis on generating knowledge in the context of practice as opposed to some artificial, experimentally contrived setting. This is a position first made prominent by John Dewey in his 1899 presidential address to the American Psychological Association, where he commented on the limitations of knowledge obtained from the laboratory: "The completer control of conditions, with resulting greater accuracy of determination, demands an isolation, a ruling out of the usual media of thought and action, which leads to a certain remoteness, and easily to a certain artificiality" (cited in Rein and White 1981:34). A more contemporary version is offered by Mishler (1979, cited in Rein and White 1981:35):

> Context-stripping is a key feature of our standard methods of experimental design, measurement, and statistical analysis.

... Our procedures are aimed at isolating variables from their functioning personal and social contexts. We try to find pure variables, measures of unitary dimensions that will be uncontaminated by other variables. . . . A prominent theme in these recent critiques is the discovery that research findings appear to be context-dependent.

The classic proposal for such context-based study was made near the turn of the century by the German philosopher Wilhelm Dilthey, who advanced the *hermeneutical approach*. Hermeneutics (derived from the Greek word *hermeneutikos*, "to interpret") is ordinarily defined as the science of interpretation and explanation (Habermas 1971; Orcutt 1990; Palmer 1969). For centuries, hermeneutics was an approach used to study the authenticity and meaning of literary works. According to this perspective, one must study human beings and social phenomena in their broad historical contexts and with keen awareness of one's own cultural, conceptual, and personal biases.

Although support is growing for the kind of inquiry promoted by the qualitative, naturalistic, heuristic, and hermeneutic approaches, it is important to note that some social work scholars have also called for a more tentative, moderate embrace of these views. Mullen (1985), for example, cautions against enthusiastic acceptance of the heuristic model in a way that would preclude the use of experimentation, quantification, and other conventional features of positivism:

> The exclusion of quantification and the descriptive or inferential type of statistical analysis from procedures that are available for scientific work would more than likely be unacceptable to most scientists, although they clearly have individual preferences. To exclude these procedures, most researchers would say, would be to discard the powerful tools of description and analysis that, in spite of frequent misfits with underlying measurement and statistical assumptions, have been found to work. On the basis of experience, they would say, important psychological and sociological qualities have been measured with knowledge, care, and skill, and many statistical procedures have been found to be robust. They would point to the remarkable advances being made in the areas of measurement and statistical analysis (such as the statistical analysis of qualitative data, Bayesian methods, multivariate procedures) that are responsive to these difficulties.

And, they might say, these quantitative procedures tend to simplify, dissect, and objectify substantive concerns, this being their function.

The heuristic perspective regarding the quantitative-qualitative dilemma is not clear. The perspective rejects much of inferential statistics and calls for an abandonment of tests of significance. Yet, it does not propose alternative procedures for arriving at generalizations. (16)

Although significant differences of opinion persist about the most viable model for social work research, it is clear that the vast majority of social work scholars now prefers an approach that relies systematically on a variety of data collection tools, sources, and methods of analysis and interpretation. Nearly all commentators on the epistemological debate acknowledge there is a place for deductive and inductive frameworks, quantitative and qualitative data collection techniques, large samples and small samples, objectivity and subjectivity, and explanation and prediction. Acknowledgment is now widespread that competent social work depends, as Wood (1990) suggests, on "the ability of practitioners to be polyocular—to have a variety of lenses through which to view their cases and the clinical judgment necessary to select the conceptual lens that fits best the data of the case. Indeed, in a given case—or even in one interview in a case—the competent practitioner may be utilizing several different descriptive and prescriptive theories in rapid succession or even simultaneously" (378).

Most social workers concur, however, that they should not view various epistemological perspectives and methodological techniques as a "grab bag" collection through which one rummages for the "approach-of-the-day." Anarchy in research and extreme forms of relativism should be avoided; rather, social workers need to draw *systematically* on various research perspectives and techniques in order to produce the most lucid, illuminating, and compelling body of information required by varying practice circumstances. Thus, formal evaluation of a long-term residential program for emotionally disturbed adolescents may call for a combination of quantitative, empirically based, self-report data from checklists, questionnaire data, and academic performance data, *and* qualitative data based on extensive observation in several naturalistic settings. A single-subject (n = 1) study of progress made by a depressed client might entail a combination of quantitative data drawn from an empirically based depression scale administered weekly *and* qualitative data drawn from nonstructured observation and interviews. No particular methodological strategy has a corner on the market. Each has its strengths and limitations. The challenge is to construct imaginative, fruitful, and ethically appropriate combinations of epistemological perspectives and methods to fit varying social work contexts and circumstances. As Allen-Meares and Lane (1990) conclude in their discussion of the use of qualitative and quantitative data collection techniques:

> The key to integration is not simply to use both qualitative and quantitative data collection techniques but rather a much more complex approach: to use the appropriate technique or combination at the right stage of the social work process. Integration is not an additive process; it is a perspective in which qualitative and quantitative data serve unique and different purposes and act to reinforce each other to strengthen the social work process. (455)

It is not enough, however, merely to promote in an abstract way more systematic, selective integration of epistemological perspectives, data collection strategies, and data analysis techniques. Effective integration requires more specific prescription, and must occur in all social work research domains, including exploratory, descriptive, and explanatory research. Effective integration must occur with respect to a variety of research goals, including theory construction, hypothesis testing, needs assessments, program evaluations, and single-subject designs.

Integration can be approached in several ways (Peile 1988). According to the "critical paradigm," which originated with Marx and Hegel, effective synthesis occurs as a result of a dialectical process. In principle, the dialectical process produces "synthesis" out of the conflict between "thesis" (for example, positivism) and "antithesis" (for example, naturalism). One might view the epistemological debate among social workers over the past ten to fifteen years as a manifestation of this dialectical process. Although full synthesis has not been achieved, much greater consensus now exists regarding the need for integration of methods than existed when the debate began in earnest.

A second model, known as the "creative view" (Peile 1988), is designed to bring together two *partial* views to provide a unified view. Thus, a creative approach would bring together elements of positivism and nonpositivism in a way that demonstrates that the two approaches are inseparable if we are truly to understand social work phenomena. Neither view by itself is a complete view (Bohm 1980, 1981; Prigogine and Stengers 1984; Sheldrake 1985).

A third approach, one that most closely resembles recent integration attempts in social work, is a product of what is generally known as the "new paradigm research group" (Burrell and Morgan 1979; Feyerabend 1975; Morgan 1983; Reason and Rowan 1981). This approach assumes that no one research framework is superior and that all perspectives and approaches are necessary and interdependent. For proponents of this school of thought, positivist and nonpositivist perspectives need to be integrated within a "multimethod epistemological approach" (Peile 1988:12).

Clearly, many participants in the debate—both positivist and nonpositivist in orientation—favor some form of methodological pluralism, although no doubt there would be some difference of opinion about the nature of the mix. Heineman Pieper (1985) concludes: "We must try everything and anything that promises to give us helpful knowledge about problems that are important to us" (6). Mullen (1985), in his critique of Heineman Pieper, also concludes that social work researchers deal with a wide range of substance and methods and that "this diversity is to social work's advantage" (18). Beckerman (1990) argues that "researchers and practitioners would be able to communicate much more effectively with each other if they agreed on a continuum of knowledge. . . ." (401) and Allen-Meares and Lane (1990) contend that "both the quantitative and the qualitative paradigms contain useful elements. The real issue facing social work is how to integrate these two perspectives effectively into a unified approach" (452). Similar sentiments are echoed by Beckerman (1990), Berlin (1990), Brekke (1986), Geismar (1982), Haworth (1984), Imre (1982, 1984), Meyer (1990), Peile (1988), Reid (1987), Rodwell (1987), Ruckdeschel and Farris (1981), Schuerman (1987), Scott (1990), Videka-Sherman, Reid, and Toseland (1990), Weick (1987), Wood (1990), and Zimmerman (1989). Most commentators on the debate acknowledge, directly or indirectly, the value of what Denzin (1978) referred to some years ago as "multiple triangulation." As Hartman (1990) said, "There are indeed many ways of knowing and many kinds of knowers" (4).

Although epistemological pluralism may be suitable in a variety of social work research endeavors—particularly needs assessments, program evaluations, and single-case designs—it may be difficult to achieve with respect to theory construction. While some theories of assessment and intervention, for instance, may invite pluralism, others are based on basic, fundamental premises that reflect an explicit theoretical bias. If a social worker sets out to develop a behaviorally oriented assessment theory or a psychodynamically oriented treatment theory—and is unwilling to incorporate alternative theoretical viewpoints—epistemological pluralism may be unrealistic. As Lakatos (1980) suggests, hard core theoretical bias provides a "protective belt" around the inquiry. If social workers hold tight to a particular theoretical perspective—and in some instances they may have good reasons to do so—we cannot reasonably expect them to embrace an ambitious form of pluralism. There may be an intimate connection between one's theoretical allegiance and certain epistemological assumptions. A hard-boiled behaviorist simply may be unwilling to entertain some qualitative, nonempirical measures (Brekke 1986). A cognitively oriented practitioner may be unwilling to use the vocabulary of intrapsychic phenomena. Whether or not these are reasonable biases is a worthwhile discussion. Without a fundamental shift in a social worker's perspective, however, epistemological pluralism may make little sense in these circumstances.

Whatever epistemological framework we operate within, it is important to acknowledge that, in the end, social workers are unlikely to generate grand theory related to practice, policy, administration, and so on. It is unlikely we will ever be in a position to make sweeping theoretical statements about the etiology of social problems, effective interventions, and so on. Far more likely is that our aim will be toward what Merton (1949) dubbed "theories of the middle range," that is midlevel theories whose main purpose is to help practitioners understand discrete aspects of social problems and interventions relevant to them (Shireman and Reamer 1986:104; Wood 1990:387).

This suggests candid acknowledgment that practical limits on social workers' knowledge-generating ability are likely to endure. While our methodological tools certainly have become more sophisticated during the profession's century-old formal existence—and we can anticipate with some confidence that over time these tools will become even more sophisticated—our ability to understand and measure the world of social work is still rather primitive. There is much we do not understand—and may never grasp—about the determinants of social problems, their correlates, and intervention. This is not to discount the impressive strides social workers have made in their various attempts to illuminate the nature and consequences of practice. We are clearly capable of conducting quite competent and valuable program evaluations, needs assessments, and descriptive studies, for example. But with respect to more ambitious explanatory research, we must acknowledge candidly the relative modesty of our advances. Popper (1950) put it well in his reflections on indeterminism in scientific inquiry:

> I suggest that this misinterpretation is due to the tendency of attributing to Science (with a capital S) a kind of omniscience; and that this theological view of science ought to be replaced by a more humanistic view, by the realization that science is the work of ordinary humans, groping their way in the dark. In doing so, we may sometimes find something interesting; we may be astonishingly successful; but we shall never get anything like "the whole truth." Our theories are not descriptions of nature, but only of some little feathers which we plucked out of nature's garb, more or less accidentally. (193)

In fact, our knowledge about etiology and the effectiveness of social work intervention is, at best, partial, or what Brodbeck (1968) aptly dubbed "imperfect knowledge." Our ability to measure adequately, control for extraneous factors, and imagine in the first place all of the relevant variables is constrained by the limits of our intellectual capacity and insight. And perhaps this is the way it ought to be if we are to live in a world that is not completely deterministic.

CHAPTER FIVE

🙟🙠

AESTHETICS

Beauty in things exists in the mind
which contemplates them.

—DAVID HUME

Social workers have always recognized that skilled practice contains artistic and aesthetic elements. Although science-based and theoretical knowledge related to social work intervention, human behavior, and social welfare policy is an essential component of competent, first-rate social work, it is widely recognized that there is an art—albeit vaguely defined—to good practice.

The concept of art, and the metaphor of the artist, appear throughout social work. We sometimes speak of a clinician's uniquely effective and novel intervention in a complex case as "artistic." We also speak of a community organizer's artistic efforts to empower neighborhood residents in their battle for enhanced municipal services.

In fact, before 1930 many definitions of social casework classified it as an art (Bowers 1949; Rapoport 1968:139). Although these references tended to be rather superficial, it is clear that social work's earliest practitioners and scholars recognized the artistic and aesthetic aspects of their vocation. In her classic *Social Diagnosis,* published in 1917, Mary Richmond commented on casework as an art:

We turn now to the details of social case work method. It will be necessary to remember that in any art the description of its processes is necessarily far more clumsy than are the processes themselves. In the last analysis moreover, the practitioner of an art must discover the heart of the whole matter for himself—it is of the essence of art that he shall win his way to this personal revelation. (103)

Several years later, Karl DeSchweinitz (1924) also characterized social work as an art in *The Art of Helping People Out of Trouble*. In 1942, Bertha Capen Reynolds published one of the most explicit characterizations of "social worker as artist" in her *Learning and Teaching in the Practice of Social Work*:

> All the arts use the person of the artist in some way as an instrument. The painter must see before he can create. The musician must hear, and also experience sound and rhythm with the whole body. The doctor must see well before he can choose the means to help the whole patient whom he sees. The actor uses his personality to portray character and action in life situations. Social work becomes dynamic only when it goes out through relationships of real meaning to people. All the arts demand a freedom of expression of the person which is rare in a society which almost automatically produces anxiety and tension. Art is the more needed in an age when many people demand escape, and all need creative relaxation. (231)

In the end, Reynolds concludes, "social work is an art, or it is worse than nothing" (232).

In 1952, Tyler's seminal essay in the *Social Work Journal* on the attributes of education for the professions also noted the central place of artistry in practice:

> For an occupation to be a profession, it should involve complex tasks which are performed by artistic application of major principles and concepts rather than by routine operations or skills. The application of these principles necessitates an analysis of the particular problem to see what are its unique aspects which will require adaptation of the principle. This adaptation is an artistic task; that is, it involves individual judgment and imagination as well as skill. (56; cited in Rapoport 1968:140–41)

Contemporary social work literature also pays considerable attention to the artistic and aesthetic aspects of practice. Most references to social work as art focus on clinical practice and casework skills, citing the artistic manner in which the profession's most proficient practitioners conduct their trade (Richan and Mendelsohn 1973; Tropp 1976; Wiegand 1979). A number of authors have commented on the ways in which social work and art share, in some noteworthy respects, perspective and method. One of the most explicit statements appears in Boehm's (1961) essay on the scientific and artistic elements of social work:

> I shall state as my major premise the proposition that the social worker in the performance of his professional activities is an artist. He is an artist in the sense that the performance of his professional tasks requires the fashioning and fusion of so many elements into the professional act that the professional effort might be likened to the creative effort of the artist. (145)

The attempt to draw connections between social work and art is particularly deliberate in Rapoport's (1968) essay, "Creativity in Social Work":

> Social work, like art, is engaged in problem solving, be it the problem of expression, communication, transformation, or change. Both deal with human materials or human themes and both require an intimate "knowing and contact." Both call for creative and imaginative use of self. Both require a special kind of distance and objectivity. Thus, in social work, we are accustomed to thinking about the need for objective appraisal as well as the compassionate response. (151)

Two unusually ambitious attempts to discuss the relationship between social work and art appear in Siporin's (1988) essay, "Clinical Social Work As an Art Form" and England's (1986) book, *Social Work As Art*. Siporin's main point is that social workers need to explore the artistic aspect of practice more thoroughly, particularly with respect to the practitioner's creative style, the helping relationship, and metaphorical communication. For Siporin, social workers who grasp the artistic and aesthetic elements of their work are likely to have enhanced understanding of and insight about social work processes:

The primary goal of art is to create beauty. The goal of social work practice is to help people resolve their problems in social functioning. Social work practice and the arts, as represented by the visual, literary, and performing arts, have many qualities in common. Both involve much more than the performance of technical skills. Both are concerned with individualization and the refashioning of material and subject matter; with creating a form that has symmetry and a balance of system components; and with the transformation and communication of subjective, personal experience. Both attempt to reveal or achieve a unique, harmonious unity of components and to communicate and share this unifying experience. Both utilize creativity and craft to envision and construct a new reality with more valued and nurturing forms. . . .

The social worker uses style in essentially the same way as does the artist. The worker attempts to design and form therapy into a clear, well-proportioned, and coherent structure. The social worker pays attention to the rhythms of therapy and assures that tasks and performances have a beginning, middle, and end. The worker also pays attention to the melodies of life themes, which are often intergenerational, such as fear of sexual intimacy or beliefs in inherent weakness, sin, or doom. The practitioner uses various technical procedures, such as sensory images and metaphors and psychosocial rituals and ceremonies, to engage, arouse, and influence the client intellectually and emotionally. (178, 179)

England's (1986) *Social Work As Art* provides one of the profession's most thorough examinations of the artistic and aesthetic elements of practice. Focusing largely on British social work and drawing extensively on British social work literature, England explores the subjective and intuitive nature of much of social work practice. For England, social workers must recognize that their "intuitive use of self" is an essential ingredient in good social work practice, the cultivation and application of which constitutes an art form:

It becomes clear that there are substantial grounds for locating social work within the tradition of art. Art offers recognition and exploration of the ephemerality which marks the subject matter of all social work; it knows the practices of selection and synthesis which social workers must undertake if their understanding is to be adequately complex and coherent; it places the same high value upon the communication of that understanding. Art strengthens social work's theory . . . . Social work thus manifestly belongs in the tradition of art, and it has a considerable potential value as a social institution practiced in striving for the "whole texture." (114, 117)

With the exception of England's unusually ambitious analysis, and a handful of briefer essays (Boehm 1961; Eaton 1958; Kaminsky 1985; Rapoport 1968; Siporin 1988), social workers' discussions of the artistic and aesthetic aspects of practice have been strikingly superficial. Although it is widely recognized—in both conversation and literature—that social work has its artistic features, few in-depth analyses exist. Rapoport (1968) reached this conclusion some years ago, when she stated: "In the literature of the social work profession . . . the conception of artistry is only given a nod. It has not been made the subject of serious inquiry, nor has it been endowed with values, dignity, and institutional supports which a genuine commitment would demand" (140). More recently, England (1986) and Siporin (1988) came to the same realization. England concluded: "A small number of social work theorists have given specific attention to the theoretical relationship between art and social work. Their work does not, in the main, look to theoretical or critical approaches to art" (94). Siporin echoed this same sentiment when he said that "the art of social work is neglected in academic pronouncements and the literature" (177):

Many innovative, creative procedures and techniques express the artistic, aesthetic dimension of social work practice. Clinicians have learned to structure the helping process as dramatic, transformative, learning experiences for clients. . . . All of these procedures improve treatment methods and techniques. However, it is unfortunate that little attention has been paid to identifying and understanding of the aesthetic elements used in these procedures or to analyzing their effects in artistic terms. The profession lacks the language and the analytic methodology for doing so. (178)

THE NATURE OF AESTHETICS

Clearly, the philosophical roots of the links between social work and art need to be explored in greater depth. For an adequate treatment of the subject, we must first consider the nature of aesthetics and the relevance of these concepts to social work practice.

Aesthetics may be generally defined as the philosophical study of beauty and taste. In the *New English Dictionary,* aesthetics is defined as "the philosophy or theory of taste or of the perception of the beautiful in nature and art." The word is derived from the Greek *aisthanesthai,* to perceive, and *aisthetica,* things perceptible.

Although Plato and Aristotle commented on the nature of beauty and art, aesthetic theory, in the formal sense, does not appear in their work (Saw and Osborne 1968). St. Thomas Aquinas included commentary on the nature of beauty in his thirteenth century *Summa Theolagiae.* Before the eighteenth century, however, discussions of aesthetics did not appear, by and large, in the works of the great philosophers. Instead, writing on aesthetics tended to be the product of relatively minor figures such as Baltasar Gracian, Jean de La Bruyere, and Georges-Louis Leclerc, comte de Buffon.

For the most part, aesthetics did not appear as an explicit focus of study until the end of the seventeenth and the beginning of the eighteenth century. It was then that concepts such as time, taste, imagination, natural beauty, and imitation came to be recognized as the central topics in aesthetics. The Third Earl of Shaftesbury and his disciples Francis Hutcheson and Joseph Addison were major influences in Britain during this period (Aesthetics 1988, 26). Hutcheson was among the first to ask questions that continue to have currency: How can we know something is beautiful? What guides our judgment and what validates it?

The term *aesthetics* was introduced into philosophical parlance about the middle of the eighteenth century by the German philosopher Alexander Gottlieb Baumgarten. Although he was clearly influenced by Baumgarten, Immanuel Kant later criticized Baumgarten's narrow application of the term to the field of taste and argued that, true to its etymological meaning, aesthetics ought to entail the study of sense perception generally. It was Kant's *Critique of Aesthetic Judgment* ([1790] 1928) that first identified aesthetic attributes as a phenomenon distinct from the study of that which is useful, pleasant, or morally good. It was during this general period that explicit interest in human taste and in the "factual aspects of the appreciation of beauty as a distinct mode of awareness and a subject for philosophical theory" first emerged, to some extent as a result of the empirical epistemology of John Locke (Saw and Osborne 1968:18).

Aesthetics, then, entails the study of the ways in which individuals perceive, judge, assess, evaluate, or comment about works of art—not art in the narrow sense, such as paintings, but creative works produced by painters, writers, poets, dancers, sculptors, artisans, and so on. As Beardsley (1970) aptly puts it, aesthetics, as a branch of philosophy, is essentially *metacriticism:* "It deals with philosophical problems that arise when we make statements about works of art and other aesthetic objects. And aesthetic theory, as a body of knowledge (or at least reasoned belief), consists of general principles that provide solutions to those problems and thus serve as theoretical underpinnings for art criticism" (3).

For aesthetics theory to be relevant to social work, then, professional practice must be recognized as having artistic qualities. Although numerous references to "social work as art" could easily be produced, social work rarely includes discussion of art in the formal sense and rarely explores the extent to which professional practice meets commonly accepted criteria for what constitutes an art form.

It is difficult, in fact, to be precise about exactly what it is that artistic forms of social work have in common with acknowledged works of art, such as Michelangelo's *David,* Dante's *Divine Comedy,* Shakespeare's *Othello,* Mozart's *Don Giovanni,* or Leonardo's *Mona Lisa.* As Sparshott (1982) says in *The Theory of the Arts,* "Poets and painters are in some sense doing the same sort of thing, and it is not easy to say in what sense this is so" (4). No doubt, no one will ever agree on what, exactly, constitutes art, just as no one will ever agree on what constitutes that which is morally good. Nonetheless, it is worth considering and applying some rigorous speculation to social work, to enhance our understanding of what constitutes artistic practice.

Although most social workers disagree about what constitutes good intervention, good outcome, and so on, many do concur that a body or "corpus" of social work values, principles, and skills exists that provides a measurable degree of unity to the profession and is an essential ingredient of its art. I shall say more about this shortly. In the meantime, however, it is helpful to consider Sparshott's (1982) useful view on the matter of what constitutes art:

An art in the traditional sense may be defined as a corpus of knowledge and skills organized for the production of changes of a specific kind in matter of a specific kind. The corpus that constitutes an art is one of knowledge and skills. It is because knowledge and skill can be transferred from an operation to other similar operations (defined as similar by this transferability itself) that arts exist. The different things that are made and done are the body of the art, but it is the skill embodied in this practice that works as a soul to make the body a single organism. If, for example, musicians no longer shared any agreed technique, the unity of the art of music would be merely extrinsic, an outcome of the circumstances of its production by accepted promoters in accepted halls in the presence of invited accredited reviewers and with the other trappings associated with music in the eyes of the musical profession and public. And it is hard to imagine that this exoskeleton of sustaining institutions could have formed itself around a body of practice that had not originally been sustained by some intrinsic unity. (26)

While this definition clearly incorporates what artists, writers, painters, dancers, and poets do, it also seems to incorporate what professionals and, more specifically, social workers do. Social workers obviously draw on a body of knowledge and skills organized for the production of changes in individuals, families, groups, communities, and organizations—such as enhanced mental health or improved living or neighborhood conditions, working climate, or interpersonal relationships. And, as I will explore more fully below, there does appear to be at least some superficial agreement about what gives social work its unique—or unifying—character (derived, in large measure, from its evolved value base).

Sparshott goes on to offer a conceptual definition of art that is particularly sympathetic to professional social work (although Sparshott certainly did not intend to comment on social work per se):

Our definition, however, does not require us to equate "matter" with material in the sense of stuff to be manipulated. The word is to be taken more generally: whenever anything is done or made, there is always something that the agent or artisan accepts at the beginning of his work as that to which, or with which, or about which, something has to be done, whether this something be a lump of rock, a fictional theme, or an awkward situation. And one of the first things that has to be said in distinguishing what authors do from what physicians do is that the former work with words and the latter work on people's bodies. One might go on from there to reflect on the difference between working *on* things and working *with* things and on how a doctor's relation to a patient's body (or bodily condition) differs from a writer's relation to words (or his theme), but such reflection would not make the crude initial distinction less important. Complexities and ambiguities in what constitutes the matter proper to any given art will answer to complexities in the practice and theory of the art itself. (27)

AESTHETICS: CONCEPTUAL FRAMEWORKS

Philosophers who have studied aesthetics have taken several broad approaches to the subject. One approach is quite abstract and involves the study of aesthetic concepts and the language of aesthetics. Such inquiry explores, for example, what we mean when we conclude that a particular painting or poem is beautiful. How should beauty be defined? Can it be defined? What constitutes beauty?

This form of inquiry has obvious relevance to social workers. Clinical social workers, for example, often make judgments about the concept of mental health and then design interventions based on these perceptions. If a social worker assumes that mental health can be defined, applies a subjectively formed definition to a particular client, and designs and implements a treatment plan, it is clear that aesthetic judgments have significant bearing on intervention. Similarly, aesthetic judgments are involved when a social worker who is a community organizer assumes that distinctions can be made between "unhealthy" and "healthy" communities, makes an evaluative judgment concerning the "health" of a particular community, and consequently designs and implements an intervention plan. Implicit in these activities is a belief that qualities or attributes, such as health and pathology, can be defined and grasped in much the same way that an artist believes that beauty can be defined and grasped.

A second approach to aesthetics focuses on the states of mind— such as individuals' responses, attitudes, and emotions—that are a part of the aesthetic experience (Aesthetics 1988:15). The emphasis here is on the observer's reaction to that which he or she observes. What is the nature of the attitudinal and emotional response we have to a particular sculpture or short story that moves us to conclude that this is a special work of art? What is the nature of the attitudinal and emotional response social workers have to a particular therapeutic intervention with a troubled family or a de-

pressed client that moves them to conclude that the skill involved
was artistic?

The third approach is perhaps the most obvious. This involves
study of the aesthetic object itself. Here philosophers study particular paintings, poems, books, plays, and sculptures to assess their
aesthetic qualities. Unlike the first approach, the goal here is to
assess their beauty, or other relevant qualities, rather than to explore whether and how beauty can be defined in the first place.

Similarly, social workers often assess what might be considered
aesthetic qualities of individual clients, families, communities, or
organizations. Although social workers do not ordinarily think of
these as aesthetic assessments, the process is very much the same.
Judgments that a particular client is "healthy," that a particular
organization is "pathological," or that a particular community is
"disorganized," are, in important respects, aesthetic judgments.

In general, then, aesthetics can involve the study of artistic
works themselves and those who produce them, or it can involve
more abstract speculation about the language and conceptual criteria individuals use to make aesthetic judgments. Aschenbrenner
(1974) refers to this as the distinction between *primary criticism*
(assessments of particular works of art) and *metacriticism* (critique
of primary criticism). This is a distinction that is roughly comparable to the one we encountered in our discussion of moral philosophy, between normative ethics (application of ethical criteria to
particular ethical questions or dilemmas) and metaethics (speculation about the nature of moral language and concepts).

Comprehensive aesthetic theories generally deal with four main
elements of the artistic situation: (1) the artist, (2) the art itself, (3)
the spectator, and (4) society (Sheppard 1987; Trilling 1970; Vivas
and Krieger 1962). With respect to the artist, one can ask two kinds
of questions: *intrinsic* and *extrinsic* (Vivas and Krieger 1962).
Intrinsic questions focus on the artist's particular gifts and skills,
how the artist's talent was developed or acquired, and how the
artist uses his or her skill to produce works of art. In contrast,
extrinsic questions concern the artist's relationship with and obligation to his or her audience and the broader society.

Although these questions have been asked mainly of painters,
sculptors, poets, and writers, they are equally applicable to social
workers. Certainly it makes sense to speculate about "intrinsic"
issues concerning a social worker's particular gifts and skills, how
the social worker's talent was developed or acquired, and how the
social worker uses his or her skill to produce "artistic" outcomes. It

also makes sense to focus on "extrinsic" issues concerning a social worker's relationship with and obligation to his or her audience (for example, supervisor or agency) and the broader society. Social workers do not produce "works of art" for their own sake; ultimately, social work interventions are designed to be of some benefit to individual clients, group members, family members, or the society at large. As a profession, social work has an established obligation to serve a broad audience that extends beyond the intrinsic self-interest of individual clients and practitioners.

Then we need to consider the object of art itself, that which the artist produces—the particular painting, poem, book, or play, for instance. Here, too, we can ask both "intrinsic" and "extrinsic" questions. The intrinsic questions concern the unique artistic qualities of the object, for example, its creative content, structure, or use of color. The extrinsic questions concern the effect the work of art has on its audience and the broader society, for example, what a painting may communicate about prevailing values, what a poem with a political message may inspire in its audience, or what a provocative book may influence its readers to do.

Such intrinsic and extrinsic questions also have obvious relevance to social work. What intrinsic qualities does skillful or artistic casework, therapy, agency administration, or community organizing have? Extrinsically, what effect does skillful social work skill have on third parties and the broader society? Clearly, artistic casework with an alcoholic or depressed client may have profound effects on the client's family members, friends, employers, and the general public. Artistic administration of a public welfare agency may have important consequences for the agency's clients and their family members, employees, and taxpayers.

Intrinsic and extrinsic questions can also be asked about the art work's spectator. What does an observer of fine art experience intrinsically, that is, emotionally and psychologically? What emotions does a beautiful poem or painting elicit? Extrinsically, what effect does this response have on an individual's subsequent values, priorities, thoughts, and behavior?

Here, too, connections to social work are evident. In social work the spectator may be the client, a family member, agency employee, community resident, or anyone else in a position to observe a practitioner's skillful intervention. Presumably, observation of a skillful intervention can evoke emotional response of varying degrees—whether positive or negative—and can have a significant effect on spectators' values, priorities, thoughts, and behavior.

Imagine, for example, a neighborhood resident who observes a social worker's artistic intervention with local gang members. The resident may experience emotional gratification and pleasure, and may, as a result, decide to remain in the community and get involved in community affairs. Or, a parent who observes a social worker's artistic intervention with his behaviorally disordered son may have a strong emotional reaction that leads him to alter his way of interacting with, managing, and disciplining his child.

Although the subject of aesthetics, in the formal sense of the term, has not been addressed extensively in social work literature, several authors have made at least passing references to it. In her seminal article on creativity in social work, for example, Rapoport (1968) commented on the aesthetic aspects of social work intervention, albeit without exploring aesthetic concepts per se:

> The artistic process involves consciously controlled and purposeful activity which is guided by various aesthetic laws and principles. The end result of this process is the artistic product. . . . While the practitioner may not be guided by aesthetic laws, it is possible to apply some principles of aesthetics to a given piece of social work practice. All of us, I am sure, have responded with a sense of deep pleasure upon hearing about or reading a particular case which we readily label as beautiful. What properties characterize the beautiful case, or any given piece of work in any realm of social work activity? (141–42, 155–56).

England (1986) also comments on the aesthetic features involved in the social work process, particularly with respect to the beginning stages of the practitioner-client relationship:

> This early stage of the social work process might be likened to "aesthetic" perception in art appreciation. In the aesthetic experience "the great concern is to let all that is present in the object appear to the self in the fullest and most vivid manner." It is similar to the disinterested respect, the empathic acceptance that social workers prize in their professional attitudes toward their clients. (103)

England, however, takes his application of aesthetic principles one step further to comment on the aesthetic aspects of the *outcome* or product of social work process. His language and conceptualization are clearly in the tradition of aesthetics theory:

Workers do use "aesthetic" terms to identify good work; in the context of an argument which locates such reference to a general "aesthetic" of social work it would become possible to outline procedures and terms which would facilitate the critical review of social work practice. If social work can really be "beautiful" we can consider whether attempts to throw light on the nature of "beauty" will also illuminate the nature of social work. (99)

In his essay on clinical social work as an art form, Siporin (1988) also comments on both the aesthetic aspects of the social work process and of individuals' reaction to artistic work. With respect to the aesthetic aspects of the social work process, Siporin observes:

Art in social work refers to developing patterns of human behavior and relationships that are original and beautiful. Human actions can be considered aesthetic when they are creatively performed with a sense of grace and elegance in style; have a clear, well-proportioned form appropriate to their setting; and are rich in color and texture. An art form refers to a medium through which art is produced and expressed. Social work practice is an art form that utilizes original, creative activities, as well as conventional ones, to help clients lead full and productive lives. The art of social work practice integrates values, knowledge of theory, practice wisdom, and expert skill. (177–78)

Siporin (1988) also regards the insight that results from skillful clinical work with a client as essentially aesthetic in nature: "The moment of sudden insight—the eureka experience—into a client's problem is often equated with an aesthetic experience. . . . The aesthetic experience in therapy is tied to major transformations in consciousness, self-concept, attitudes, beliefs, and cognitive schemata as well as to individual behavior and interpersonal relationships" (182).

Thus, a small number of social work scholars has recognized the relevance of aesthetics to social work practice. Scholars such as Boehm, Rapoport, Reynolds, Richmond, England, Hollis, and Siporin have highlighted aesthetic aspects of practice and alerted practitioners to their importance. These occasional references to aesthetics and social work, however, do not include in-depth analysis of aesthetics theory and concepts. For social workers to fully appreciate the relevance of aesthetics, we must examine more closely the philosophical underpinnings of aesthetical inquiry, particularly with respect to the nature of criticism in social work and evaluation of social work process and outcome; the attributes of social workers as artists; and social work as art and as science.

CRITICISM AND EVALUATION IN SOCIAL WORK

Recently, my family and I took a long hike while on vacation on Block Island, off the coast of mainland Rhode Island. As we approached a hollow, my wife and I simultaneously remarked at the breathtaking view of landscape enveloped by a scintillatingly blue sky. We stopped and stared, as did another family wandering along the same path. As we absorbed the scene, it was evident to us all that we were observing something inherently beautiful. There was no doubt in our minds. I said, in fact, that it was impossible to imagine that anyone would not find the view compellingly beautiful.

Most of us would probably agree that life occasionally produces such immanent beauty—perhaps in the form of a striking sunset, a moving passage in a novel, or a gripping sculpture. Once we move beyond this sort of scenery and artistic work, however, consensus is much harder to achieve. Take, for example, conflicting and controversial reaction to various forms of modern art, avant-garde film, and obscenity-laced drama. We know by now that nearly every form of art is bound to have its aficionados and its detractors.

What about the products of social work? Is there anything in social work that is comparable to the Block Island hollow, where everyone, it seems, would be struck by its awesome beauty? Are there certain clinical interventions, community organizing skills, or administrative strategies that would strike nearly every observer as artistic? Or are social work phenomena much more like what we encounter with controversial paintings, film, and drama, where a cross section of spectators is likely to produce diverse reactions and impressions, both positive and negative? Are there any objective criteria to distinguish between that which is truly artistic and that which is not?

THE NATURE OF CRITICISM. The study of such evaluative criteria traditionally falls within the field of *criticism*, whether it concerns literature, art, music, poetry, dance, drama, or film. The word *criticism* derives from the Greek word meaning judgment and dates as far back as Plato (see his *Ion, Meno, Phadeus,* and *Republic*) and Aristotle (see his *Poetics* and *Rhetoric*). Criticism generally refers to the analysis, interpretation, justification, description, evaluation, or judgment of literary, artistic, musical, or dramatic works (Harris and Levey 1975; Krieger 1976; Trilling 1970). Much of the criticism literature speculates about criteria for assessing the quality of artistic works and the intentions of the artist (Ellis 1974; Hobsbaum 1970). As Sparshott (1982) says: "The process of analyzing the ceaseless stream of an intelligent being's activity into performances and discussing whether, to what extent, and in what way they have been successfully performed goes by the generic name of criticism" (57).

The phenomenon of criticism has obvious relevance to social work, particularly with respect to our need to evaluate the quality of practitioners' work and the outcome of their efforts. As England (1986) aptly notes:

> Criticism . . . is an integral though unrecognized element in the practice of social work. Its proper development will lead directly to the improvement of the general standard of practice. It will also serve a wider end, for the development of an adequate criticism will make social work "visible" and will thus allow for its much broader understanding. It will be the means to a real exploration and analysis of social work. . . .
> The discussion of art and criticism makes possible a more rounded consideration of social work, and allows a grasp to be gained of the steps the social worker takes in integrating his learned theory and in integrating theory with practice. The discussion offers the route to a legitimate "practice theory" for social work, and consequently a means of identifying and evaluating good practice. (119, 125)

Several styles of criticism are particularly relevant to any attempt to judge or assess social work activities and outcomes. *Theoretical criticism* refers to attempts to derive general principles, criteria, and tenets to evaluate a particular work of art. Thus, those who lean toward theoretical criticism are inclined to ask whether objective criteria can be identified to determine whether any work of art is beautiful, skillfully produced, and so on. The same question, of course, can be asked about social work skills and outcomes, such as assessment techniques, treatment plans, and administrative style.

In contrast, *practical criticism* refers to the application of general principles, criteria, and tenets—produced as a result of theoretical criticism—to individual works of art. Thus, although one may accept a certain set of criteria for the evaluation of artistic works, it is yet another challenge to apply these criteria to the evaluation of a particular work. (Note that this distinction is also reminiscent of the division between metaethics—the study of general principles or moral criteria for determining that which is morally right or wrong— and normative ethics—the application of general principles or moral criteria to particular ethical cases or dilemmas.) Social workers may, for example, agree that demonstration of accurate empathy is a necessary, though perhaps not sufficient condition for artistic clinical skill (at the level of theoretical criticism), yet disagree about whether such accurate empathy is in evidence in a particular interview conducted by a particular practitioner (at the level of practical criticism).

It is also useful to distinguish between what is often called *Aristotelian criticism* and *Platonic criticism*. Aristotelian criticism tends to emphasize the *in*trinsic value of a given artistic work; that is, the Aristotelian approach asks whether and in what ways a work of art has inherent value. The same question may also be asked about psychotherapeutic intervention, for example.

Platonic criticism, on the other hand, tends to judge a work by its *ex*trinsic value or its social impact; that is, the Platonic approach emphasizes the extent to which a particular book, poem, or play affects society at large, in the form of public opinion, social movements, a community's values, and so on.

This Platonic perspective is, of course, especially relevant to social work. While some may argue that social work activities and interventions have some intrinsic value, more likely social workers will focus on debate about their extrinsic value, that is, their effect on the individuals, families, groups, communities, or organizations served, along with society at large.

AESTHETIC EVALUATION. Theories of aesthetics have focused to a great extent on ways to evaluate, judge, interpret, and analyze works of art. Three sets of issues related to such aesthetical assessment pertain to social work: (1) whether objective standards can be established to assess the nature and quality of social work activities and outcome; (2) what criteria ought to be used to make such assessments; and (3) the process involved in aesthetic assessment in social work.

Some scholars—though relatively few, it seems—have argued that works of art contain certain attributes that objectively, and uniformly, produce certain responses among those who observe them. As David Hume asserted in his eighteenth-century essay, "Of the Standard of Taste," in which he discusses the permanent, objective value of Homer's works: "Some particular forms or qualities from the original structure of the internal fabric are calculated to please, and others to displease. . . . It must be allowed that there are certain qualities in objects which are fitted by nature to produce those particular feelings" (in Morawski 1974:126). Sheppard (1987) presents a similar view in her *Aesthetics:*

> Might there be some elusive quality possessed by all the different objects we appreciate aesthetically which explains our interest in them? . . . Such objects, it might be said, do not all represent something else, they are not all expressive, they are not all appreciated for their formal features, but they all have one crucial quality which elicits aesthetic admiration. English lacks a satisfactory term for this quality but we may call it "beauty" so long as we remember that it is a quality which may be found in men and wine and even cows as well as in landscapes, women, horses, and flowers, in plays, novels, and concertos, as well as in paintings, buildings, and songs. (61)

A more common view, however, is that our perceptions and evaluations of any scene or work of art are necessarily subjective, shaped by our respective biases, vantage points, vested interests, training, and experiences. Sheppard's (1987) sentiments are representative of this view:

> In the case of natural objects, no one else is guiding the way we look, listen, or feel but as beholders we can provide our own guidance. We can choose to look at a landscape from a particular angle or go to a viewpoint from which the shapes of hills are particularly striking. In so doing we are, as it were, "framing" the landscape. We are looking at it as if it were a painting designed for our inspection. (60)

Although it is tempting to believe that objective criteria exist to determine whether works of art are beautiful, pleasure-producing, or of high quality (again, consider, for example, the considerable consensus that exists concerning the quality of certain of Shakespeare's, Mozart's, and Michelangelo's works, or of the beauty of a glowing sunset), by now relatively few scholars argue that true objectivity exists (Gert 1970:53–54). Ultimately, it seems, we bring to bear our own subjective judgments and perceptions when we assess any work of art, whether in the form of a painting or family therapy. As Sparshott (1982) concludes: "It need not be implied that there is only one such way of identifying or interpreting anything" (108).

In this regard, philosophers sometimes refer to the distinction between the *intentional* and *material* object of aesthetic experience—a distinction that stems from the Scholastic philosophers of the Middle Ages. In short, the material object is the actual work one observes—the physical sculpture, the novel, or, in the case of social work, the behavior of a client following some intervention. The intentional object, in contrast, is the product of one's perception of the work as a function of one's state of mind (Aesthetics 1988:17). The intentional object, of course, can vary from person to person based on their varying (and subjective) perception of the nature and quality of that which they observe. As Trilling (1970) argues:

> As for objectivity itself, although it is indeed a quality which we look for in criticism and prize when we find it, Aristotle's *caveat* against demanding more exactness than the subject-matter permits is here most relevant. We expect of the critic that he will make every possible effort, in Matthew Arnold's famous words, "to see the object as in itself it really is" and to describe it accordingly. But we know that what is seen by one critic with the best possible will to see accurately is likely to be different from what is seen by another critic from an equally good will. There comes a point at which description becomes interpretation. There is no help for this failure of perfect objectivity, if that is indeed what we ought to call it. It is in the nature of the case that the object as in itself it really is will not appear wholly the same to any two minds. Perhaps this is properly a cause for rejoicing. Mozart as interpreted by Toscanini is not the same as Mozart interpreted by Munch, but both interpretations give us pleasure and win our admiration. And if, apart from either interpretation, there is a Mozart as in himself he really is, we shall never know him: there can only be other interpretations. (15)

To what extent do we accept this conclusion in social work? On the one hand, most social workers appear to agree that some forms of practice are objectively "bad" or inferior, at least based on prevailing standards in the profession. Imagine a clinical social worker who has sexual contact with a series of clients. Or imagine a casework supervisor in a public welfare agency who berates a minority client for being "shiftless" and who tells this client that her ethnic group is "subhuman" and needs to be socialized to be responsible citizens. Is it possible that subjective impression has any place in the assessment of the quality of this sort of social work "practice"? Could any observer possibly conclude that this is sound, acceptable practice? Are there not at least some objective criteria for making such a determination? Could not the same "objectivity" be applied in a case where a community organizer helps a local "white supremacist" group devise illegal ways to prevent minorities from renting apartments or buying homes in the neighborhood? Or an agency administrator who falsifies records to conceal his embezzlement of agency funds? The fact that objectivity is difficult to achieve in all instances does not mean that it cannot be achieved in any instance. As Sheppard (1987) says in her *Aesthetics:*

> It is all too easy to leap from the evident fact that many works of art are susceptible of more than one interpretation, and the recognition that different interpretations of a work may conflict with one another, to the wild claim that there is no limit to the possible interpretations. Yet experience suggests that while there may be no one right interpretation of a work there can be wrong interpretations, that we cannot be persuaded of just *anything,* that some critical assessments can be shown to be mistaken. (87)

But how common are such blatant examples of poor (or, conversely, superior) practice? Much more common, it seems, are displays of practice skills that are far more debatable, controversial, and open to interpretation. Experienced social workers know that even their most skilled interventions are likely to be praised and valued by some colleagues and criticized by others. Given the diversity of social workers' training, backgrounds, theoretical orientations, and values, it is unlikely that objective criteria can be established for assessment of social work process and outcome with individuals, families, groups, communities, or organizations.

In spite of this inevitable subjectivity, however, our efforts to identify a conceptual framework for the conduct of criticism in social work, and to reach at least some reasonable agreement about relevant criteria for critical assessment, can be productive. They can lend discipline and order—and a common vocabulary—to discussion and debate among social workers about the quality of their work. As England (1986) concludes:

> Good social work rests upon the process of criticism, a process of experience and understanding, of analysis and comparison. A critical faculty is integral to the very practice of social work. ... A widespread and detailed critical dialogue is the only means whereby any canons of professional judgment and evaluation can be established in social work, through the establishment of common professional meanings and a common professional culture. This criticism, like art, and like life, is subjective, but it is the apparent fallacy of social work to assume that this precludes the possibility of inquiry, intellectual precision and impersonality. (125)

And as Gert (1970) notes, although we may not always agree that any given form or expression of practice is superior to all others, it is quite possible for us to agree that a certain *group* of practice activities or interventions is superior to nearly all others:

> So it may not always be possible to decide which one of a set of tools is best. Each of them might be better in one characteristic, with no way of deciding which combination is best. All informed rational men [sic] may agree that A, B, and C are good tools, and that D, E, and F are bad ones. Further A and B may be preferred to C. Nonetheless there may be no agreement on whether A or B is better. .... But the lack of complete agreement does not mean that there will not be substantial agreement. There is no agreement about whether Ted Williams, Stan Musial, or Willie Mays was the best baseball player. This does not mean that there is no agreement that all three of them are better than 99 percent of all baseball players, past or present. (53)

If we accept that a critical assessment of the quality of social work activities and outcomes has value, what criteria should we employ? As I noted above, aestheticians often distinguish between *intrinsic* and *extrinsic* theories of valuation. According to the intrinsic view, works of art or aesthetic objects are to be judged by their inherent value. According to the extrinsic view, works of art or aesthetic objects are to be judged by their effect or influence on an external audience—whether an individual, group, or the broader society (Aesthetics 1988:24). This distinction is somewhat akin to that made by Kant, in his *Critique of Aesthetic Judgment*, between *free beauty*, ascribed to an object in virtue of its form alone, without consideration of any end to which the object may be directed, and *dependent beauty*, which depends on the end to which the object is directed (Sheppard 1987:41). (Note the similarity between this distinction and that between deontological ethics—where certain actions are considered inherently right or wrong in the moral sense—and teleological ethics—where actions are judged to be right or wrong by virtue of their consequences.)

This is an important distinction for social workers to consider. Can we say, for example, that a social worker who mounts a comprehensive job training program in a low-income community is, based on the extrinsic view, involved in a more valuable activity than the social worker who provides insight-oriented psychotherapy to a well-functioning, affluent client who is preoccupied with family-of-origin issues? Is there some intrinsic value to the latter activity that makes it comparable in worth to the former? Can we say that some social work activities are, by their nature, more valuable than others because of their relative extrinsic or intrinsic value? This is an essential debate for the profession, particularly given social work's normative mission to enhance both individual and communal well-being. And given that mission, the measuring rod in social work would seem to obligate us to embrace, primarily, the extrinsic perspective of aesthetic evaluation.

Not surprisingly, virtually no one in the art world agrees on what precise criteria ought to be used to evaluate works. Some critics emphasize such attributes as "form" and "unity," while others stress "coherence," "completeness," and "realism" (Beardsley 1970; Morawski 1974).

There is, however, considerable accord on the need for standards and debate about standards, in order to avoid aesthetic anarchy or an evaluative free-for-all. As Daiches (1981) observes with respect to evaluating the quality of literature: "If we believe in literary criticism at all—as distinct from literary history and from mere explanation and description—we must believe that there are criteria of literary excellence derived from the nature of literature itself" (355). And as Sparshott (1982) asserts with respect to evaluating the quality of art:

> Where there is art there are standards, and where there are standards there must be people to formulate, impose, and

imply them. . . . The organization of an art shows in the development and applications of a set of standards specific to the art, by which one measures how closely the relevant perfection has been approximated. But any knowledge and skill, once developed into a body of accepted practice, can be judged in abstraction from whatever ends the technique was devised to serve. (30, 40)

In her *Aesthetics,* Sheppard (1987) provides a useful framework for thinking about critics' ability to evaluate and judge by standard criteria. Although her focus is on the concept of "beauty" in art, Sheppard's approach to the problem can be applied very usefully to social work.

Sheppard suggests several possible answers to the question, "What is beauty?" (Social workers, of course, might simply substitute "good practice" for "beauty.") One possible answer is that beauty is a "simple quality" that is not susceptible to further definition or analysis. For social workers, then, good practice is a simple quality; either we apprehend it when we observe practice activities or we do not (this is roughly comparable to so-called intuitionism in moral philosophy, embraced by those who believe that right or wrong action is something we grasp merely through intuition, not through more complex cognitive analysis). According to this view, it is futile to attempt more ambitious definition or analysis. [In this regard, one of the luminaries in contemporary aesthetics, Benedetto Croce, distinguishes between the use of *expression* or *intuition* in aesthetic judgments—grasping the uniqueness of an object without classifying it as an object of some particular kind—and *representation* or *conceptual thought*—using concepts to descriptively classify and generalize about aesthetic objects (Aesthetics 1988; Sheppard 1987).]

A second possible answer is that beauty may be defined in terms of other more specific aesthetic qualities, such as grace, elegance, and daintiness. From this perspective, social workers would define good clinical practice in other aesthetic terms. An example appears in Siporin (1988), where he states that in good clinical work: "The social worker uses style in essentially the same way as does the artist. The worker attempts to design and form therapy into a clear, well-proportioned, and coherent structure" (179). Of course, as Sheppard notes, one has to decide where to draw the line concerning which other aesthetic qualities to consider: "In exchanging one term, 'beauty,' for a family of terms, we exchange one problem for a family of interlocking and interrelated problems" (63).

A third possible answer is to define beauty in terms of other nonaesthetic qualities, such as its impact on the broader culture. In social work, this might take the form of judging the aesthetic quality of an intervention by its "effectiveness," that is, the extent to which it enhances mental health, reduces poverty or delinquency rates, and so on.

The principal problem here is drawing logical connections between aesthetic concepts (such as beauty or artistic practice) and nonaesthetic concepts (such as efficacy or efficiency). As Hume noted in the eighteenth century, a similar difficulty occurs in moral philosophy with respect to the well-known "is-ought" problem, according to which descriptive statements of fact about an action do not lead, logically, to normative conclusions about its moral rightness or wrongness; that is, no logical connection exists between descriptive and normative statements (Searle 1969). And as Sheppard concludes with respect to judging beauty in works of art:

> Attempts to define beauty in terms of particular non-aesthetic qualities are always open to counter-examples; suggested definitions are always both too narrow, in failing to include instances of beauty, and too wide, in failing to exclude instances which have the relevant non-aesthetic qualities and yet are not beautiful. (63)

Finally, a fourth possible answer to the question "What is beauty?" is to abandon any effort to come up with precise standards or criteria to determine beauty (or good practice) and, instead, shift the focus to examining the *process* involved in making such judgments (metacriticism, in contrast to primary criticism). Here the emphasis is on the psychology of such judgments and the cognitive processes involved in making them.

THE AESTHETIC PROCESS. How social workers assess the process and outcomes of their work is critical. All of us have had the experience of sitting in a staff meeting where the participants discuss their reactions to some event they have experienced in common—contact with a particular client or a site visitor from a funding agency, perhaps. It is not at all unusual to discover that these various people who were witness to the very same events, and auditory and visual stimuli, walked away with very different impressions of what took place, who said what, and the implications of the occurrence. What may appear to one observer to be a display of irreconcilable conflict in an enmeshed family that is without clear boundaries may seem to a second observer to be a functional release of constructively stored anger that may lead to wholesome resolution of protracted tension. Similarly, what may appear to one observer to be a site visitor's hostile critique of an agency's administrative practices may appear to a second observer to be useful, tactfully worded feedback that can promote much-needed reorganization. In research we refer to this as the problem of interrater or interobserver reliability (Rubin and Babbie 1989:144), where observation and interpretation of a subject's behavior vary from person to person.

What we have here, of course, is the understandable human tendency for individuals to perceive the world uniquely depending on their backgrounds, training, experience, and so on. This is not a particularly novel insight. The well-worn phrase, "beauty is in the eye of the beholder" may be hackneyed, but it also rings true.

What this raises, of course, is the question of whether social workers can achieve reasonable consistency in the criteria they use to observe, and whether such consistency is even desirable. Is there any point in trying to objectify and make more uniform the way social workers interpret what they do and see, or is a perceptual free-for-all perfectly acceptable? In the research domain, social workers have extolled the virtues of consistency and attempted to minimize the sources of "noise" in data gathering that introduce bias and threaten objectivity. In the ethics domain, however, social workers have virtually abandoned any hope of producing objective standards to determine, in all cases, what is ethically right and wrong (setting aside those uncomplicated instances referred to above where no reasonable person would argue the ethics of the situation, such as when a social worker becomes sexually involved with a client).

Some argue that the best one can hope for in aesthetic judgment is a considerable degree of neutrality in observation; that is, observers should, as much as possible, strip away preconceived biases that may affect their judgment, and approach a work of art with a conceptually clean slate. This is somewhat akin to the concept of the "ideal observer" introduced in the eighteenth century by Adam Smith with respect to judgments about morality. For Smith, an ideal observer is one who is informed, impartial, fair, dispassionate, calm, willing to universalize, able to consider the good of everyone, and so on (Baier 1965; Donagan 1977; Frankena 1973). As Morawski (1974) notes:

> In fact, aesthetics has been struggling for years with the notion of an ideal observer and can still find no way out of the vicious circle in which either the ideal observer is determined by public taste and judgment, or else some values are first acknowledged as artistic and whoever expounds them is recognized as a final authority. Aesthetics, thus, has continual difficulties with its standards of value and judgment, and competing views still leave the field contested as it has been for centuries. (177)

The concept of an ideal observer is not unlike Kant's view that an aesthetic attitude is one "divorced from practical concerns, a kind of 'distancing,' or standing back, as it were, from ordinary involvement" (Aesthetics 1988:17). Kant described the observer of a work of art "not as distanced but as disinterested, meaning that the recipient does not treat the object of enjoyment either as a vehicle for curiosity or as a means to an end. He contemplates the object as it is in itself and 'apart from all interest'" (Aesthetics 1988:18).

Even if such an ideal is desirable, however, it is doubtful it could ever be achieved in social work. It is one thing to walk up to a painting one has never seen before or hear a poem for the first time and render an aesthetic judgment as to its quality. Critics engage in this sort of activity all the time; media critics, in fact, are paid to make such judgments about works with which they have had no prior contact.

Social workers, in contrast, are rarely in such an unspoiled position. Although an outside consultant or site visitor can occasionally make what amounts to aesthetic judgments about some aspect of social work practice, far more common are situations where the observer, by necessity, has some familiarity—often considerable—with the relevant context, including the participants, the relevant history, or organizational and political environment. An involved clinical supervisor can hardly be expected to suspend his or her considerable familiarity with the clinician's style, theoretical orientation, the client's diagnosis, and treatment history. And an agency administrator who is expected to produce an annual evaluation of a subordinate's work can hardly be expected to be completely uninfluenced by her prior work experience with the individual involved and informal comments that circulate in the agency. The context cannot be ignored.

Moreover, nothing suggests that the criteria ordinarily attached to the "ideal observer" are as neutral as they appear to be. Even these criteria, despite their apparent objectivity, are value-based. They are not value-neutral. One can argue, in fact, that any aesthetic judgment *ought* to be influenced by contextual ingredients, that these backdrop elements provide the warp and woof for any meaningful, informative assessment. Instead, the ultimate challenge—and obligation—is to identify the contextual factors that exert influence and to speculate about the implications of this influence.

Some aestheticians argue (Matthew Arnold, for example) that such context—particularly in relation to the contexts that surround comparable works—is essential, that no amount of detailed analysis of an individual work in a vacuum can possibly convey the true quality of that work. From this point of view, a "context of relevant comparisons" is necessary to be able to draw a meaningful comparison between like works: "Critical reasoning is an attempt to place works of art in relation to one another, so that the perceived greatness of the one will provide the standard of measurement for the other" (Aesthetics 1988:25–26). This suggests that individual plays, poems, and, by extension, social work processes (for example, therapeutic interventions or organizational change strategies) cannot be judged solely on their own merits; instead, the observer must place the work within the relative context created by the existence of other works in the profession in order to make meaningful judgments. The value we attach to any given work is dependent, at least in part, on this sort of relevant comparison. This sentiment is echoed by England (1986), particularly with respect to enhancing the development of evaluative consistency in social work:

> The greatest gain from the practice of an adequate criticism in social work . . . and the legitimating basis for any professional culture, would be the achievement of some clearer standard, some viable measure, to be used in professional practice. Such a measure in fact flows from the process of creating real community. Shared meanings are clearly relative and based upon value; indeed social reality requires such constant affirmation and confirmation precisely because it *is* based upon value. (124)

There is at least some agreement that aesthetic judgments ought to include attention to an object's *form* as well as *content*. In the art world, content typically refers to the subject matter or the particular message conveyed, for example, the meaning of a certain facial expression in a painting, the topic broached in a poem, or the social issues addressed in a play. Form, in contrast, refers to the way in which the work is expressed and composed.

This, of course, is a familiar, and useful, distinction for social workers. Clinical social workers are trained, for instance, to tune into the content of clients' communications *and* the form of the communication, including relevant nonverbal cues, the timing of a particular communication, terminology, and affect. The form of the communication often carries with it clinically meaningful data that must be considered in addition to relevant content.

The same, of course, applies to aesthetic judgment of social workers' activities. A supervisor who conducts an evaluation of a social worker's performance must pay attention to the form of the worker's display of duties (for example, therapeutic and communication style, collegial interaction, affect) as well as the content (for example, the number of cases opened and closed during the year, the content of new projects inaugurated in the agency, the issues addressed in a treatment group).

There is also considerable agreement that aesthetic judgments of any work necessarily incorporate both *intellectual* and *sensory* elements. Social workers know full well that assessments of their work cannot separate cognitively derived or purely intellectual impressions from more subjective sensory impressions. If social workers view a tape of a therapeutic session, aesthetic judgment cannot rely entirely on some gridlike checklist of "objective" criteria of "elements of good practice" (for example, the social worker's eye contact, posture, empathic communications, use of silence). Inevitably, an observer of the tape is likely to have a sensory-based response to what he or she sees that accompanies any form of purely intellectual evaluation. As England (1986) argues in his comments about the need to supplement cognitively oriented evaluative criteria with a considerable degree of sensory, intuitive, or aesthetic assessment:

> The concepts of coherence and complexity may sound unfamiliar to the social worker, but they are relevant because the social worker aspires to that same understanding as the artist. They are also relevant because of their use for evaluation, *for*

although social work has sought for evaluative criteria which have more apparent precision than "coherence and complexity," it has sought in vain. If social work is to be seen as art, then such concepts may help social work construct a genuinely viable approach to the criticism and assessment of practice. (108; emphasis added)

Although sensory or intuition-driven responses are difficult to characterize with much precision and exactness, all of us, I suspect, have some understanding of what this means. Based on our sensory impressions, a therapy session, a meeting of neighborhood residents, or a staff meeting is or is not going well. It "works" or "it does not work," a vaguely defined, but essential distinction that is well accepted in art:

Whether such [aesthetic] theories can cast light on the mysterious unity between the intellectual and the sensory that we observe in aesthetic experience remains doubtful. The argument for saying that there is a single process of imagination involved in all perception, imagery, and remembering seems to consist only in the premise (undoubtedly true) that in these mental processes thought and experience are often inseparable. But to suppose therefore that there is some one "faculty" involved in forging the connection between them is to fail to take seriously the fact that they are inseparable. (Aesthetics 1988:19)

THE SOCIAL WORKER AS ARTIST

Certainly it is useful to speculate about the ways in which social workers can appreciate aesthetic concepts and draw on them to enhance their understanding of social work process and outcome. Distinctions between concepts such as free and dependent beauty, expression and representation, form and content, and intellectual and sensory response can add considerable depth, substance, and clarity to our efforts to grasp the nature of social work practice.

This perspective, however, places most of its emphasis on social workers' efforts to understand, assess, and interpret practice—how social workers *think* about practice and its outcomes. It neglects an additional, vitally important aspect of the relationship between social work and aesthetics: the social worker as artist. Here the focus is on the artistic skill involved in practice, what the worker actually *does*. The distinction is roughly analogous to that between art appreciation and painting; the former entails ways of thinking about and understanding art, while the latter entails the actual production of art.

As I have noted earlier, social workers are occasionally described as artists, the most skilled of whom know just how and when to introduce a novel intervention, reorganize an agency staff, or develop local community leadership. These skills are often described as an artistic gift. It is commonly believed that some social workers have the gift and some do not. And as with painters and sculptors, there is considerable debate about whether such a gift is innate or can be cultivated and learned.

Some aestheticians believe that gifted artists (however "gifted" is understood)—whether authors, painters, playwrights, poets, or musicians—have in common some hard-to-define, intangible qualities. In aesthetic works one often encounters references to unique attributes of "style," "creativity," "sensibility," "feeling," "intelligence," or "imagination" that set the gifted artist apart from the ordinary artist or nonartist. Aschenbrenner (1974) suggests that the skilled artist's unique gift pertains to his or her ability to creatively bring out and effectively mix hard-to-reveal qualities in the artistic object. Although Aschenbrenner's comments focus exclusively on traditional art, they are easy to apply to social workers' efforts to intervene with individuals, families, groups, communities, and organizations:

> I would argue that this capacity is really *creative receptivity*. The visual artist can mix, cut, burn, chisel, melt, break, join and reorder his materials in a limitless number of ways (and there will be analogies of these physical operations for all the arts), but what he cannot do, what no one but God or nature can do is to create a quality. The artist can break or join or mix to reveal a quality: the qualities of things are their own. The artist's ingenuity lies in the power to *reveal* qualities. (70)

One finds similar rhetoric in a handful of social work essays on the subject of art and social work. Rapoport (1968) and Siporin (1988) both note the essential role of creativity in artistic social work. Rapoport writes, "It would seem that in social work we could appropriately use the terms creative, artistic, and craftsmanlike (or skillful). By 'creative,' I mean thought and action which are innovative, which lead to the forging of something new. This may apply to the development of a theory, or to the development of new therapeutic approaches or techniques, or to the novel organization and delivery of services" (142). In a similar vein, Siporin highlights what he describes as prerequisities for creativity and the creative process in social work:

> Creativity is the dominant characteristic of the art of social work practice. Clients come to social workers feeling frustrated or trapped in stressful, overwhelming situations. New interpretations and creative solutions of problems are required to help clients deal with their problems. Good clinical social work involves creative assessment, planning, intervention, and evaluation. . . . Creatively applied, social work helps clients develop new insights into their problems, generates alternative solutions to these problems, and creates new patterns for interpersonal relationships utilizing the client's internal and social resources. (180)

Many aestheticians also believe that artists' individual backgrounds and personalities are significant determinants of their creative capacities. How and why painters, authors, and poets select their subject matter, medium, and style of expression have a great deal to do with their personal experiences in the world. As Sparshott (1982) says, "Every artist, after all, is an individual whose personal history and training are different from those of any of his colleagues and any member of his public. His work cannot have the same meaning for them as it does for him any more than it can have the same significance" (261). With particular respect to social work, Siporin (1988) argues that certain personality traits are essential to produce the truly creative practitioner:

> An effective and creative style that is able to produce art in clinical social work requires that the practitioner have certain personality attributes, talents, and abilities. . . .
>   A creative person is adventurous, playful, humorous, curious, and insightful. He or she has an open mind and a fertile imagination, as well as a moral sensibility that is concerned about behaving rightly in particular areas of life. Yet such a person can be a nonconformist, disturbed, and deviant in areas of life. The creative person needs to be capable of both divergent and convergent thought. He or she needs to possess associative fluency and flexibility, be able to shift perspec-

tives, and use different frames of reference to develop original ideas and solutions. The creative person uses the right and left brain and employs logical as well as nonrational, parallel, lateral, analogical, and intuitive kinds of reasoning. (180)

Volumes have been written about the ways in which such phenomena as personal trauma, interpersonal relationships, geographic location, and political climate have influenced and shaped artists (Daiches 1981). Aschenbrenner (1974), for example, stresses: "In art we are always interested in persons and not just in products: we care about the chef and waiter, not only about what they feed us. Just as the argument of criticism is indefeasibly *ad hominem* so our attention to the artwork must lead us back to the artist" (74).

Speculation about the influence of personal biography and personality is especially common in the literary world. For example, in the introduction to his *Literary Criticism,* Trilling (1970) notes the historic connection between personal background and artistic style:

In highly developed cultures an admired work of literature has always been associated with the man [sic] who wrote it and its qualities accounted for by his temperament. Buffon's famous statement, "Style is the man himself," made in 1753, was perhaps, in its being made at all, a portent of the emphasis that Romanticism was to place on the personality of the author, but it expresses what readers have always felt without saying so. For the earlier readers, however, the equation of man and style was a satisfying tautology; for later readers it settled nothing—on the contrary, it opened the way to questions. If the style is the man himself, how did the man become himself, the person who is signalized by this style and no other? And since style is at the service of, and controlled by, the man's emotion seeking expression, would not the emotion be the better understood if its occasion in the author's actual experience were known?

In his *Critical Approaches to Literature,* Daiches (1981) makes a similar observation with respect to writers:

Perhaps more fruitful than general psychological and psychoanalytic theories of the origin of art are the particular applications to particular cases. . . . One could analyze a particular work and draw from the analysis inferences about the psychology of its author; one could take the whole body of an

author's writing and derive from it general conclusions about
his state of mind which could then be applied to elucidate
particular works. One could take the biography of a writer, as
illustrated by the external events of his life and by such things
as letters and other confessional documents, and construct
out of these a theory of the writer's personality—his conflicts,
frustrations, traumatic experiences, neuroses, or whatever they
happened to be—and use this theory in order to illuminate
each one of his works. Or one can work back and forth between the life and the work, illuminating each by the other,
noting from the biography certain crises reflected in the works,
and seeing from the way they are reflected in the works what
their real biographical meaning was. (334)

To social workers, of course, this is a familiar and congenial form
of speculation. Throughout social work's history, practitioners have
been cognizant of, probably more than most other professionals,
the intimate connections between practitioners' personal histories
and personalities and their chosen field of work, the settings in
which and the populations with which they work, their theoretical
biases, and intervention techniques. Examples include conjecture
about the influence of practitioners' intrapsychic dynamics on their
work, the influence of agency directors' upbringing on their administrative style, and the influence of community organizers' political
history on their intervention approaches.

A relatively recent strain of thought concerning the "practitioner
as artist" focuses on the unique kind of reflection skilled professionals engage in during their work. Much of this speculation is contained in Schon's (1983, 1987) pioneering writings on the concepts
of "knowing-in-action" and "reflection-in-action." For Schon (1987),
professional work necessarily entails complex problem solving involving "indeterminate zones of practice" characterized by uncertainty, uniqueness, and value conflicts—problems that "escape the
canons of technical rationality" (6). Schon describes technical rationality as an

epistemology of practice derived from positivist philosophy,
built into the very foundations of the modern research university. Technical rationality holds that practitioners are instrumental problem solvers who select technical means best suited
to practical purposes. Rigorous professional practitioners solve
well-formed instrumental problems by applying theory and

technique derived from systematic, preferably scientific knowledge. . . .

But, as we have come to see with increasing clarity over the last twenty or so years, the problems of real-world practice do not present themselves to practitioners as well-formed structures. Indeed, they tend not to present themselves as problems at all but as messy, indeterminate situations. (3–4)

Schon's discussion of knowing-in-action and reflection-in-action is quite reminiscent of social workers' age-old speculation about practice wisdom in the profession (DeRoos 1990; Scott 1990). Knowing-in-action, Schon (1987) says, is an ingredient in professional artistry and entails knowing how to perform some practice function without even thinking about it, essentially instinctively, and does not "depend on our being able to describe what we know how to do or even to entertain in conscious thought the knowledge our actions reveal" (22); that is, one does not have to think about one's actions and judgments prior to or during the performance, one may be unaware of having learned to do these things and simply finds oneself performing them, and one may be unable to describe the understanding one's action reveals (DeRoos 1990:282; Schon 1983:54).

Reflection-in-action, in contrast, entails consciously thinking about and evaluating an action during its performance. The process involves active reflection on what one is doing, how one is doing it, and how well it is going—a familiar activity and priority in social work: "It is this entire process of reflection-in-action," Schon (1983) says, "which is central to the 'art' by which practitioners sometimes deal well with situations of uncertainty, instability, uniqueness, and value conflict" (50).

Schon clearly sees the use and cultivation of knowing-in-action and reflection-in-action as expressions of artistic professional practice, particularly when faced with situations of uncertainty, indeterminacy, and what he dubs professional "messes":

The artistry of painters, sculptors, musicians, dancers, and designers bears a strong family resemblance to the artistry of extraordinary lawyers, physicians, managers, and teachers. It is no accident that professionals often refer to an "art" of teaching or management and use the term *artist* to refer to practitioners unusually adept at handling situations of uncertainty, uniqueness, and conflict. (16)

Schon's observations about knowing-in-action and reflection-in-action have particularly important implications for social work education. First, to the extent that these are attributes we value, it is important to consider their place in social work education. Ideally, social work students begin their education with some notable predisposition toward the sort of practice wisdom suggested by Schon's concepts. The task of social work education is, then, to enhance these qualities, polish and refine them. This is not an easy task, of course, although educators share a deep-seated belief that practice wisdom—the creative, artistic conduct of social work—can in many, although perhaps not all, instances be taught and learned.

Siporin (1988), for example, argues with respect to clinical social work skills that while teaching fledgling practitioners these skills can be daunting, an "effective and creative style that is able to produce art in clinical social work requires that the practitioner have certain personality attributes, talents, and abilities." Apparently with a bit of realism and humility in his voice, Siporin adds, "It is important to note that most of these personality characteristics can be taught and learned" (180). Schon (1983) reinforces this belief with respect to the professions in general, recognizing that educators are not always able to convey these skills routinely and not all students are able to learn them:

> If it is true that there is an irreducible element of art in professional practice, it is also true that gifted engineers, teachers, scientists, architects, and managers sometimes display artistry in their day-to-day practice. If the art is not invariant, known, and teachable, it appears nonetheless, at least for some individuals, to be learnable. (18)

Schon's principal—and appropriate—concern is that, as a group, educators in the professions may not be sufficiently convinced of the need to focus on the teaching of professional artistry, along with a more science-based, positivistic approach to professional education. The tension between those who view practice as science and as art, Schon (1987) notes, suffuses professional education, even to the point of challenging the assumption that artistic practice can be taught in formal professional schools:

> Where the core curriculum of professional education is relatively diffuse, unstable, and insecure, as in Nathan Glazer's "minor professions," the problem of education for artistry tends to take a different form. In social work, city planning, divinity,

and educational administration, for example, educators tend to ask more open-endedly what competences ought to be acquired, through what methods, and in what domains of practice and even to wonder aloud whether what needs most to be learned can best be learned in a professional school. Here education for artistry becomes embroiled in the larger question of the legitimacy of professional education. (15)

On the basis of his extensive participant observation of styles and patterns of learning in a range of professions—including architecture, psychiatry, engineering, town planning, and management—Schon concludes that what social workers call practice wisdom, and what is akin to Schon's knowledge-in-action and reflection-in-action, can best be taught by coaching, in the context of the unique relationship that can develop between a tutor and student, especially in a studio or conservatory environment. Although Schon (1987) does not explicitly refer to social work field settings as an example of such a conducive learning environment, the implication is clear:

Perhaps, then, learning *all* forms of professional artistry depends, at least in part, on conditions similar to those created in the studios and conservatories; freedom to learn by doing in a setting relatively low in risk, with access to coaches who initiate students into the "traditions of the calling" and help them, by "the right kind of telling," to see on their own behalf and in their own way what they need most to see. We ought, then, to study the experience of learning by doing and the artistry of good coaching. We should base our study on the working assumption that both processes are intelligent and—within limits to be discovered—intelligible. And we ought to search for examples wherever we can find them—in the dual curricula of the schools, the apprenticeships and practicums that aspiring practitioners find or create for themselves, and the deviant traditions of studio and conservatory. (17)

SOCIAL WORK AS ART AND SCIENCE

In my discussion of various epistemological issues in social work, I noted practitioners' increasing recognition that the application of positivist assumptions and the scientific method has limits. Although a wide range of empirically based inquiries has considerable value in social work—including experimental, descriptive, and exploratory studies of individual clients, families, groups, communities, and organizations—we now have a much better grasp of empiricism's limits. Difficulty operationalizing complex and abstract social work concepts, producing research designs that adequately control for a multitude of extraneous factors, and eliminating sources of bias and error that interfere with objective measurement constrains what empirical research methods have contributed and can contribute to what we know about people's problems and the most effective ways to respond to them. Devising precise measures for the artistic aspects of social work is difficult.

Although he overstates the case somewhat, Schon (1983) captures the mood of many contemporary social workers when he asserts: "Among philosophers of science no one wants any longer to be called a Positivist, and there is a rebirth of interest in the ancient topics of craft, artistry, and myth—topics whose fate Positivism once claimed to have sealed" (48). In a later work, Schon (1987) takes his argument a step further, claiming that attempts at scientific or empirical understanding of practice should be secondary to initial inquiry about the artistic nature of practice:

> The question of the relationship between practice competence and professional knowledge needs to be turned upside down. We should start not by asking how to make better use of research-based knowledge but by asking what we can learn from a careful examination of artistry, that is, the competence by which practitioners actually handle indeterminate zones of practice—however that competence may relate to technical rationality. (13)

In the end, however, this is not a very constructive way to forge a relationship, or even clarify the nature of the relationship, between science and art in social work. This sort of critique of the limits of science does not, by itself, produce a particularly strong foundation for claims that much of social work practice reduces to an art form. While it may be that the nature of some, or even many, artistic aspects of practice will continue to elude even the most skillful of social work researchers, scientific inquiry and data gathering undoubtedly have their place in the profession and are likely— in a modest way, at the very least—to continue to enhance the quality of professional services. Instead of this kind of backhanded characterization of the relationship between science and art in social work we need a more constructive view, one that acknowledges the respective value and contribution of each domain and that understands their interdependence.

We especially need to resist the occasional suggestion that there is an enduring contest between science and art in social work or that science has little or nothing to add to the profession's corpus of knowledge and expertise. It is one thing to say, with conviction, that scientific methods cannot adequately capture all of what good social work practice is about; it is quite another, however, to conclude that science has nothing of value to add. In his compelling essay, "Clinical Social Work as an Art Form," for example, Siporin (1988) suggests such an adversarial relationship:

> The current emphasis on the scientific aspects of social work practice is unrealistic, distorting, and has negative consequences that the profession should avoid. Moreover, this overemphasis on the scientific aspects of social work leads to the use of misleading criteria for effectiveness, for example, statistical difference tests for treatment outcomes. (178)

Although those who view social work only through scientific lenses are certainly shortsighted about the nature of practice, empiricism surely has a useful place. The relationship between science and art in social work should not be viewed as adversarial, mutually exclusive, or zero-sum in nature; instead, it must be viewed as both supplementary and complementary.

What is particularly needed in the profession, then, is a clearer demarcation of the boundaries, a deeper, richer grasp of the proper place of science and art. As Rapoport (1968) observed insightfully some years ago: "Social work traditionally has been defined as both science and art. This dual nature is an attribute of all helping professions" (139).

In what ways can science and art supplement and complement each other in social work? First, it seems clear that neither domain has a monopoly on a true understanding of social work practice. As I have discussed at length, positivism and empiricism are always likely to fall short of being able to measure and gather data about some aspects of social work. Some of the artistic aspects of social work reduce to aesthetic phenomena that can be measured, if at all, only crudely. I doubt that even the most ambitious empirical efforts will ever be able to grasp what a client experiences when chronic depression lifts or a remarkable insight occurs. Certainly researchers can ask questions that elicit verbal or written descriptions of these experiences, but it is unlikely that clients' articulated expressions of these events or researchers' detailed recordings of them will come very close to capturing what actually occurs. The same applies to other aesthetic moments in social work, for example, when an agency's staff members finally gel after much administrative intervention and group process or when a neighborhood reaches a magical moment of empowerment partly as a result of an organizer's efforts. As Bertha Reynolds (1942) noted a half-century ago in her classic, *Learning and Teaching in the Practice of Social Work:*

> Social work is not accurately described, however, as a field of scientific knowledge applied to human problems. It is more than that, because the application of knowledge to the social relationships of human beings calls for the perception and sensitivity of the artist. . . . The art of social work is learned by experience illumined by theory, but it is experience in which the worker learns to see and hear and feel more than he can explain. (51)

But attempts at aesthetic understanding of social work also have their limits. At best, aesthetic description and interpretation are vague and highly subjective. Although aesthetics provides social workers with a rich vocabulary and collection of concepts to enhance understanding of good practice, in the end some precision, consistency, and generalizability may be missing. In this sense, the respective strengths of science and art need to supplement each other in social work. The rigor of science can add discipline and fine-grained detail to what might otherwise be amorphous, cloudlike aesthetic descriptions of practice. An aesthetic framework, however, can add conceptual, emotional, and contextual depth, along with a multidimensional view, to empirically based measures that might otherwise be mechanically fact-filled, sterile, unidimensional, and stripped of context. Vivas and Krieger (1962) characterize this complex relationship eloquently in their introductory passage in *The Problems of Aesthetics:*

> The aesthetician seeks clarity, and to the best of his ability he tries to keep his eyes on the facts. But the facts in aesthetics cannot be exhibited unambiguously, nor can they be discovered by those who lack training and sensibility of a highly specialized kind. Nor is the aim of the aesthetician to discover

invariant relations which can be formulated in such a way as to be open to test in terms of prediction. He seeks something else—something which seems much more refractory to satisfactory definition and which may remain, after our best efforts, ineradicably vague: he seeks an intellectual grasp, a comprehension, in the almost literal sense of the word, a gathering together in a single picture, of the various solutions to his several problems in their complex interrelations. If his results lack the quality of those achieved by the positive scientist, he can console himself by remembering what Aristotle said. There are some subjects, he said, that "admit of much variety and fluctuation of opinion," and in them "We must be content . . . to indicate the truth roughly and in outline," since we are "speaking about things which are only for the most part true and with premises of the same kind to reach conclusions that are no better." (5)

Regrettably, and surprisingly, throughout social work's history relatively few voices have called for such a constructive, realism-based relationship between aesthetic and scientific understanding. In 1958, Eaton made a rather quiet plea in his essay, "Science, 'Art,' and Uncertainty in Social Work," in which he juxtaposed the artistic and scientific approaches to social work. In 1970 Hollis also called for assertive integration of science and art in practice, when she said: "An underlying premise of this approach is that casework is both art and science. Intuitive insights and spontaneity are combined with continuous effort to develop and systematize knowledge and understanding of objective truths about man and his social expressions, relationships, and organizations" (38). And in his 1986 work England echoed a similar sentiment: "An assessment of the nature of social work must necessarily include examination of social work as art as well as social work as science; both are clearly integral and essential parts of the whole. Without this duality, no inquiry into social work can have an adequate framework for analysis, nor can analysis be complete" (115).

Clearly, social workers as a group need to deepen their understanding of the complex relationship between the scientific and artistic aspects of practice. The tension that currently characterizes the relationship, at least in the minds of many practitioners, must yield to a mature, open-minded willingness to recognize how these contrasting views of the practice world can, indeed, supplement and complement one another. Boehm (1960; cited in Boehm

1961:147) is among the few social work scholars who have articulated this need in a compelling way:

> As the painter's strokes reflect at one and the same time his knowledge of perspective and his aesthetic conception of the object he paints, so does the social worker's skill reflect his scientific knowledge and the values which underlie it. In quite the same sense as the painter's, our calling is an art and our sense of identity might be heightened if we can think of ourselves as artists.
>
> We are artists not only because we blend science and values but also because the expression of this blending in the form of skill is an achievement that belongs to us and to us alone, for the performance of our skills is the expression of our creativity, the creativity of the artist. (5)

Certainly, one of social work's principal virtues is its simultaneous concern with intellectual, scientifically based rigor and value-based commitment to human rights and justice, directed, ultimately, to the alleviation of human suffering. Effective integration of these concerns, and their expression through skillful practice, constitutes social work's most unique art form.

ℰℱ

THE PLACE
OF PHILOSOPHY
IN SOCIAL WORK

Early in the twentieth century, there was some doubt as to whether social work was indeed a profession. Abraham Flexner's oft-cited assertion in 1915, at the National Conference of Charities and Correction, was that social work was not yet a full-fledged profession. Although Flexner conceded that social work then met several of the criteria necessary for status as a profession—a learned character, practicality, a tendency toward self-organization, and altruistic motivation—he concluded that at least one essential ingredient was missing: individual responsibility.

If we take the concept of individual responsibility in social work seriously, it entails considerably more than mere autonomy in practice settings; at its foundation, individual responsibility depends on a *philosophical* framework that is indigenous to the social work profession. Such a framework should provide practitioners with the intellectual rootage necessary to inform and sustain autonomous practice. It is the contours of this philosophical framework that I have tried to define.

At its foundation, social work is organized around a collection of deep-seated, philosophical issues. Social workers' preoccupation with welfare rights, the role of the state, and distributive justice is grounded in enduring issues that have drawn the attention of political philosophers for centuries. The omnipresent ethical issues social workers face in practice are variations on themes addressed by moral philosophers at least since Socrates' time. The arguments and claims social workers make concerning the nature and effectiveness of professional practice must, ultimately, be measured against rigorous standards of logic. Contemporary debate about the role of science in social work reflects enduring epistemological controversy that challenges our beliefs about what and how we know. Social workers' widespread assumptions about the artistic aspects of practice, and ways of critiquing practice, are extensions of traditional questions of aesthetics.

My hope is that this survey and analysis of philosophical issues in social work will help members of the profession appreciate, more than they might otherwise, the many fundamental questions we face in our persistent efforts to address the needs of vulnerable individuals. Social workers have an understandable tendency to forego or postpone in-depth inquiry into complex philosophical concerns that may seem, at best, to have only thin connections to the heart of professional practice. After all, a social worker who provides services in a locked psychiatric unit or in a shelter for battered women can hardly afford to carve out much time during working hours to ruminate about the abstract, and occasionally abstruse, sorts of ideas I have addressed here. Typically, more pressing matters are at hand, such as preventing a suicide or locating affordable housing for a client.

Nonetheless, at some points in our professional lives we must be willing to make room to reflect on the larger issues. These are the ideas that helped to inaugurate social work and give it shape and meaning. While the profession's principal impetus must always be focused on the delivery of services to individuals, families, groups, communities, and so on ("working retail," one might say), we cannot afford to neglect the enduring philosophical concerns that launched the profession in the first place and that have served as its compass. For example, social workers' mission and role in state agencies—public welfare, child welfare, mental health, criminal justice, and so on—should not be taken for granted or carried out uncritically. They ought to be continually defined, examined, and redefined in light of answers we provide to complicated questions about the concept of welfare, the duty to aid, the responsibility of the public and private sectors for welfare, distributive justice, and so forth. Moreover, we must recognize that both the questions we address and the answers we produce may change over time, as a function of shifting political contexts and contemporary events.

Similarly, social workers' judgments about what constitutes "good" practice should not be formed or conveyed uncritically. Even if their arguments conform to accepted canons of logic—and this in itself is a substantial challenge—social workers must be willing to critique the conceptual and methodological tools they use to gather information, determine effectiveness, and render opinions about the quality of their work.

In this sense, the topics surveyed in this book may provide a useful template to enable social workers' periodic return to questions of enduring importance. As professionals' careers unfold, priorities shift and issues that attract their attention recede and emerge. As these inevitable changes occur, it is essential that social workers revisit basic questions about core aims, mission, and methods. Otherwise, we risk losing the normative bearings that ultimately infuse social work with its essential meaning.

In two respects, what I have offered here is only a beginning. First, it is a beginning in that a number of additional questions remain to be asked and answered. With regard to political philosophy, social workers need to be clearer about the most appropriate division of responsibility between the public and private sectors for welfare, particularly with respect to the responsibility government should assume for welfare benefits and social service programs. More thought must also be given to the appropriateness of government interference with market conditions to enhance citizen well-being and to prevent social, psychological, or economic vulnerability.

Concerning moral philosophy, the profession is only at the beginning stages of its grasp of ethical theory and its relevance to social work practice. Although social workers now have a reasonably good grasp of the diverse ethical dilemmas that arise in practice, much work remains to be done to enable practitioners to appreciate ethical nuance, dissect ethical issues that are embedded in practice, and apply ethical theories. In addition to mastering the rudiments of moral philosophy and ethical theory, social workers need to enhance their ability to identify and analyze ethical concepts, and construct compelling arguments to support their views, especially when moral duties conflict.

Social workers also need to gain a greater appreciation of the canons of logic and their relevance to practice. Although the apparatus of formal logic does not need to be integrated in the daily workings of the typical social worker, systematic introduction to principles of logic and common fallacies can strengthen social workers' ability to present sound, forceful, and compelling arguments and to detect and challenge flawed claims presented by others.

In the epistemological realm, contemporary social workers need to gain a better understanding of the evolution of debate about the role of science in practice. This is a provocative controversy that, in recent years especially, has changed the way many social workers think about and evaluate practice. The conclusions we reach about the place of empiricism and other forms of knowledge in social work will have considerable bearing on the way social workers are trained and attempt to demonstrate the process and outcome of their interventions.

Finally, social workers are also only at the beginning stages of comprehending the relevance of aesthetics to practice. We are not entirely clear about the aesthetic elements in practice, the relationship between the artistic and scientific aspects of practice, or ways to evaluate and critique our work using aesthetic concepts.

In these respects, then, the framework I have offered here can, by necessity, only be a beginning, a beginning of a constant cycle of constructive questioning and debate. I hope I have at least introduced a useful vocabulary and conceptual map to enable social workers to pursue these issues and cultivate these ideas further.

But the content of this book constitutes a beginning in another important respect as well. As I stated in my opening comments, I do not claim that this book broaches every imaginable philosophical issue that is germane to social work. Such a claim would be both arrogant and naive. Instead, what I claim is that *The Philosophical Foundations of Social Work* presents an overview and initial analysis of a wide range of what are among the most central, compelling, and enduring philosophical issues facing the profession.

This is, then, not an exhaustive treatment of the topic. Under each of the five major headings, one could reasonably argue that additional topics could have been included. I have no doubt about this. As I also suggested earlier, one could also reasonably argue for the inclusion of additional areas of philosophy.

I recognize that some social workers may find in these comments only further confirmation of their suspicions about the merits (or demerits) of philosophical exploration and inquiry. After all,

I seem to be saying that the important questions may never get answered and the boundaries may be forever blurred.

I do not think, however, that these are, in any way, fatal flaws. I do not think that this sort of inherent uncertainty diminishes the value of the philosophical enterprise. Few areas of true importance in life serve up crystal-clear answers to complex questions. That is certainly the case with respect to debate about matters such as abortion, termination of life, and the existence of a deity. Although actual consensus on these matters may never be achieved, something compelling about the issues manages to pull our attention.

In my view, this ought to be the case with the sorts of issues I have broached here. The philosophical topics raised in these pages are far from trivial. They rivet our attention to the intellectual and normative foundation of social work, a profession whose daunting mission is to enhance the quality of life, particularly for those who are most vulnerable. Social workers' continual concern with these enduring philosophical issues can go a long way toward ensuring that the profession's principal mission will be preserved.

REFERENCES

Abramovitz, M. 1986. The Privatization of the Welfare State: A Review. *Social Work* 31(4): 261–62.

Abramovitz, M. 1988. *Regulating the Lives of Women*. Boston: South End Press.

Aesthetics. 1988. *The New Encyclopaedia Britannica*, 15th ed. Chicago: Encyclopaedia Britannica.

Allen-Meares, P. and B. A. Lane. 1990. Social Work Practice: Integrating Qualitative and Quantitative Data Collection Techniques. *Social Work* 35(5): 452–58.

Aschenbrenner, K. 1974. *The Concepts of Criticism*. Dordrecht, Holland/ Boston: D. Reidel.

Atherton, C. R. 1989. The Welfare State: Still on Solid Ground. *Social Service Review* 63(2): 167–79.

Austin, D. M. 1976. Research and Social Work: Educational Paradoxes and Possibilities. *Journal of Social Service Research* 2(4): 172.

Baier, A. 1988. Theory and Reflective Practices. In D. M. Rosenthal and F. Shehadi, eds., *Applied Ethics and Ethical Theory*, pp. 25–49. Salt Lake City: University of Utah Press.

Baier, K. 1965. *The Moral Point of View*. New York: Random House.

Barry, B. 1973. *The Liberal Theory of Justice*. New York: Oxford University Press.

Beardsley, M. C. 1970. Aesthetic Theory and Educational Theory. In R. A. Smith, ed., *Aesthetic Concepts and Education*, pp. 3–20. Urbana, IL: University of Illinois Press.

Beckerman, A. 1978. Differentiating Between Social Research and Social Work Research: Implications for Teaching. *Journal of Education for Social Work* 14(2): 9–15.

Beckerman, A. 1990. Thoughts on Epistemological Issues in Social Work. In L. Videka-Sherman and W. J. Reid, eds., *Advances in Clinical Social Work Research*, pp. 400–404. Silver Spring, MD: National Association of Social Workers.

Bentham, J. [1789] 1948. *An Introduction to the Principles of Morals and Legislation*. New York: Hafner.

Berlin, Sir I. 1969. *Four Essays on Liberty*. Oxford: Oxford University Press.

Berlin, Sir I. 1975. Two Concepts of Liberty. In F. E. McDermott, ed., *Self-Determination in Social Work*, p. 149. London: Routledge and Kegan Paul.

Berlin, S. 1990. Dichotomous and Complex Thinking. *Social Service Review* 64(1): 6–59.

Berofsky, B., ed. 1966. *Free Will and Determinism*. New York: Harper and Row.

Beveridge, Sir W. 1942. *Social Insurance and Allied Services*. New York: Macmillan.

Biestek, F. 1975. Client Self-Determination. In F. E. McDermott, ed., *Self-Determination in Social Work*, p. 19. London: Routledge and Kegan Paul.

Black, P. N., E. K. Hartley, J. Whelley, and C. Kirk-Sharp. 1989. Ethics Curricula: A National Survey of Graduate Schools of Social Work. *Social Thought* 15(3/4): 141–48.

Blau, J. 1989. Theories of the Welfare State. *Social Service Review* 63(1): 26–38.

Block, F., R. Cloward, B. Ehrenreich, and F. F. Piven. 1987. *The Mean Season*. New York: Pantheon.

Bloom, M. and J. Fischer. 1982. *Evaluating Practice: Guidelines for the Accountable Professional*. Englewood Cliffs, NJ: Prentice-Hall.

Boehm, W. W. 1960. The Need for Courage. *Revue de l'Université d'Ottawa* 30 (January–April): 5.

Boehm, W. W. 1961. Social Work: Science and Art. *Social Service Review* 35(2): 144–52.

Bohm, D. 1980. *Wholeness and the Implicate Order*. London: Routledge and Kegan Paul.

Bohm, D. 1981. Insight, Knowledge, Science and Human Values. *Teachers College Record* 82(3): 380–402.

Bowers, S. 1949. The Nature and Definition of Social Casework. *Social Casework* 30: 311–17, 369–75, 412–17.

Brekke, J. S. 1986. Scientific Imperatives in Social Work Research: Pluralism is not Skepticism. *Social Service Review* 60(4): 538–54.

Brennan, W. C. 1973. The Practitioner as Theoretician. *Journal of Education for Social Work* 9 (Spring): 7.

Briar, S. 1979. Incorporating Research into Education for Clinical Practice in Social Work: Toward a Clinical Science in Social Work. In A. Rubin and A. Rosenblatt, eds., *Sourcebook on Resource Utilization*, pp. 132–140. New York: Council on Social Work Education.

Briar, S. 1980. Toward the Integration of Practice and Research. In D. Fanshel, ed., *Future of Social Work Research*, pp. 3–37. Washington D.C.: National Association of Social Workers.

Brodbeck, M. 1968. Explanation, Prediction, and Imperfect Knowledge. In M. Brodbeck, ed., *Readings in the Philosophy of the Social Sciences*, p. 368. New York: Macmillan.

Bronowski, J. 1973. *The Ascent of Man*. Boston: Little, Brown.

Bruce, M. 1965. *The Coming of the Welfare State*. London: B. T. Botsford.

Buchanan, A. 1978. Medical Paternalism. *Philosophy and Public Affairs* 7: 370–90.

Buchanan, A. 1982. *Marx and Rawls: The Radical Critique of Justice*. Totowa, NJ: Rowan and Allanheld.

Burrell, G. and G. Morgan. 1979. *Sociological Paradigms and Organizational Analysis*. London: Heineman.

Callahan, D. and S. Bok, eds. 1980. *Ethics Teaching in Higher Education*. New York: Plenum Press.

Carter, R. 1977. Justifying Paternalism. *Canadian Journal of Philosophy* 7: 133–45.

Cohen, M. R. and E. Nagel. 1934. *An Introduction to Logic and Scientific Method*. New York: Harcourt, Brace and World.

Copi, I. M. 1986. *Introduction to Logic*, 7th ed. New York: Macmillan.

Covey, H. C. 1982. Basic Problems of Applying Experiments to Social Programs. *Social Service Review* 56(3): 424–37.

Daiches, D. 1981. *Critical Approaches to Literature*, 2d ed. New York: Longman.

Daniels, N., ed. 1975. *Reading Rawls*. New York: Basic Books.

Denzin, N. K. 1971. The Logic of Naturalistic Inquiry, *Social Forces* 50: 166–82.

Denzin, N. K. 1978. *Research Act: A Theoretical Introduction to Sociological Methods*. New York: McGraw-Hill.

DeRoos, Y. S. 1990. The Development of Practice Wisdom through Human Problem-Solving Processes. *Social Service Review* 64(2): 276–87.

DeSchweinitz, K. 1924. *The Art of Helping People Out of Trouble*. Boston: Houghton Mifflin.

Donagan, A. 1977. *The Theory of Morality*. Chicago: University of Chicago Press.

Dostoevsky, F. 1914. *Crime and Punishment*. London: William Heinemann.

Dunn, W. and I. Mitroff. 1981. The Obsolescence of Evaluation Research. *Evaluation and Program Planning* 4: 207–18.

Dworkin, G., ed. 1970. *Determinism, Free Will and Moral Responsibility*. Englewood Cliffs, NJ: Prentice-Hall.

Dworkin, G. 1971. Paternalism. In Richard A. Wasserstrom, ed., *Morality and the Law*, pp. 107–26. Belmont, CA: Wadsworth.

Dworkin, R. 1981. What is Equality? Part 2: Equality of Resources. *Philosophy and Public Affairs* 10: 283–345.

Eaton, J. 1958. Science, "Art," and Uncertainty in Social Work. *Social Work* 3(3): 3–10.

Elliott, M., comp. 1984. *Ethical Issues in Social Work: An Annotated Bibliography*. New York: Council on Social Work Education.

Ellis, J. M. 1974. *The Theory of Literary Criticism*. Berkeley: University of California Press.

Elster, J. 1988. Is There (or Should There Be) a Right to Work? In A. Guttman, ed., *Democracy and the Welfare State*, pp. 53–78. Princeton, NJ: Princeton University Press.

Emmet, D. 1962. Ethics and the Social Worker. *British Journal of Psychiatric Social Work* 6: 165–72.

England, H. 1986. *Social Work As Art*. London: Allen and Unwin.

Epstein, W. E. 1986. Science and Social Work. *Social Service Review* 60(1): 145–60.

Fanshel, D., ed. 1980. *Future of Social Work Research*. Washington D.C.: National Association of Social Workers.

Feinberg, J. 1970. *Doing and Deserving: Essays on the Theory of Responsibility*. Princeton, NJ: Princeton University Press.

Feinstein, A. R. 1967. *Clinical Judgment*. New York: Krueger.

Feyerabend, P. 1975. *Against Method*. London: New Left Books.

Fischer, D. H. 1970. *Historian's Fallacies*. New York: Harper and Row.

Fischer, J. 1981. The Social Work Revolution. *Social Work* 26(3): 199–207.

Fischer, J. 1984. Revolution, Schmevolution: Is Social Work Changing or Not? *Social Work* 29(1): 71–74.

Fottler, M., H. Smith, and W. James. 1981. Profits and Patient Care Quality in Nursing Homes: Are They Compatible? *The Gerontologist* 21(5): 532–38.

Frankena, W. 1973. *Ethics*, 2d ed. Englewood Cliffs, N.J.: Prentice-Hall.

Frankfurt, H. 1973. Coercion and Moral Responsibility. In Ted Honderich, ed., *Essays on Freedom of Action*, p. 79. London: Routledge and Kegan Paul.

Fried, C. 1978. *Right and Wrong*. Cambridge: Harvard University Press.

Friedman, M. 1962. *Capitalism and Freedom*. Chicago: University of Chicago Press.

Furniss, N. and T. Tilton. 1977. *The Case for the Welfare State*. Blooming-ton, IN: Indiana University Press.

Gambrill, E. 1990. *Critical Thinking in Clinical Practice: Improving the Accuracy of Judgments and Decisions about Clients*. San Francisco: Jossey-Bass.

Geismar, L. L. 1982. Debate with Authors: Comments on "The Obsolete Scientific Imperative in Social Work Research." *Social Service Review* 56(2): 311–12.

Geismar, L. L. and K. M. Wood. 1982. Evaluating Practice: Science or Faith? *Social Casework* 63(5): 266–72.

George, V. and P. Wilding. 1976. *Ideology and Social Welfare*. London: Routledge and Kegan Paul.

Gert, B. 1970. *The Moral Rules*. New York: Harper and Row.

Gewirth, A. 1978a. *Reason and Morality*. Chicago: University of Chicago Press.

Gewirth, A. 1978b. Ethics. In *Encyclopedia Britannica*, 15th ed. Chicago: University of Chicago Press.

Gibbs, L. E. 1991. *Scientific Reasoning for Social Workers*. New York: Macmillan.

Gilbert, N. 1983. *Capitalism and the Welfare State*. New Haven: Yale University Press.

Gilbert, N. and B. Gilbert. 1989. *The Enabling State: Modern Welfare Capitalism in America*. New York: Oxford University Press.

Gilder, G. 1981. *Wealth and Poverty*. New York: Basic Books.

Ginet, C. 1962. Can the Will Be Caused? *Philosophical Review* 71(1962): 49–55.

Goldstein, H. 1986. Toward the Integration of Theory and Practice: A Humanistic Approach. *Social Work* 31(5): 352–57.

Goodin, R. E. 1988. *Reasons for Welfare*. Princeton: Princeton University Press.

Gordon, W. 1965. Knowledge and Value: Their Distinction and Relation-ship in Clarifying Social Work Practice. *Social Work* 10(3): 32–39.

Gordon W. E. 1983. Social Work Revolution or Evolution? *Social Work* 28(3): 181–85.

Gordon, W. E. 1984. Gordon Replies: Making Social Work a Science-Based Profession. *Social Work* 29(1): 74–75.

Gough, I. 1979. *The Political Economy of the Welfare State*. New York: Macmillan.

Grinnell, R., ed. 1981. *Social Work Research and Evaluation*. Itasca, Il.: F. E. Peacock Press.

Gutmann, A., ed. 1988. *Democracy and the Welfare State*. Princeton, NJ: Princeton University Press.

Guzzetta, C. 1980. Untitled paper presented at meeting of the Group for the Advancement of Doctoral Education, Hunter College, p. 8.

Gyarfas, M. 1969. Social Science, Technology, and Social Work: A Case-worker's View. *Social Service Review* 43(3): 259–73.

Gyarfas, M. G. 1983. Debate with Authors: The Scientific Imperative Again. *Social Service Review* 57(1): 149–50.

Habermas, J. 1971. *Knowledge and Human Interests*. Boston: Beacon Press.

Harre, R. 1970. *Principles of Scientific Thinking*. Chicago: University of Chicago Press.

Harris, W. H. and J. S. Levey, eds. 1975. *New Columbia Encyclopedia*. New York: Columbia University Press.

Hartman, A. 1990. Editorial: Many Ways of Knowing. *Social Work* 35(1): 3–4.

Hawkes, T. A. 1982. Cost Control in Government Supported Social Service Programs. Prepared remarks of the Director of the Office of Program Coordination and Review, U.S. Department of Health and Human Services, delivered at a conference, "Paying for Maryland's Social Services," University of Maryland at Baltimore, May 14.

Hawkesworth, M. 1985. Workfare: The Imposition of Discipline. *Social Theory and Practice* 2: 163–82.

Haworth, G. O. 1984. Social Work Research, Practice, and Paradigms. *Social Service Review* 58(3): 343–57.

Hayek, F. A. 1944. *The Road to Serfdom*. Chicago: University of Chicago Press.

Hayek, F. A. 1976. *Law, Legislation, and Liberty, Vol. 2: The Mirage of Social Justice*. London: Routledge and Kegan Paul.

Heineman, M. 1981. The Obsolete Scientific Imperative in Social Work Research. *Social Service Review* 55(3): 371–96.

Heineman, M. B. 1982. Debate with Authors: Author's Reply. *Social Service Review* 56(1): 146–48.

Heisenberg, W. 1958. *Physics and Philosophy*. New York: Harper.

Higgins, J. 1981. *States of Welfare: A Comparative Analysis of Social Welfare*. New York: St. Martin's Press.

The History of Western Philosophy. 1989. In *Encyclopedia Britannica*, 15th ed., p. 742. Chicago: University of Chicago Press.

Hobsbaum, P. 1970. *Theory of Criticism*. Bloomington: Indiana University Press.

Holland, T. 1983. Debate with Authors: Comments on "Scientific Imperatives in Social Work Research and Practice." *Social Service Review* 57(2): 337–39.

Hollis, F. 1970. The Psychosocial Approach to the Practice of Casework. In R. W. Roberts and R. H. Nee, eds., *Theories of Social Casework*, pp. 33–75. Chicago: University of Chicago Press.

Hollis, F. 1975. Principles and Assumptions Underlying Casework Practice. Lecture delivered at United Nations seminar for the advanced study of social work; cited in R. F. Stalley, Determinism and the Principle of Client Self-Determination, in F. E. McDermott, ed., *Self-Determination in Social Work*, p. 93, 106–7. London: Routledge and Kegan Paul.

Hospers, J. 1966. What Means This Freedom? In B. Berofsky, ed., *Free Will and Determinism,* pp. 6, 40. New York: Harper and Row.

Hudson, W. H. 1982. Scientific Imperatives in Social Work Research and Practice. *Social Service Review* 56(2): 246–58.

Hudson, W. H. 1983. Debate with Authors: Author's Reply. *Social Service Review* 57(2): 339–41.

Hume, D. 1739. *A Treatise of Human Nature,* bk. 2, pt. 3, sec. 2.

Hunt, L. 1978. Social Work and Ideology. In N. Timms and D. Watson, eds., *Philosophy in Social Work,* pp. 7–25. London: Routledge and Kegan Paul.

Imre, R. W. 1982. *Knowing and Caring.* Lanham, Md.: University Press of America.

Imre, R. W. 1984. The Nature of Knowledge in Social Work. *Social Work* 29(1): 41–45.

Ingle, D. 1976. *Is It Really So? A Guide to Clear Thinking.* Philadelphia: Westminster Press.

Jansson, B. S. 1988. *The Reluctant Welfare State.* Belmont, CA: Wadsworth.

Jayaratne, S. and R. Levy. 1979. *Empirical Clinical Practice.* New York: Columbia University Press.

Jennings, B., D. Callahan, and S. M. Wolf. 1987. The Professions: Public Interest and Common Good. *Hastings Center Report* 17(1)(Supplement): 3–10.

Jonsen, A. R. 1984. A Guide to Guidelines. *American Society of Law and Medicine: Ethics Committee Newsletter* 2: 4.

Judge, K. and M. Knapp. 1985. Efficiency in the Production of Welfare: The Public and Private Sectors Compared. In R. Klein and M. O'Higgins, eds., *The Future of Welfare,* pp. 130–49. Oxford: Basil Blackwell.

Kaelin, E. F. 1989. *An Aesthetics for Art Educators.* New York: Teachers College Press.

Kahane, H. 1990. *Logic and Philosophy: A Modern Introduction,* 6th ed. Belmont, CA: Wadsworth.

Kaminsky, M. 1985. Daily Bread: Or, the Marriage of Art and Social Work. *Social Work with Groups* 8(1): 17–23.

Kant, I. [1790] 1928. *Critique of Aesthetic Judgment,* tr. J. C. Meredith. Oxford: Clarendon.

Kant, I. [1797] 1959. *Foundations of the Metaphysics of Morals,* tr. L. W. Beck. New York: Liberal Arts Press.

Karger, H. J. 1983. Science, Research, and Social Work: Who Controls the Profession? *Social Work* 28(3): 200–205.

Kass, L. R. 1990. Practicing Ethics: Where's the Action? *Hastings Center Report* 20(1): 5–12.

Keynes, J. M. 1960. *The General Theory of Employment, Interest, and Money.* London: Macmillan.

Kirk, S., M. Osmalov, and J. Fisher. 1976. Social Workers' Involvement in Research. *Social Work* 21: 121–24.

Krieger, M. 1976. *Theory of Criticism*. Baltimore: Johns Hopkins University Press.

Krouse, R. and M. McPherson. 1988. Capitalism, "Property-Owning Democracy," and the Welfare State. In A. Gutmann, ed., *Democracy and the Welfare State*, pp. 79–105. Princeton, NJ: Princeton University Press.

Kuhn, T. S. 1962. *The Structure of Scientific Revolutions*. Chicago: University of Chicago Press.

Lakatos, I. 1980. Falsification and the Methodology of Scientific Research Programmes. In J. Worral and G. Currie, eds., *Philosophical Papers: The Methodology of Scientific Research Programmes*, vol. 1, pp. 8–10. New York: Cambridge University Press.

Levins, R. 1966. The Strategy of Model Building in Population Biology. *American Scientist* 54: 421–31.

Lewis, C. S. 1947. *The Abolition of Man*. New York: Macmillan.

Lincoln, Y. S. and E. G. Guba. 1985. *Naturalistic Inquiry*. Beverly Hills, CA: Sage.

Lofland, J. 1976. *Doing Social Life: The Qualitative Study of Human Interaction in Natural Settings*. New York: Wiley.

Maas, H. S. 1968. Social Work Knowledge and Social Responsibility. *Journal of Education for Social Work* 4(Spring): 45.

Maas, H. S. 1977. Research in Social Work. In *Encyclopedia of Social Work*, 17th ed. Washington, D. C.: National Association of Social Workers.

MacDonagh, O. 1961. *A Pattern of Government Growth, 1800–1860*. London: MacGibbon and Kee.

Macklin, R. 1988. Theoretical and Applied Ethics: A Reply to the Skeptics. In D. M. Rosenthal and F. Shehadi, eds., *Applied Ethics and Ethical Theory*, pp. 50–70. Salt Lake City: University of Utah Press.

Marshall, T. H. 1981. *The Right to Welfare and Other Essays*. London: Heinemann.

Martin, G. R., Jr. 1990. *Social Policy in the Welfare State*. Englewood Cliffs, NJ: Prentice-Hall.

Marx, K. and F. Engels. 1955. *The Communist Manifesto*. New York: Appleton-Century-Crofts.

Mendelsohn, M. 1974. *Tender Loving Greed*. New York: Knopf.

Merton, R. K. 1949. Social Theory and Social Structure. In R. K. Merton, ed., *Social Structure and Anomie*, pp. 125–49. Glencoe, IL: Free Press.

Meyer, C. H. 1990. The Forest or the Trees? In L. Videka-Sherman and W. J. Reid, eds., *Advances in Clinical Social Work Research*, pp. 395–99. Silver Spring, MD: National Association of Social Workers.

Mill, J. S. [1863] 1957. *Utilitarianism*. Indianapolis: Bobbs-Merrill.

Mishler, E. 1979. Meaning in Context. *Harvard Education Review* 49: 1.

Moon, J. D. 1988. The Moral Basis of the Democratic Welfare State. In A. Gutmann, ed., *Democracy and the Welfare State*, pp. 27–52. Princeton, NJ: Princeton University Press.

Morawski, S. 1974. *Inquiries into the Fundamentals of Aesthetics*. Cambridge, MA: MIT Press.

Morgan, G. 1983. *Beyond Method*. Beverly Hills, CA: Sage.

Mullen E. J. 1985. Methodological Dilemmas in Social Work Research. *Social Work Research & Abstracts* 21(4): 12–19.

Murray, C. 1985. *Losing Ground: American Social Policy, 1950–1980*. New York: Basic Books.

Nagel, E. 1970. Determinism in History. In G. Dworkin, ed., *Determinism, Free Will and Moral Responsibility*, p. 55. Englewood Cliffs, NJ: Prentice-Hall.

Narveson, J. 1988. Is There a Problem About "Applied" Ethics? In D. M. Rosenthal and F. Shehadi, eds., *Applied Ethics and Ethical Theory*, pp. 100–115. Salt Lake City: University of Utah Press.

Nickel, J. W. 1978–1979. Is There a Human Right to Employment? *Philosophical Forum* 10: 149–70.

Nickel, J. W. 1988. Philosophy and Policy. In D. M. Rosenthal and F. Shehadi, eds., *Applied Ethics and Ethical Theory*, pp. 139–48. Salt Lake City: University of Utah Press.

Noble, C. N. 1982. Ethics and Experts. *Hastings Center Report* 12(3): 5–9.

Nozick, R. 1974. *Anarchy, State, and Utopia*. New York: Basic Books.

Nozick, R. 1989. *The Examined Life: Philosophical Meditations*. New York: Simon and Schuster.

Orcutt, B. A. 1990. *Science and Inquiry in Social Work Practice*. New York: Columbia University Press.

Orne, M. 1969. Demand Characteristics and the Concept of Quasi-Controls. In R. Rosenthal and R. Rosnow, eds., *Artifact in Behavioral Research*, pp. 143–79. New York: Academic Press.

Palmer, R. E. 1969. *Hermeneutics*. Evanston, IL: Northwestern University Press.

Peile, C. 1988. Research Paradigms in Social Work: From Stalemate to Creative Synthesis. *Social Service Review* 62(1): 1–19.

Perlman, H. H. 1965. Self-Determination: Reality or Illusion? *Social Service Review* 39: 410–21.

Pieper, M. H. 1982. Debate with Authors: Author's Reply. *Social Service Review* 56(2): 312.

Pieper, M. H. 1985. The Future of Social Work Research. *Social Work Research & Abstracts* 21(4): 3–11.

Pinker, R. 1979. *The Idea of Welfare*. London: Heinemann.

Piven, F. F. and R. Cloward. 1971. *Regulating the Poor*. New York: Vintage.

Piven, F. F. and R. Cloward. 1982. *The New Class War*. New York: Pantheon.

Plant, R. 1985. Welfare and the Value of Liberty. *Government and Opposition* 20: 297–314.

Plant, R., H. Lesser, and P. Taylor-Gooby. 1980. *Political Philosophy and Social Welfare*. London: Routledge and Kegan Paul.

Polansky, N. A., ed. 1960. *Social Work Research*. Chicago: University of Chicago Press.

Polansky, N. A. 1971. Research in Social Work. In *Encyclopedia of Social Work*, 16th ed. New York: National Association of Social Workers.

Political Philosophy. 1988. In *Encyclopedia Britannica*, 15th ed., pp. 972–84. Chicago: University of Chicago Press.

Popper, K. 1950. Indeterminism in Quantum Physics and in Classical Physics, Part 1. *British Journal for the Philosophy of Science* 1: 117–33.

Popper, K. R. 1965. *Of Clouds and Clocks: An Approach to the Problem of Rationality and the Freedom of Man*, annual Holly Compton Memorial Lecture. St. Louis: Washington University.

Popper, K. 1966. *The Open Society and Its Enemies*, 5th ed. London: Routledge and Kegan Paul.

Prigogine, I. and I. Stengers. 1984. *Order out of Chaos*. Boston: Shambhala.

Primus, W. 1989. Background Material and Data on Programs Within the Jurisdiction of the Committee on Ways and Means. Washington, D.C.: U.S. Government Printing Office.

Rae, D. 1981. *Equalities*. Cambridge, MA: Harvard University Press.

Rapoport, L. 1968. Creativity in Social Work. *Smith College Studies in Social Work* 38(3): 139–61.

Ratcliffe, J. W. 1983. Notions of Validity in Qualitative Research Methodology. *Knowledge: Creation, Diffusion, Utilization*, 5(2): 161–62.

Rawls, J. 1971. *A Theory of Justice*. Cambridge, MA: Harvard University Press.

Reamer, F. G. 1979. Protecting Research Subjects and Unintended Consequences: The Effects of Guarantees of Confidentiality. *Public Opinion Quarterly* 43: 497–506.

Reamer, F. G. 1983a. Social Services in a Conservative Era. *Social Casework* 64(8): 451–58.

Reamer, F. G. 1983b. The Concept of Paternalism in Social Work. *Social Service Review* 57(2): 254–71.

Reamer, F. G. 1983c. The Free Will-Determinism Debate in Social Work. *Social Service Review* 57(4): 626–44.

Reamer, F. G. 1987. Values and Ethics. In A. Minahan et al., eds., *Encyclopedia of Social Work*, 18th ed., pp. 801–809. Silver Spring, MD: National Association of Social Workers.

Reamer, F. G. 1989. Toward Ethical Practice: The Relevance of Ethical Theory. *Social Thought* 15(3/4): 67–78.

Reamer, F. G. 1990. *Ethical Dilemmas in Social Service*, 2d ed. New York: Columbia University Press.

Reamer, F. G., ed. 1991. *AIDS and Ethics*. New York: Columbia University Press.

Reamer, F. G. 1992. Social Work and the Public Good: Calling or Career? In P. Reid and P. R. Popple, eds., *The Moral Purposes of Social Work*, pp. 11–33. Chicago: Nelson-Hall.

Reamer, F. G. and M. Abramson. 1982. *The Teaching of Social Work Ethics*. Hastings-on-Hudson, NY: The Hastings Center.

Reason, P. and J. Rowan. 1981. On Making Sense. In *Human Inquiry: A Sourcebook for New Paradigm Research*, p. 130. New York: Wiley.

Reich, R. 1983. *The Next American Frontier*. New York: Penguin.

Reid, W. J. 1987. Social Work Research. In A. Minahan et al., eds., *Encyclopedia of Social Work*, 18th ed., pp. 474–87. Silver Spring, MD: National Association of Social Workers.

Reid, W. J. and A. Smith. 1981. *Research in Social Work*. New York: Columbia University Press.

Rein, M. and S. H. White. 1981. Knowledge in Practice. *Social Service Review* 55(1): 1–41.

Reisman, D. 1977. *Richard Titmuss: Welfare and Society*. London: Heinemann.

Reynolds, B. C. 1942. *Learning and Teaching in the Practice of Social Work*. New York: Russell and Russell.

Richan, W. and A. Mendelsohn. 1973. *Social Work: The Unloved Profession*. New York: New Viewpoints.

Richmond, M. 1917. *Social Diagnosis*. New York: Russell Sage Foundation.

Riecken, H. W. 1962. A Program for Research on Experiments in Social Psychology. In N. F. Washburne, ed., *Decisions, Values and Groups*, vol. 2, pp. 25–41. New York: Pergamon Press.

Rimlinger, G. 1971. *Welfare Policy and Industrialization in Europe, America, and Russia*. New York: Wiley.

Rodwell, M. K. 1987. Naturalistic Inquiry: An Alternative Model for Social Work Assessment. *Social Service Review* 61(2): 231–46.

Rosenberg, M. J. 1969. Conditions and Consequences of Evaluation Apprehension. In R. Rosenthal and R. Rosnow, eds., *Artifact in Behavioral Research*, pp. 279–349. New York: Academic Press.

Rosenthal, R. and R. Rosnow, eds. 1969. *Artifact in Behavioral Research*. New York: Academic Press.

Ross, W. D. 1930. *The Right and the Good*. Oxford: Clarendon Press.

Rubin, A. and E. Babbie. 1989. *Research Methods for Social Work*. Belmont, CA: Wadsworth.

Ruckdeschel, R. A. 1985. Qualitative Research as a Perspective. *Social Work Research & Abstracts* 21(2): 17–21.

Ruckdeschel, R. A. and B. E. Farris. 1981. Assessing Practice: A Critical Look at the Single-Case Design. *Social Casework* 62(7): 413–19.

Ruckdeschel, R. A. and B. E. Farris. 1982. Science: Critical Faith or Dogmatic Ritual? *Social Casework* 63(5): 272–75.

Saleeby, D. 1979. The Tension Between Research and Practice: Assumptions for the Experimental Paradigm. *Clinical Social Work Journal* 7(Winter): 267–69.

Salmon, W. C. 1963. *Logic*. Englewood Cliffs, NJ: Prentice-Hall.

Sapolsky, H. M. and S. Finkelstein. 1977. Blood Policy Revisited—A New Look at "The Gift Relationship." *Public Interest* 46(Winter): 15–27.

Saw, R. and H. Osborne. 1968. Aesthetics as a Branch of Philosophy. In
H. Osborne, ed., *Aesthetics in the Modern World*, pp. 15–32. London:
Thames and Hudson.

Schon, D. A. 1983. *The Reflective Practitioner*. New York: Basic Books.

Schon, D. A. 1987. *Educating the Reflective Practitioner*. San Francisco:
Jossey-Bass.

Schuerman, J. 1982. Debate with Authors: The Obsolete Scientific Imperative in Social Work. *Social Service Review* 56(1): 144–46.

Schuerman, J. 1987. Passion, Analysis, and Technology: The *Social Service Review* Lecture. *Social Service Review* 61(1): 3–18.

Schumpeter, J. A. [1942] 1950. *Capitalism, Socialism, and Democracy*, 3d
ed. New York: Harper and Row.

Schumpeter, J. A. 1963. *History of Economic Analysis*. London: Allen and
Unwin.

Scott, D. 1990. Practice Wisdom: The Neglected Source of Practice Research. *Social Work* 35(6): 564–68.

Searle, J. R. 1969. How to Derive "Ought" from "Is." In W. D. Hudson,
ed., *The Is/Ought Question*. New York: St. Martin's Press.

Sheldrake, R. 1985. *A New Science of Life*. London: Paladin.

Sheppard, A. 1987. *Aesthetics*. Oxford: Oxford University Press.

Shireman, C. H. and F. G. Reamer. 1986. *Rehabilitating Juvenile Justice*.
New York: Columbia University Press.

Siegel, D. H. 1984. Defining Empirically Based Practice. *Social Work* 29:
325–31.

Siegel, D. H. and F. G. Reamer. 1988. Integrating Research Findings,
Concepts, and Logic into Practice. In R. M. Grinnell, Jr., ed., *Social
Work Research and Evaluation*, 3d ed., pp. 483–502. Itasca, IL: F. E.
Peacock.

Simon, H. A. 1957. *Models of Man: Social and Rational*. New York: Wiley.

Simon, H. A. 1966. Scientific Discovery and the Psychology of Problem
Solving. In R. Colodney, ed., *Mind and Cosmos: Essays in Contemporary Science and Philosophy*, pp. 22–40. Pittsburgh: University of Pittsburgh Press.

Singer, P. 1988. Ethical Experts in a Democracy. In D. M. Rosenthal and
F. Shehadi, eds., *Applied Ethics and Ethical Theory*, pp. 149–61. Salt
Lake City: University of Utah Press.

Siporin, M. 1988. Clinical Social Work as an Art Form. *Social Casework*
69(3): 177–83.

Smart, J. J. C. 1970. Free Will, Praise and Blame. In G. Dworkin, ed.,
Determinism, Free Will and Moral Responsibility, p. 197. Englewood
Cliffs, NJ: Prentice-Hall.

Smart, J. J. C. 1971. Extreme and Restricted Utilitarianism. In Samuel
Gorovitz, ed., *Mill: Utilitarianism*. Indianapolis: Bobbs-Merrill.

Smart, J. J. C. and B. Williams. 1973. *Utilitarianism: For and Against*.
Cambridge: Cambridge University Press.

Smith, J. D. 1986. The Concentration of Wealth in the United States:

Trends in the Distribution of Wealth Among American Families. Washington, DC: Joint Economic Committee, U.S. Congress.

Smullyan, A. 1962. *Fundamentals of Logic*. Englewood Cliffs, NJ: Prentice-Hall.

Soyer, D. 1963. The Right to Fail. *Social Work* 8: 72–78.

Sparshott, F. 1982. *The Theory of the Arts*. Princeton, NJ: Princeton University Press.

Spicker, P. 1988. *Principles of Social Welfare*. London: Routledge.

Stroll, A. and R. H. Popkin. 1979. *Introduction to Philosophy*, 3d ed. New York: Holt, Rinehart and Winston.

Sudman, S. and N. M. Bradburn. 1974. *Response Effects in Surveys*. Chicago: Aldine.

Suppes, P. 1957. *Introduction to Logic*. Princeton, NJ: D. Van Nostrand.

Tawney, R. H. 1964. *Equality*. New York: Barnes and Noble.

Taylor, R. 1963. *Metaphysics*. Englewood Cliffs, NJ: Prentice-Hall.

Titmuss, R. 1958. *Essays on the "Welfare State."* London: Unwin University Books.

Titmuss, R. 1972. *The Gift Relationship*. New York: Vintage Books.

Trattner, W. I. 1979. *From Poor Law to Welfare State*, 2d ed. New York: The Free Press.

Trilling, L., ed. 1970. *Literary Criticism*. New York: Holt, Rinehart and Winston.

Tropp, E. 1976. The Challenge of Quality for Practice Theory. In B. Ross and S. K. Khinduka, eds., *Social Work in Practice: Fourth NASW Symposium*. New York: National Association of Social Workers.

Tyler, R. 1952. Distinctive Attributes of Education for the Profession. *Social Work Journal* 33(April): 56.

Videka-Sherman, L., W. J. Reid, and R. W. Toseland. 1990. "Themes, Issues, and Prospects." In L. Videka-Sherman and W. J. Reid, eds., *Advances in Clinical Social Work Research*, pp. 409–21. Silver Spring, MD: National Association of Social Workers.

Vigilante, J. L. 1974. Between Values and Science: Education for the Profession During a Moral Crisis or Is Proof Truth? *Journal of Education for Social Work* 10: 107–15.

Vivas, E. and M. Krieger, eds. 1962. *The Problems of Aesthetics*. New York: Holt, Rinehart and Winston.

Weick, A. 1987. Reconceptualizing the Philosophical Perspective of Social Work. *Social Service Review* 61(2): 218–30.

Weisbrod, B. 1988. *The Nonprofit Economy*. Cambridge, MA: Harvard University Press.

Wiegand, C. 1979. Using a Social Competence Framework for Both Client and Practitioner. In F. W. Clark, M. L. Arkava, and Associates, eds., *The Pursuit of Competence in Social Work*. San Francisco: Jossey-Bass.

Wilensky, H. 1975. *The Welfare State and Equality*. Berkeley: University of California Press.

Willems, E. P. and H. L. Raush, eds. 1969. *Naturalistic Viewpoints in Psychological Research.* New York: Holt, Rinehart and Winston.

Williams, J. A., Jr. 1964. Interviewer-Respondent Interaction: A Study of Bias in the Information Interview. *Sociometry* 27: 338–52.

Wimsatt, W. G. 1981. Robustness, Reliability, and Overdetermination. In M. B. Brewer and B. E. Collins, eds., *Scientific Inquiry and the Social Sciences*, pp. 151–53. San Francisco: Jossey-Bass.

Witkin, S. L. 1991. Empirical Clinical Practice: A Critical Analysis. *Social Work,* 36(2): 158–63.

Wolff, R. P. 1977. *Understanding Rawls: A Reconstruction and Critique of "A Theory of Justice."* Princeton, NJ: Princeton University Press.

Wood, K. M. 1990. Epistemological Issues in the Development of Social Work Practice Knowledge. In L. Videka-Sherman and W. J. Reid, eds., *Advances in Clinical Social Work Research,* pp. 373–90. Silver Spring, MD: National Association of Social Workers.

Wooden, K. 1976. *Weeping in the Playtime of Others.* New York: McGraw-Hill.

Zimbalist, S. E. 1977. *Historic Themes and Landmarks in Social Welfare Research.* New York: Harper and Row.

Zimmerman, J. H. 1989. Determinism, Science, and Social Work. *Social Service Review* 63(1): 52–62.

INDEX